Give and Go

Give and Go

Basketball as a Cultural Practice

Thomas Mc Laughlin

State University of New York Press

An earlier version of Chapter 2 was originally published as "The Ethics of Basketball" in *Continuum*, April 1999, volume 13, no. 1, pp. 13–28.

An earlier version of Chapter 3 was originally published as "Man to Man: Basketball, Movement, and the Practice of Masculinity" in *South Atlantic Quarterly*, volume 103, no. 1, pp. 169–191. Copyright 2004, Duke University Press. All rights reserved. Used by permission of the publisher.

Published by
State University of New York Press, Albany

For information, contact State University of New York Press, Albany, NY
www.sunypress.edu

Production by Diane Ganeles
Marketing by Michael Campochiaro

Library of Congress Cataloging-in-Publication Data

Mc Laughlin, Thomas, 1948–
   Give and go : basketball as a cultural practice / Thomas McLaughlin.
     p. cm.
   Includes bibliographical references and index.
   ISBN 978-0-7914-7393-1 (hardcover : alk. paper)
   ISBN 978-0-7914-7394-8 (pbk. : alk. paper)
   1. Basketball—Social aspects—United States. I. Title.

GV889.26.M35 2008
796.3230973—dc22   2007025406

10 9 8 7 6 5 4 3 2 1

Contents

Acknowledgments

"Give and go" is my favorite basketball phrase. You pass the ball and move on the expectation that if the situation calls for it you will get the ball back. You have to give the ball up in order to make the play work. The phrase speaks of trust and gratitude—you believe your teammate knows the right move to make, and you give thanks to the game and all of its human interplay. I want to thank all of the players, colleagues, friends, and family members who were willing to play ball with me in the long process of writing this book.

The experience at the center of this project was over twenty years of playing in the faculty-staff community game in Broome-Kirk Gym at Appalachian State University in Boone, North Carolina, the "oldguygame," as I call it throughout this book. I am proud to be one of the founding members of this noontime "run," which has been in operation since the early 1980s and still flourishes. I had to retire from it a couple of years ago, after my feet gave out, but I am still with it in spirit. I have been playing pickup basketball since I was a kid, but I learned how to think about the game in Broome-Kirk, so I would like to thank all of the old guys who played in that game over the years. I will name some of them here, but there are plenty more: Emory Maiden, Gene Miller, Dan Hurley, Tom McGowan, Bill Ward, James Ivory, Alex Pitofsky, Chris Harris (all colleagues in the English Department), Michael Dale, Tim Silver, Jim Goff, Mark Estepp, Dick Riedl, Greg Reck, Bud Gerber, Kinny Baughman, Brad Berndt, Terry Combs, Tim Smith, Bill Baker, Mike Evans, Dave Nieman, John Cougar Hegeseth, Mike Schellinger, Steve Millsaps, Ray Russell, Mike Mayfield, Joe Pollock, Tim Huelsman, Tim Ludwig, Morris Cox, Martin Moore, Rob Norris, Tom Van Gilder, Bob Richardson, David Durham, Roland Moy, "John Bob," "Big George," and the late Jimmy Smith. I also learned a lot about basketball from Gene Gallagher, Jim Harkins, Jim Greway, Bob Byrne, Charley Teague, and Billy McGovern.

I would also like to thank the colleagues who read portions of this manuscript, who put up with more basketball talk than they might have wanted, or who helped with connections in the scholarly world, including

Leon Lewis, Jim Winders, Chip Arnold, Joan Woodworth, Tina Groover, Susan Staub, Joseph Bathanati, Kathryn Kirkpatrick, and Marianne Adams, as well as Alan McKee, Stanley Fish, Henry Jenkins, and Frank Lentricchia. Dave Haney, and Jeanne Dubino have been great and supportive department chairs, and Dean Bob Lyman and Provosts Harvey Durham and Stan Aeschleman provided personal and institutional support. Thanks also to graduate research assistants Erin Zimmerman and Catherine Talley.

I owe great thanks to all of my family—a lot of serious basketball fans—for their love and support. Thanks to Nora and Ben and Rebekah, Kate and Ryan and Sean, Julia and Joe, and especially my wife Joan, with whom I fell in love the moment I saw her jump shot.

Chapter 1

Introduction

Basketball as a Cultural Practice

In the late 1960s I played a lot of pickup basketball with a group of friends on courts in and around Philadelphia. One of them was a gifted 6'5" center, Jim Greway. Jim liked to play the high post because he had a good turnaround jump shot, and I liked to drive the baseline because I had a football body and pretty good quickness. If I beat my man and forced the defender covering Jim to help out, then Jim would always move down the lane and be ready for a pass. We *killed* people with that simple play. We never talked about it or planned to use it. It just developed out of our styles of play and our understanding of the options available in the moment. Jim knew how to deploy his body to make himself available for the pass, and I knew how to slip the ball through the defenders to give him an open shot. I think back on those game moments with great pleasure—moments when players thought together, moved together, intuited each other's actions, played the game as it was supposed to be played. How did we do that? No coach taught it to us, no strategy session planned it out, no x's and o's. We could make that play because like all other pickup basketball players we were so immersed in the culture of the game, so caught up in its daily practice, that it seemed second nature, obvious and inevitable. We had learned in the game a way of thinking, a way of moving, a way of relating to others distinctive to the practice of basketball. We did not often reflect on it or discuss it explicitly, but we knew that we were experiencing something valuable in itself, something that would become part of who we were and how we lived our lives.

The goal of this book is to articulate the culture that made that play possible, the culture inherent in the practice of the game. Basketball is played by millions of people around the world, and its elite performances are watched by millions more. For many of those millions the game is a central part of their identity. They play every day, they watch as much as they can, they read about basketball in the paper, they talk about it with their friends, they wear clothes inspired by the style of the game, they rearrange their life schedules so they can participate, and they think about themselves as players and as members of a community centered around the game. The energy and interest these players and fans give to basketball produces a cultural return. They learn from their active engagement in the practice a set of values, beliefs, ways of thinking and feeling, and ways of moving, connecting, and creating communities—a rich, extensive culture. Every time they play or watch the game, they operate inside the culture of the practice, with its habits and inclinations, and in the moment of play, in the negotiations on the court, they recreate and renew the culture that in turn shapes their bodies and minds.

Because it is played by a huge and global community, and because of its media visibility, basketball is a significant and powerful *cultural practice*. I use this term, so common in the discourse of cultural studies, to designate any activity engaged in by people who derive from it a distinctive cultural style that then becomes a significant element in their own personal identity. In this sense cultural practices include jobs and professions, crafts and hobbies, daily tasks, sports and games, religious and spiritual exercises, and arts and sciences—any activities through which complex cultures are produced and consumed. All of us engage in *many* such practices, constructing for ourselves complex identities that derive from our distinctive ensemble of practices. Basketball is just one among many such practices, but it is one of my own, one that I have participated in and been shaped by throughout my life. I am a lifelong pickup ball player, with modest skills but serious intent. Like all players, I have internalized and embodied the culture of the game, especially the local games I have played in for years. I write this book as a participant in the basketball community, as a subject inside the practice, trying to put into words what my body already knows.

Pickup basketball teaches contradictory lessons about the culture of practices. On the one hand, the culture preexists any given player or game. The actions and interactions of players are shaped by the history of the game as it is passed down to them. But on the other hand, players are constantly recreating and altering the practice in their on-court negotiations. Pickup basketball is a living culture that responds to the local circumstances and personal histories of its players. Pickup ball in a Harlem park is not pickup ball in an Indiana church hall, and pickup ball tomorrow will not be a simple repetition of pickup ball today. The culture of the game is not a rigid template that determines the actions of its practitioners. To use the language of Pierre Bourdieu, it is a set of habits and predispositions open to the improvisations of players reacting to the exigencies of the moment.

The word "practice," which I will use so frequently in this book, produces many shades of meaning, both in ordinary language and in the theoretical terminology of cultural studies. In the world of sports, of course, "practice" is part of the vernacular—it refers to the process of preparing for competition. It is used in the same way that theater people refer to "rehearsal," as opposed to "performance." In this sense, "practice" is precisely *not* the thing itself; it is *merely* preparation, the repetitive, daily dues that must be paid in order to sharpen skills that will one day be put to use that matters. But in other cultural contexts, "practice" is often used to refer to activities that matter in themselves, not just as preparation, as in the usage that refers to the "practice" of medicine or law or teaching. These professions use the term *practice* because it suggests that they can never be mastered but must be pursued in their daily exercise, in which abstract ideas are put into unpredictable, real-life action in a process of endless learning. My use of the term is certainly closer to the second of these meanings; in pickup ball there is no performance other than the daily practice. It is not preparation for a future, high-stakes performance, it is the living game itself. In order to become so immersed in the culture of basketball that intuitive play becomes second nature, one has to invest years in the practice so that reactions and decisions become embodied and "instinctive."

"Practice" suggests, on the one hand, the daily grind of practical action and, on the other, spiritual exercises that transcend the everyday. Thus one develops the mundane "practice," say, of mowing the lawn once a week, but one also "practices" yoga or meditation, ways of rising above the mundane or finding spiritual enlightenment within it. In fact, "practice" often suggests a spiritual dimension. People refer to themselves as "practicing" Catholics or Jews, asserting by the use of the word that their religion is not just an inherited tradition but rather a preoccupation that affects the daily activities of their lives. My use of the term embraces both of these shades of meaning. To "practice" basketball is to make it a part of everyday life, a habit of ordinary action and attention. But I also will argue throughout this book that the "practice" of basketball can become a physical and spiritual discipline, an opportunity for personal growth and discovery.

I am attracted as well to the usages of "practice" that refer to informal habits of operation, as opposed to formal, institutionalized rules. Thus an organization might have as its "practice" the habit of granting preferences to workers with seniority, even if there are no official rules that mandate the action. Daily life operates, of course, within the constraints of formal rules and laws, but it also proceeds by unspoken assumptions, habits of thought and action, and rules of thumb, expectations that go without saying. Pickup basketball is particularly characterized by such informal and tacit agreements, but all cultural practices involve this tacit dimension, which is created by the actions and decisions of participants. In sum, then, the ordinary meanings of the word "practice" suggest an action that becomes part of everyday life, that proceeds by informal codes of behavior, and that carries with it powerful moral and spiritual consequences. To see basketball as a "practice" in these terms is to see it as a site where a culture is created and learned.

The term *practice* has been investigated extensively by theorists of society and culture. This attention comes as a reaction, I think, to cultural theories that deny agency to individual subjects either by characterizing culture as an impersonal system or by reducing individual subjects to victim status, manipulated by the dissemination of cultural commodities in mass media. The idea of a cultural "practice," with its emphasis on the daily activities of ordinary people, turns attention to the practical embodiment and creative consciousness of individuals, without the illusion of unfettered freedom implicit in the concept of the autonomous subject. To engage in a practice is to act as an individual, but to act within a social context, since the habits of a practice are always constructed cooperatively by many individuals in complex social relationships. The agent of the practice may be in total isolation at the moment of action, a single kid shooting a basketball at a backyard hoop, but he or she has already internalized the habits and the mind-set of the practice. The term *practice* has therefore attracted theorists interested in questions of individual agency and identity, but always in social and historical situations.

One such theorist, whose work I make use of especially in thinking about the ethics of basketball, is philosopher Alasdair MacIntyre. MacIntyre is interested in practices because he sees them as situations in which the virtues are enacted. He defines "practice" as

> Any coherent and complex form of socially established cooperative human activity through which goods internal to that form of activity are realized in the course of trying to achieve those standards of excellence which are appropriate to, and partially definitive of, that form of activity, with the result that human powers to achieve excellence, and human conceptions of the ends and goods involved, are systematically extended. (1994, 187)

In this sense, a "virtue" for MacIntyre is "an acquired human quality the possession and exercise of which tends to enable us to achieve those goods which are internal to practices" (1994, 191). For the individual involved in a practice, the achievement of virtue accrues to his or her own personal endowment, but it involves a profound engagement in social relations. MacIntyre asserts that the goods of a practice "can only be achieved by subordinating ourselves within the practice in our relationship to other practitioners" because "the virtues are those goods by reference to which, whether we like it or not, we define our relationship to those other people with whom we share the kind of purposes and standards which inform practices" (ibid.). The social nature of practices is a function of their need for pedagogy; practices must be acquired by conscious effort, learned in a social context from more expert practitioners:

> To enter into a practice is to accept the authority of those standards and the inadequacy of my own performance as judged by them. It is to subject my own attitudes, choices, preferences, and tastes to the standards which currently and partially define the practice. . . . If on starting to play baseball, I do not accept that others know better than I when to throw a fast ball and when not, I will never learn to appreciate good pitching let alone to pitch. (MacIntyre 1994, 190)

In MacIntyre's analysis, individuals make moral sense only as members of communities constructed around shared activities directed at shared goals. The moral culture of these communities is a function of the practice that they pursue—the practice itself generates the virtues necessary for its own successful functioning. The individual either submits to those self-evident requirements or ceases to be useful to the practice.

I take from MacIntyre the conviction that the practice itself generates ethical norms. Players learn to behave in ways that enhance the pleasure of play. But I also believe that in basketball at least, the norms of behavior are not as *given* as MacIntyre makes them appear. That is, the ethics of basketball as a practice are generated by negotiations at the local level among practitioners of the game. The process is not impersonal, with habits of behavior deriving via a pragmatic logic from the needs of the game. Basketball ethics, I will argue, are interpersonal, deriving from the shared histories of the real subjects engaged in the practice. For me, MacIntyre underestimates the agency of practitioners as the source of the culture of practice. They do more than choose whether or not to submit to norms—they generate the norms themselves, in part as a function of the needs of the practice but also as a function of their own desires and their complex relationships with other members of the community. Practices do not call only for obedience, as MacIntyre suggests, but for a shared creativity, a willingness to negotiate the practice even as it unfolds.

Among social and cultural theorists, the great proponent of creativity in practices is Michel de Certeau, for whom the practices of everyday life are the "tactics" of the people, their ways of countering the "strategies" of the powerful institutions that seek to discipline and regulate their lives. De Certeau sees cultural life as a struggle between the forces of control that Michel Foucault described so persuasively in *Discipline and Punish* and the subjects of those disciplinary schemes, whom de Certeau sees as possessing resources of resistance that Foucault does not extensively enough address. In the rhetoric of his discourse, de Certeau is the poet of practices, describing these "tactics" in stirring terms. "Many everyday practices," he says, "are tactical in character . . . victories of the 'weak' over the 'strong' . . . clever tricks, knowing how to get away with things, 'hunter's cunning,' maneuvers, polymorphic simulations, joyful discoveries, poetic as well as warlike" (1984, xix). As a lover of pickup basketball, I am strongly attracted to de Certeau's language, which could well describe any game in any schoolyard. A "tactic," de Certeau says, "operates in isolated actions, blow by blow. It takes advantage of 'opportunities' and depends on them." A tactic must "accept the chance offerings of the moment, and seize on the wing the possibilities that offer themselves at any given moment" (1984, 37). Basketball happens precisely "on the wing," with players constantly making use of the "maneuvers" and "clever tricks" by which a smart player can overcome a physically stronger opponent. I try a move, an opponent reacts, I react to his reaction—together we make up the game on the fly, improvising every decision, deploying our bodies in unpredictable tactics that make sense only in that unfolding temporal process. De Certeau depicts cultural life itself in terms that recall a pickup game—rules are established by powerful institutions, but what matters most are the improvisations, the clever practices that allow the weak to make their own use of the rules or to slip between the cracks in their jurisdiction.

But despite my attraction to the aptness of de Certeau's language for basketball, I cannot accept his conflation of "practices" with "tactics." He may begin by saying that "*many* everyday practices . . . are tactical in character," but he often is carried away by his own rhetoric into speaking as though they were one and the same, as though all of the practices of everyday life were acts of resistance to power—tiny, local, momentary insurrections. One of de Certeau's favorite examples of a "tactic" is *la peruque*, the act of using the time and equipment of the owner to do the worker's own personal work. Thus a woodworker might use the boss's machines on the sly in order to fashion a chair for his own home, or a bookstore clerk might find time to read the shop owner's books while pretending to do inventory. No doubt such maneuvers are the everyday practice of workers everywhere, and they *are* small victories, which de Certeau calls "the guileful ruses of *different* interests and desires" (1984, 34) that "elude discipline without being outside the field in which it is exercised" (1984, 96). But de Certeau has little to say about the practices of everyday life that do not "remain heterogeneous to the systems they infiltrate" (1984, 34), but simply perform and fulfill the task they are assigned. Bookstore clerks as part of their everyday life in fact do the inventory. Woodworkers turn out chairs for the factory. Everyday practices do not necessarily resist power. They are often as "docile" as Foucault describes, reproducing systems of power rather than challenging them. In fact, without the daily background of such compliant, uncritical practices, the clever defiance of "tactics" would have no force. It is true, to use de Certeau's famous metaphor, that consumers of mass culture act as "poachers," making their own use of the media products made available by an alien, detached power elite, but consumers also routinely take in the messages and products of mass culture just as they were intended to. Practices are not inherently revolutionary, and the fact that they *can be* must be maintained without being exaggerated.

Therefore, I will argue throughout this book that basketball is simultaneously a vehicle for the inculcation of conventional cultural values and an opportunity to explore alternatives. Especially in organized basketball and in its media representations, the game is a mainstream cultural practice, an educational tool designed to create well-disciplined young men and women. Listen to any television basketball commentator or any big-time coach and you will inevitably hear about the conventional virtues of the game, life lessons in hard work, sportsmanship, team play, and self-sacrifice. You will hear, that is, the "strategies" of power rather than the "tactics" of resistance. Players who practice basketball in these contexts are not encouraged to put the game to their own subversive uses. In the pickup game, where there is no obvious authority structure, there is more room for "tactical" maneuver, and I will certainly argue that playing pickup ball encourages resistance to the mainstream culture of sports. But that is not to say that pickup basketball is a radical or an anarchistic practice. Even in the absence of authority figures, the game imposes conventional rules of behavior and patterns of thinking. I will only argue that the culture of pickup ball is looser, less restrictive, and more open to the creative and even subversive play of participants.

This *potential* for resistance in pickup basketball and other everyday practices is important to remember as we turn our attention to Pierre Bourdieu, who has described such practices more thoroughly than any other theorist, but who sometimes implies that such resistance is impossible. Bourdieu sees practices as socially significant actions made possible and meaningful by habits of mind, presuppositions, and shared ways of looking at the world—what he calls a *habitus*. The habitus of a practice develops historically as a cultural reaction to the objective "conditions of existence" faced by a social group. It is a "system of structured, structuring dispositions" (1990, 52), "structured" in the sense of being produced by the conditions of existence, and "structuring" in the sense that it produces the particular actions and perceptions of the practice itself. The habitus is the tacit set of assumptions accepted without reflection by practitioners. Their actions make sense because they are agents who have accepted the mind-set of the habitus as "what goes without saying" (1990, 92). As such, their actions put the habitus into play without ever drawing it into critical reflection. Jim and I could make that play, to use Bourdieu's terms, because we shared the same habitus.

In his thinking about practices, Bourdieu is literally a "poststructuralist." That is, the relationship between practice and habitus clearly derives from Saussure's distinction in structural linguistics between *parole* and *langue*, but Bourdieu adapts and revises the concept for his own less rigid and abstract purposes. Saussure understands parole, or individual utterances, as a function of langue, the abstract system or set of laws that structures the language. No parole has meaning unless it conforms to those laws and makes sense within that system. Speakers of a language internalize the system of langue—the laws of syntax and semantics—and it allows them to produce infinite and novel paroles, but only those that work within the system. In Bourdieu's thought, by analogy, "practices" are paroles and the habitus is langue. But Bourdieu defines the habitus in a much less systematic and abstract way. The habitus is not a system of laws or norms; it is a loose set of dispositions, habits of mind, typical emotional responses, ways of making sense of experience. Bourdieu resists all attempts to reduce the habitus to a rigid system, because he wants to emphasize the adaptability of the habitus, its ability to enable the improvisations required by the practices it makes possible. Practices do not simply derive from the logic of the habitus; they are responses in the moment to the needs of real social interactions, but they still find their meaning within the habits of thought encouraged by the habitus, or they find no meaning at all.

Bourdieu emphasizes the flexibility of the habitus, which allows "agents to generate an infinity of practices adapted to endlessly changing situations" (1977, 16). The only interest of these agents is to respond effectively to the opportunities and challenges that face them. They are not interested in consistency or logic but only in the pragmatic outcomes of their actions. They need to "cope with unforeseen and ever-changing situations" (1977, 72), so they must be open to the present, capable of "the intentionless invention of regulated improvisations" (1990, 57). Practices are inherently temporal, which is why they are misrepresented by abstract theorization, which prefers timeless laws and systems. Bourdieu himself uses the improvisations of the athlete, creating the practice in the moment of play, as his example of that temporality. The athlete's " 'feel' for the game is the sense of the immanent future of the game, the sense of the direction of the history of the game that gives the game its sense" (1990, 82). A player, like any practitioner, must be responsive to other players in the temporal flow of the game: "Each move triggers off a counter-move, every stance of the body becomes a sign pregnant with a meaning that the opponent has to grasp while it is still incipient, reading in the beginnings of a stroke or a sidestep the imminent future" (1977, 11). The practitioner is a master of "the art of living," "the art of the necessary improvisation" (1977, 10). What matters to the practitioner are not rules and models but "tact, dexterity, or savoir-faire" (ibid.), which allow maximum flexibility for the practice.

These are, of course, the virtues of the basketball player. In strategy decisions, movements of the body, and even ethical judgments, the game rewards the ability to improvise, to create in the moment in response to the creative actions of other players. Especially in pickup basketball, in which all strategy decisions are made by the players within the flow of the game, there is nothing but practice as temporal process. Every thought and movement occurs in real time, with almost no anticipatory plans or set plays. Bourdieu's account of practice, therefore, is richly applicable to basketball, which in turn comes to seem a perfect symbol for practice itself. Basketball happens "on the run," "in the open court," with ten independent agents making decisions and moving in a process so complex that chaos and confusion are always possible. What makes their play cohere, and even at times attain a magical psychic synchronicity, is the fact that they share a habitus. Because they have internalized the strategic and kinetic dispositions of the game, they are capable of "the conductorless orchestration which gives regularity, unity, and systematicity to practices" (1990, 59).

Bourdieu is clear that although practices are flexible, they are not absolutely free, since they are always governed by the dispositions of the habitus, which is in turn governed by the objective conditions that generate it. The practitioner has the freedom of the improviser, but the range of improvisations never includes moves that are unthinkable within the habitus. Bourdieu says, "The habitus makes possible the free production of all the thoughts, perceptions, and actions inherent in the particular conditions of its production—*and only those*" (1990, 55, emphasis added). The habitus is inherently conservative; Bourdieu calls it "a present past that tends to perpetuate itself into the future" (1990, 54). Thus in a basketball game, among the myriad choices open to players, it is *unthinkable* that a player would take a baseball bat to the ball, or tackle an opposing player, options perfectly thinkable within other athletic practices. Bourdieu's ideas in this context recall Marx's famous dictum that "men make their own history, but they do not make it just as they please; they do not make it under circumstances chosen by themselves but under circumstances directly encountered, given and transmitted from the past." The habitus of a practice sets up as an outer circumference within which infinite but not total diversity is possible.

The limits of the habitus have their power because they are embodied in the practitioner. That is, unlike Saussure's langue, the habitus is not an abstract system. It is not primarily intellectual, though it controls the practitioner's thinking as much as his or her emotions or movements. The habitus is so deeply internalized that it becomes embodied, worked into the neural networks and habitual movements of the practitioner. It becomes, Bourdieu says, "a way of walking, a tilt of the head, facial expressions, ways of sitting and of using implements, always associated with a tone of voice, a style of speech, and (how could it be otherwise) a certain subjective experience" (1977, 87). As Susan Brownell says in *Training the Body for China*, the habitus of any given sport works as a means of "obtaining from the body an adherence that the spirit could refuse" (1995, 12). Paradoxically, this structured embodiment is necessary for improvisation in the moment, which happens so fast that systematic thought is useless. The fine muscle control at breakneck speed and the instantaneous decision making that basketball requires can only occur when players have played the game long enough so that their bodies make decisions while their minds plot strategy. A player may *think* "I need to pass the ball to my teammate who's open for an easy shot," but it is the educated body of the player that puts the necessary spin on the ball so it is delivered to the right hand of the other player, just barely eluding the grasp of the defender. It is in the context of this embodiment that the habitus can be said to be "unconscious," taken for granted by the practitioner interested only in the outcome of the move, not the set of dispositions that makes it possible.

Bourdieu is adamant in his conviction that because the habitus is embodied and unconscious, it is invisible to the practitioner, who processes it as simply the way things are rather than as a specific cultural formation. The habitus is "history turned into nature, i.e. denied as such": "The 'unconscious' is never anything other than the forgetting of history which history itself produces by incorporating the objective structures it produces in the second nature of the *habitus*" (1977, 78–79). The result is a lack of understanding that Bourdieu sees as necessary to the practice, which has no time to question its own operation. Theory, which Bourdieu defines as a systematic, abstract knowledge of the habitus, is both impossible and useless to the practitioner. Bourdieu argues that "the necessities of practice never require such a synoptic apprehension but rather discourage it through their urgent demands" (1990, 83). "Caught up in 'the matter at hand,' totally present in the present and in the practical functions that it finds thus in the form of objective potentialities, practice excludes attention to itself (that is, to the past). It is unaware of the principles that govern it and the possibilities they contain; it can only discover them by enacting them, unfolding them in time" (1990, 92). As a result, the practitioner's account of the practice is unreliable, "quasi-theoretical": "Simply because he is questioned, and questions himself, about the reasons and the *raison d'etre* of his practice, he cannot communicate the essential point, which is that the very nature of practice is that it excludes this question" (1990, 91).

It is on this point that my understanding of practices differs from Bourdieu's. In my earlier book *Street Smarts and Critical Theory*, I argued for the existence of "vernacular theory," theory produced by practitioners themselves. My case studies examined the theoretical questioning produced by elementary schoolteachers, advertising professionals, popular culture fans, adherents of various New Age practices, anti-pornography activists, and others who would never think of themselves as "theorists" but who asked fundamental questions about the premises of their practices. On one level my differences with Bourdieu are terminological—we mean very different things by "theory." Bourdieu characterizes theory as abstract and totalizing, while I think of theory as the act of raising fundamental questions rather than the production of systematic answers. But the difference is not simply semantic. Bourdieu famously says, "It is because subjects do not, strictly speaking, know what they are doing that what they do has more meaning than they know" (1977, 79), and while I agree that our practices have more meaning than we know, I do not accept that subjects do not know what they are doing. Bourdieu does remark that "reflexive attention" sometimes occurs when "the automatisms have broken down" (1990, 91), but I would argue that, for many reasons, the automatisms routinely do break down. Sometimes practitioners encounter others within the practice who operate with different assumptions, as when basketball players from different local runs with different local customs are thrown into a pickup game together. At that point, just so the practice can proceed smoothly, they have to confront their presuppositions, the obvious truths that they can usually take for granted. Or perhaps a practitioner is asked to defend the practice, explain it to an outsider, or teach it to a newcomer. All of these situations lead to reflection on the premises of the practice, and all of them are routine moments *within* any practice. This is not to say that at these moments the practitioner steps outside of the practice into an abstract, theoretical state. No such step is necessary or desirable. Only an insider, intimately familiar with the fine details of the practice, would bother to raise such questions, and raising such questions can only occur inside of the practice.

Here is a basketball example: Some players are putting together a game at a backyard basket, a place where most of them have never played before. In such circumstances, none of the official rules that regulate court space can apply. There are no out-of-bounds markers, no foul line, no three-point arc, no lines to define the lane under the basket, so local ground rules must be created by the negotiation of the players. Maybe one of them owns this backyard, so he has to explain to the others that the boundaries of the court are by convention the end of the blacktop and the rear wall of the kitchen, or whatever. In the midst of the game, one of the players may just camp out under the basket, taking advantage of the absence of a clearly defined lane, where during an official game a player can stay only for a three count. If there is no lane, it might seem obvious to him, then there is no rule in play. But one of the others might gripe about "three seconds," on what seems to *him* the obvious grounds that the spirit of the rule should be in play, even if the lines are not on the court. The offender might refuse to listen, secure in his own "obvious" interpretation. One of my friends in such a situation would begin to count—loudly—"six, seven, eight, nine," calling out the offending player and embarrassing him into compliance. Such negotiations are of the essence of the practice. They occur, as de Certeau and Bourdieu would say, "on the wing," in the temporal flow, the give and take, of the practice. But in my terms they are moments of theory, moments when the habitus is being brought into question by the practitioners themselves. Not only are they thinking about and discussing the relationship between official rules and local customs, they are negotiating questions of interpersonal power and practice-specific fairness. They know what they are doing.

This is an important point for me, of course, because this study is based on the proposition that one can give an account of a practice from within it, relying on insider experience. Cultural practices have a strong personal dimension, since they are the sources from which individuals learn the cultural styles that they identify as their *personal* styles. Individuals commit so much of themselves and their daily lives to certain cultural practices that these practices become central to their personal identities. And if we remember the sheer number and diversity of cultural practices, then we can see the power they have in shaping subjectivity. For several years now as a writing teacher I have been encouraging students to write about the practices of everyday life that matter most to them, on the conviction that they will learn much about themselves as well as their social behavior and relationships. For me, then, this exploration of the culture of basketball begins in my own experience of the game, my own engagement with its practices, and my relationship with hundreds of other players that I have encountered, enhanced, I hope, by years of reading on the cultural issues that the game raises but never straying from the insights produced by direct engagement.

I have been involved with basketball as a player or fan since the 1950s. My earliest memory of the game is going with my father to the outdoor courts near Overbrook High School in West Philadelphia to see a young player who was dominating the older guys in a summer league—Wilt Chamberlain. Almost since the beginning of the game, Philadelphia has produced great players and great teams on every level of the game. I went to high school games, college games, and professional games throughout my childhood. When I was seven I went with my older sister and her boyfriend to see our West Catholic High School team get blown out in the city championship by Chamberlain in his senior year at Overbrook. I went with my dad to see the Philadelphia Warriors at the smoky, crowded Convention Hall when they played the Boston Celtics with Bob Cousy and Bill Russell. I remember standing at the end of the court as the Boston players came through the crowd to start the game, booed and cursed at every step. As these early memories suggest, I was a fan before I was a player, and the experience of being in a crowd, energized by the game, immersed in the group emotion, remains very powerful for me.

The most exciting basketball in Philadelphia in the 1950s and 1960s was the "Big Five"—Villanova, Penn, LaSalle, St. Joseph's, and Temple—all of which were national collegiate powers during this era. Growing up as a Catholic schoolboy, it was inevitable that I would attend one of the local Catholic colleges, and I do not exaggerate when I say that I chose LaSalle in great part because I saw that it was assembling a dominant team. By the time I was a junior in college, it was ranked second in the country (the next year it was put on probation by the National Collegiate Athletic Association [NCAA], but that is another story). All of the Big Five teams at the time played their home games at The Palestra, the arena on the University of Pennsylvania campus in West Philadelphia. When they played against each other, half the crowd was for one team and half for the other, so the noise never stopped, and the emotional pitch of the games was very high. The Palestra developed a legendary status as a basketball arena, and as a fan I feel privileged to have been a part of that experience. I remember being a lovesick twenty year old, recently broken up with the woman who would later become my wife, going to a LaSalle-Villanova game and completely forgetting my sorrow, caught up in the frenzy of the game and the crowd. Just recently, my daughter, whose fiance was serving in Iraq, went to a North Carolina-Duke game and experienced the same emotions. These fan experiences of my childhood and youth taught me about the *local* nature of basketball practice. For me basketball was a matter of neighborhood, school, ethnic affiliation, religious identity, and city loyalties. I grew up around people who identified strongly with the teams that represented them, and who saw in the game an ethical, cultural character that in turn defined their own identities.

My experience as a basketball player has always been in the pickup game. I was never good enough to play for a school team, but I played endlessly on courts in backyards, schoolyards, recreation centers, church halls, and school gyms. I played intramural ball in high school and college and later in industrial leagues as an adult, but never on elite-level teams in highly competitive organized basketball. As a teenager and college student, with whichever friends wanted to play at a given moment, we roamed from court to court looking for games. I still think of an outdoor court on a hot summer night as the ideal situation for basketball. I always liked to play with and against players who were better than I was, so I had to survive on muscle and intelligence against their talent and skill. In and around Philadelphia, pickup games were highly sophisticated, with players who had internalized the mental game, so there were picks away from the ball, lots of help on defense, and uncanny passes. I was never better than mediocre, but I played a lot of good ball.

As an adult, I had the great fortune to find a game that has kept me playing into my fifties. All too often players think of basketball as a young person's game, to be abandoned for golf or tennis when adulthood settles in. But around the country there are now hundreds of local runs in which players into their sixties and even their seventies are still playing full-court basketball. As a college teacher, I have been part of a noontime "oldguygame" since the early 1980s. About a year ago I finally had to retire from the full-court game, because of bone spurs and chronic weak ankles. Now I am limited to half-court games, which I hope I can play as long as I live. At the core of the experience that is the foundation of this book are my more than twenty years of playing in the noontime game in the Broome-Kirk gym on the campus of Appalachian State University. Similar games are found on almost all college campuses, open to faculty, staff, and community players. An internet search with the key words "noontime basketball," will reveal scores of sites that suggest the extent and variety of the phenomenon. They are classic local "runs," many of them with long histories, and all of them with distinct local cultures. As I discuss in the chapter on basketball communities, there are many other kinds of runs, at workplaces, churches, prisons, military installations, YMCAs, and health centers. My own experience with the local culture in Broome-Kirk certainly colors my view of basketball culture in general, but it also is a constant reminder that there are *many* local basketball cultures, as many as there are local runs.

The quality of play at Broome-Kirk is relatively high. Over the years there have been ex-college players, ex-high school stars, and even one guy who played for about three games in the National Basketball Association (NBA). There are many lifelong pickup players like myself, and some people who play more for the workout than for the basketball. Ages range from the mid-twenties to mid-sixties, and most players are in good physical condition. The game is full-court, with a lot of running, though the number of fast breaks decreases as the hour or so winds down. The games are fairly competitive, but the fact that many of us work together keeps down the level of physical intensity. Because of the years of experience most players bring to the game, the cognitive level of play is very high. Players know each others' moves and tendencies, so there are a lot of clever passes and subtle interactions. Players are able to anticipate others' moves, leading to constant adjustments and readjustments on offense and defense. Good young players who join the run often enjoy the high level of the mental game, the moves and countermoves. That is, it is a fairly typical oldguygame, one in which many players can stay happy for a long time.

The game also has a very positive affect. It includes faculty, administrators, coaches, staff, and a few local players from off campus who know about the game. As I will discuss later, the game therefore breaks down some barriers, bringing together in this practice people who would otherwise never meet. There are occasional animosities, usually between players who perceive the level of competition differently. But there is a general consensus that we want a competitive game but not a hyperaggressive game—competitive enough to generate a sense of commitment, but without damaging the fabric of the community. This consensus is in part a function of the fact that we all live in a fairly small town and therefore have other points of social connection, and in part a function of our age. Younger players with an excess of testosterone and adrenaline quickly become socialized into the prevalent playing style, or they decide to leave the game.

The extended group of players frequenting the game is fairly homogeneous. Currently all of the players are male, though over the years several women have played comfortably and successfully. Reflecting the racial composition of our university and town, the players are mostly white, though there have always been black players, almost all of whom have felt at home in the game. The game has tended to retain players for very long periods, so players tend to know each other well, over many years. Strands of diversity exist in the community of players, especially in terms of social class, which has ranged from senior administrators and successful business professionals to groundskeeping and housekeeping staff. There also is a religious diversity in the group, especially because several ministers from the town have found the game. Players are therefore faced with the challenge of interacting and cooperating with representatives of different social groups and lifestyles, but they can rely on some social commonalities that ease cooperation.

From my experience in this game I have learned a number of lessons that I have put into play in this book. I have learned to look past the macho bluster of elite-level, televised basketball to find a much more complex form of masculinity at work in the game. I have learned to appreciate the beauty and complexity of even the most ordinary game. I also have learned to appreciate the "localness" of basketball, recognizing that every game develops its own unique ethical style, movement patterns, and cognitive habits. I have understood the emotional intensity of the game and the many ways that it depends on shared interpersonal histories and relationships. All of these themes play a role in this study, shaping my observations of the game's details.

Most importantly, my experience in this game and in the many others in which I have played over the years has convinced me that the essence of basketball is not the NBA or the NCAA tournament but the pickup game, even the most casual session of putting up a few shots at a picnic or a family gathering. Unlike football, for example, which requires for its ideal form of play the organization and institutional support that only a formal game can provide, basketball is inherently a simple game that needs only a rim and a ball. Of course there is sandlot football, touch football, but they are only pared-down versions of the real thing, which requires referees, timekeepers, helmets and pads, and coaches and boosters. Basketball, on the other hand, is the purest when it is the simplest, when the least institutional apparatus is in force. No coaches, no referees, no clock, no spectators, no general managers or athletic directors. Just a court, a few players, some time to play. It is under those conditions that the creativity and flow of the game exist in their ideal state. Pickup basketball is made up in the moment, by the players themselves, with no one to tell them how to do it, what decisions to make, or how to relate to each other. They have to improvise it all, in the real-time experience of the game. At its best, organized, elite-level ball aspires to that creative flow, despite the efforts of coaches and officials and media packagers to submit it to their disciplines. Pickup basketball is a rough democracy, created by the players and for the players, and in that sense the game finds its purest expression on the schoolyard, in the driveway, in the church hall, or at the Y, not at Madison

Square Garden or the Staples Center. Almost all players, even at the NBA level, would agree with this assessment, romantic as it seems.

In pickup ball the players themselves make all of the important decisions. In the absence of coaches, they create strategy on the run and make the million micro-decisions necessary for the simplest of maneuvers. They play off of each other's decisions, keeping up a keen awareness of the emerging situation on the floor. In the absence of referees, they make all of the calls in the game, including foul calls, out-of-bounds decisions, and rule violations. There is no authority figure on the court, so all calls must be negotiated instantaneously by the players. In the absence of league commissioners and general managers, players decide how teams will be selected, how substitutes will be used, how the court will be configured, how many points the game will total, and how the next team to enter the game will be constituted. And in the process of making these decisions, they construct the culture of the game, the habitus of their practice.

The differences between pickup ball and organized, elite basketball become an important theme in this study. Although I enjoy watching professional and college basketball on television, I recognize that organized basketball is a disciplinary structure in which players are subject to the power of coaches, bureaucrats, and team owners. Bero Rigauer, in his trenchant study *Sport and Work*, defines modern sport in the following terms: "discipline, authority, competition, achievement, goal-oriented rationality, organization, and bureaucratization" (1981, 1), and therefore he sees it as an embodiment of the norms of industrial society. In contrast, Michael Novak's *The Joy of Sports*, which sees the primal source of sports as "a deep natural impulse that is radically religious: an impulse of freedom, respect for ritual limits, a zest for symbolic meaning, and a longing for perfection" (1976, 19), seems hopelessly romantic, a willful denial of the role that sports can play in disciplining young people, training them to accept authority and follow orders. When I think about organized basketball, Rigauer's point seems undeniable, but when I think about pickup ball, I am willing to risk Novak's romanticism. Pickup ball is not bureaucratized; it is organized and disciplined only by the players present at the moment of play, and "goal-oriented rationality" is foreign to its spirit. Pickup ball really is *play* rather than organized sport, and although its culture is determined in part by its social circumstances, its players engage in a rough cultural democracy, creating their own practice right there on the court. In a disciplined, hierarchical society, pickup ball offers a real alternative—not a radical rejection of modern structures of authority but at least a momentary evasion, a model of the improvisations that de Certeau admires, the tactics by which power can be faked out, set aside for the moment of play.

I should note that many of the features I see in basketball as a
cultural practice are not unique to basketball. For example, the improvised, real-time decision making of basketball is also present in soccer. The
grace and beauty of basketball movement also can be seen in football and
in many other sports. The fan communities that arise around basketball
have arisen around almost all sports, but the *array* of practices making up
the game is unique. The culture of basketball communities is a function of
the characteristics of the game itself. As players construct a culture around
the game, they extend its array of practices into the infrastructure that
supports it. Thus, for example, the endless interpersonal negotiation that the
game itself requires extends into the openness to negotiation that characterizes basketball culture. Every ongoing pickup game, for example, has to
create its own method for choosing sides. There is no rule book to decide
the process—it must be negotiated over time, and it constantly adapts to the
needs of the players present. The game creates habits of mind and body
unlike any other sport, and it is surrounded by its own unique culture.

Because I rely so much on my own experiences of the game, there
are some limits to this study that I should acknowledge. First, I have little
to say about the experience of organized teams in official leagues. Obviously there is an entire cultural experience in such environments, but my
only knowledge of that culture is as a fan who has read the usual newspaper and magazine articles about locker room politics and the complex
relationships between coaches and players. I have certainly learned much
about the practices of the game by watching television coverage of elite
ball, but because television abstracts the performance from its context, the
culture of the elite game is almost invisible to outsiders. Also, I do not
write directly about the women's game, which I follow as a fan but with
which I have little direct experience. I can and do make a few guesses
about whether my understandings of basketball culture would apply to the
women's game, but I do not claim any great expertise. Finally, this book is
limited by my own limits of experience in the game. I have not played
overseas, I have not played often in majority black games, I have not
played in prisons or on military bases or in church leagues, and so on. I
have visited many games and talked to players with a vast array of experiences, but I base my insights on my own experience, realizing, I hope,
that the game is different in all of those different circumstances. In fact,
that *difference* is one of my central points. There is no such thing as a
basketball culture—there are *many* basketball cultures, as distinct as the
local practices that create them. This book, then, is the product of one
player with one history in the practice, trying to articulate the complex
local constructions of many players with their many histories.

The first chapter of the book examines the ethical practices of the game. Discussions of the *rightness* of play are remarkably common in basketball, at every level of the game, from the elite to the most casual. The ethical tone of the game is the result of a complex mix of official rules that govern play, virtues that arise out of the pursuit of the pleasure proper to the game, and locally negotiated ethical decisions that reflect players' personal relationships and histories. Every single game evolves its own ethical tone—some are bitterly competitive and cutthroat, while some are easygoing and mild—and local basketball cultures develop over time a characteristic ethical style, assented to tacitly by all who play in that local run, and maintained quite consciously by the leading players in the community. This chapter demonstrates that basketball communities are self-governing, creating their own moral constraints and policing their own practice. The ethical dimension of the habitus of the practice clearly demonstrates that the players themselves are responsible for the values and moral dispositions of the game.

The second chapter considers the physical culture of the game—its articulation of space and its characteristic kinetic styles. Once again the theme of negotiation arises, in that the rules regulating space are often worked out on the local level. The game of basketball moves ten large bodies at high speed through a limited and demarcated space and thus encourages physical grace and cooperative movement. The chapter emphasizes the beauty of the game, comparing it to dance and other movement systems. It also considers the physical intimacy of the game, which requires close and intense physical contact among players. This deployment of bodies in the game constructs a complex experience of masculinity for the men who play it. I argue that basketball, despite the often vivid hypermasculinity of its media images, has the potential to provide a more progressive, less predictable enactment of gender identity. In a culture that often encourages men to be intensely competitive and homophobic in their relationships with other men, basketball encourages nonviolent and nonsexual physical contact and creates strong affective ties. The spatial, physical, and kinetic habits of the practice tell us much about the culture of basketball.

The third chapter turns to the mental dispositions of the practice. Just as basketball teaches habits of the body, it teaches habits of the mind. Both de Certeau and Bourdieu use sports as an example of the way that practices unfold in time, and basketball certainly does operate as a mental game in the unfolding of temporal exchanges among the players. Especially in pickup ball, where there are no coaches and no efforts to establish a "game plan," decisions happen in real time, in reaction to events within the game. This improvisation involves ten people, each unaware of the mental process of all the others, yet all making decisions that react to the cues sent out by every player at every moment of the game. Basketball has a high decision frequency, with many independent agents making many decisions simultaneously. Yet even players who have never met each other before can collaborate in successful play. And players who have learned each other's moves and mental habits over time are routinely capable of minor miracles, anticipating reactions that have not yet occurred to the other players. I characterize the mental disposition of the game as "group, real-time, improvised decision making," and I therefore see basketball as a rich and complex cognitive practice.

Because players move and think together on the court, connecting cognitively, physically, and emotionally, they are capable of creating rich and meaningful communities. The fourth chapter of this book looks closely at these communities, ranging from intense local groups to the global phenomenon that is contemporary basketball. Using Etienne Wegner's work on "communities of practice," I argue that the practice of basketball generates communities that in turn produce the culture of the game. The most vital of these communities are "runs," ongoing local games that attract a shifting but stable group of players, often over many years. These groups make the decisions that create the habitus for their practice, internalized by all of the members of the group and taught to newcomers. I also argue that basketball creates looser "communities of interest" around the practice among fans and followers of the sport. These fan communities also develop distinctive cultural formations, habits of interpretation, and evaluation. These local communities of players and fans have in recent years become a global phenomenon, as television and other forms of cultural contact have spread this American game to virtually every country on the planet. The chapter therefore considers the relationships between local and global communities focused around a shared practice. I make the argument that communities of practice and communities of interest have the potential to cut across the divides created by identity communities organized around race, gender, sexual orientation, ethnicity, nation, religion, and so on. A practice such as basketball becomes an important element in personal identity for many people, but it does not bring with it the deep commitments that these identity communities require. Communities of practice can therefore connect individuals from diverse groups in a meaningful but nondivisive way.

The fifth chapter takes up the controversial issue of race within the basketball community. Because elite levels of the sport are dominated by African American players, race is an important issue within the community. The dominance of black players has led some white racist sport fans to shun the game or to see it in simple, stereotyped terms, and it has led many black cultural critics to analyze the game as an element in the African American cultural tradition. This chapter argues that television and other media coverage of the game tend to reinforce racial stereotypes, casting the black player as the natural athlete and the white player as the hard-working coach on the floor. However, within the basketball community, such simple oppositions often are brought into question. Fans can and do easily refer to players who are counterexamples and who defy racial expectations. And players themselves quickly find that the stereotypes must be abandoned in the face of the actual players in a given game, players whose strengths and weaknesses cannot be reduced to simple racial categories. I therefore argue that basketball is one of the few cultural sites in which a healthy discourse and debate about race is possible within American society. Basketball as a cultural practice does not overcome racial divides, but it does bring people with diverse racial identities together around a shared practice that raises complex questions about racial identity itself.

The sixth and seventh chapters of the book deal with media representations of basketball. No local basketball community is immune to the representations of the practice current in mass media. Those representations become elements in the identity of members of the community, in part because they constitute the public face of the practice, the images that are available to outsiders and casual observers. The sixth chapter therefore focuses critical attention on television coverage of the game, which domesticates and submits it to the powerful gaze of its spectators, reinforcing conventional ideologies of gender and race for a mainstream audience. The chapter looks at the visual style of TV coverage, in terms of camera work, editing, and composition, as well as the discursive practices of play-by-play announcers and analysts, all of which operate to place simplifying frames of reference around a complex culture. Television removes basketball from its local contexts, reducing the variety of the game to a bland sameness in which every game in every context is framed within the same visual and verbal patterns.

If television coverage therefore radically simplifies the practice, then basketball films are more successful in representing the cultural diversity of the game. The seventh chapter examines recent films about basketball, noting the ways in which their richer narrative context allows them to get at the local cultures and idiosyncratic personal textures that the game takes on in its varied manifestations. Because of the conventions of realistic film narrative, which require individualized characterization and specific physical and social settings, basketball culture is better served by film than by the decontextualizing tendencies of television coverage. Taken together, recent basketball films provide a rich ethnographic account of basketball as a cultural practice.

Throughout this book I write not only as a member of the basketball community but also as a lover of the game. Sports rightly have their cultural critics, and I cite many of them in this study. Sports can teach cruelty and encourage a hypercompetitive mentality. They can be used to reinforce a spurious and narrow nationalism, male dominance, homophobia, racism, and violence. They can be integrated into media marketing systems that use them as little more than narcotic diversions or opportunities to advertise the latest snack food or athletic shoe. But when you get away from organized sports and media images, you come into contact with a much richer cultural phenomenon. Pickup basketball is not about advertising hype or political power or ideological manipulation. It is about friendly competition, rich relationships, local communities, and the pleasure of play. People engaged in that practice create in it and get from it a culture that sustains them and becomes part of their everyday life. Much of this cultural work occurs under the radar of sociological and cultural analysis, because it is apparently so casual and mundane. Not much appears to be at stake when some kids shoot hoops in their backyard, or when coworkers decide to start an after-work pickup game. No grand cultural policy enters into their thinking. No media coverage calls them to the public's attention. But it is in these almost invisible practices of everyday life that cultures are created. Basketball is just one of those practices, but the closer you look at it the more you can see it as an instance of how ordinary people quietly create the fabric of our cultural life.

Chapter 2

The Ethics of Basketball

"Sports build character" is a shopworn, often hypocritical phrase. I associate it with sober-minded YMCA directors and sleazy college coaches trying to sound like "educators." It is our culture's official excuse for allowing ourselves to indulge in the joy of play and its cover-up of the often abusive disciplines of organized sport. But there is an inescapable truth to the cliche. Anyone who plays a sport, especially for a long time, learns from it particular habits of mind, modes of decision making, and strategies of moral judgment. Different sports provide different opportunities for learning and thus tend to produce different kinds of "character." Golf, for example, has a strict ethic of personal accountability—serious players will turn themselves in for small procedural infractions. Football imposes strict limits on what it defines as acceptable violence. Mixed-doubles tennis teaches exquisite forms of courtesy and aggression. So what are the moral lessons of basketball? What judgments are required, and how are those judgments made? What is the ethical dimension of the culture of basketball?

The answers to these questions move us beyond basketball itself into the popular culture of which it is an important part. According to the Sporting Goods Manufacturing Association, 35 million Americans play basketball, making it the most popular team sport in the country. Millions more are avid fans who follow the game through media coverage, which often focuses on its ethical dimension—think of the fan radio and journalistic laments over the flamboyant styles of the game's young gangsta millionaires. Basketball also has become a central element in other forms of popular culture—in films, television shows, advertising, youth fashion, and popular music. The NBA, Nike, and ESPN are the most visible of the

23

economic forces that have pushed basketball to the center of the national consciousness and made the game into an international icon for American youth and prosperity. The "character" that basketball encourages is thus a major factor in the "character" of American and, increasingly, global culture.

Basketball is a rigorously ethical game. Physical contact is more controlled than in football, and though there is a lot of pushing and jockeying for position, there is surprisingly little outright violence, even though the elite game now attracts bigger and stronger players than ever in its history. Certain specific acts of violence are outright despised. One is "undercutting," taking the legs out from under a jumping player. Jumps in basketball leave a player vulnerable, and though it is okay to bump someone in the air, it is never okay to undercut him. The risk of injury is too high, and the fear of falling is too primal. The result is almost always a fight. "No undercutting" is as close to a universal rule as there is in basketball, but subtle ethical issues around it produce less unanimity. One way to unsettle a hot shooter is to *pretend* to undercut him. You can dip your shoulder and take a first step toward the player, and as you shy away you can create enough anxiety to distract the shot. The "morality" of this move is more ambiguous and situational. In organized ball you see it regularly, though even there it seems questionable, a slick move to cover up poor defense—beneath a good player's dignity. In some highly competitive pickup games it is ordinary practice, along with a whole array of elbows, pushes in the back, and hacks on the arm. In my "oldguygame" it has all but disappeared. We have tacitly agreed that we can do without what now seems like a childish trick. We do not talk about this issue, but we could if we needed to. As a community of basketball players we have negotiated our own ethic, just as other communities of players have devised their own, from the NBA down to the most casual driveway game. The subtle and coherent but various and changing ethics of the game define basketball as a cultural practice, one that reveals much about contemporary American culture and maybe something about ethics as such.

Since the ethic of basketball has this strong *local* quality, every game develops its own distinctive ethical style. In my oldguygame the key to the ethical tone is the fact that we all know each other outside of the game and all have to live together in our work and civic lives. Despite the intensity of the contest, there is restraint and tolerance, and as a result serious infractions against the code of the game are rare. But a book such as Michael Moran's (1991) *Nothing but Net: An Essay on the Culture of Pickup Basketball* tells a very different story about the ethical tone of a game at an outdoor court in a public park, where no one knows the other players outside of the context of the game. There the level of violence is higher, and selfish, showboat play is more common. This is not to say that there is no ethic in their game, just a different ethic encouraged by a different situation. In our game, with older players and with social constraints in place, the ethic discourages violence and encourages selfless play.

The ethic of basketball is not just a set of negative rules regulating violence. It also is a set of positive encouragements to play the game as the game seems to want to be played, as a team game, a game of passing and cutting and picks and rolls and precision alleyoop passes, moves that require subtle communication and anticipation. This pursuit of excellence in the practice of the game is encouraged by an array of microspecific, informal rules that guide every move and countermove. These rules are drilled into players on organized teams by coaches, and they are learned by pickup players from experience and from the models set by other players. They are not universals, since they are always subject to local adaptations and revisions, but they are widely shared general guidelines. Some examples follow:

Call the pick. A pick is a maneuver in which an offensive player gets in the way of a defensive player who is covering another man. If the player you are guarding is setting the pick, then it is your job to yell "watch right" or "pick right" so your teammate will know he is about to be blocked. If you do not call the pick, then your teammate will get clobbered, and he will let you know about it. "Call the pick, dammit" is a pretty common phrase on the court. The penalty for this failure is that your teammate will start feeling the pick before it gets there and will stop playing tough defense as his man cuts to the basket.

Find the open man. One of the most discouraging kinds of players is the gunner who will force up a shot after attracting two or three defenders. Most of these shots are wild and worthless, and they waste the efforts of teammates. Nobody likes to stand around and watch while a selfish player takes shot after shot, even if a fair number of them go in. Really good offensive players feel the double-team and find the man left open. Though this rule is widely accepted, there are some subtleties and local variants. First of all, some players *can* score consistently against the double-team, so in certain situations all you can do is say "good take" and hope they remember to pass now and then. And some players are so weak offensively that you would not pass it to them even if they were *wide* open. If Michael Jordan can beat the double-team, then he is not going to pass to some stiff. In my game, on the other hand, even the stiff feels comfortable taking the open shot. After all, we are out there to have fun and enjoy the game, so the ethic is, If you have an open shot, take it! We tend to compliment even the poorest shooters for taking the right shot.

Rest on offense. This is a rule that coaches have been preaching for generations. If you are tired, then it is more ethical to rest when your team has the ball. If you rest on defense then you hurt the whole team, but if you rest on offense then maybe you hurt only your own stats. This rule is a subset of the general feeling in basketball that defensive play is more virtuous than offensive play. On offense you get to score, to make your move, to show your skill. On defense your efforts are reactive rather than creative, and they often are overlooked. Coaches and television analysts will say that defense requires character. Defense is "blue collar"; it requires a good "work ethic." It shows dedication and team loyalty. The ethical player is a good defensive player.

If you're cold, stop shooting. Much of the force of the basketball ethic is directed at overly selfish play. If you are missing your outside shot on a given day, then the ethic requires you to start making good passes, setting picks, posting up under the basket, fighting for offensive rebounds—all of the ways other than shooting that a player can contribute to the team's offensive success. The exception to this rule applies to the *great* shooter: Even if a great shooter misses a few in a row, he has the right and duty to keep on shooting until the slump is over. As this last example suggests, part of the ethic involves ruthless honesty about your own abilities. You have to play your role, and it is foolish to try to be any kind of player other than the one you are.

Reward the player who hustles. If a big guy makes a great defensive play and then runs the court on the fast break, it is the duty of the point guard to get the ball back to the big guy in position for a shot. Running hard on the break, especially for a big player, is a tribute to conditioning and to the ethic that produced it. A point guard who ignores this gesture and takes the ball to the basket himself loses the confidence of his teammates because he does not acknowledge the reciprocity, the mutual giving, that is the unique pleasure of the game.

Examples could be multiplied indefinitely. The ethic of basketball is extensive and specific, and, remarkably, it is an ethic in motion. In the midst of fast and contested movement, with players making the instantaneous strategy decisions necessary in an improvisatory game, moral decisions are made with equal speed, guided by the ethical culture that the players tacitly share. It would be very rare that any player would articulate the rules as an organized system, but players routinely invoke specific rules and expectations, with full confidence that they will be understood by the other players. The *speed* of these moral decisions suggests an ethic so deeply held that it can be applied instantly, even in subtle or borderline situations. I have felt the shaping power of this ethic in my own life, even or especially at the times when I was not living up to it. And though I am not a professional ethical philosopher, I believe that the ethic of basketball can teach us something about ethics in general. Reflecting on the origin of this ethic and its modes of enactment might add to our understanding of how ethics operate in all of our cultural practices.

The ethics of basketball are a complex mix of official rules, sanctioned by governing bodies, ethical norms that arise out of the desire to maximize the pleasure of the practice, and local negotiations among players as to how the game will be played at this very moment, among the actual players gathered there. The ethical tone of every game is created by the players themselves, out of their histories in the game, their personal experiences, their ethical styles. Ongoing games, or *runs*, in basketball slang, in which roughly the same players play together in different combinations for years, certainly do develop distinct ethical cultures, even though all of them have internalized roughly the same general ethical norms. In most pickup games there is a lot of overt discussion of ethics. There is no referee present, so decisions about what is a foul and who knocked the ball out of bounds and whether that was traveling have to be made by the players themselves, in instantaneous negotiating sessions. Certainly there are official rules of the game, but in pickup ball what matters is how the local decisions tend to go. One of the distinctions between organized sports and more informal games is that, as Alan Ingham says, "games are democratic. They require inter-subjective negotiation to constitute rules that give us pleasurable satisfaction even if we get some bumps and lumps in the process" (2004, 16). Pickup games are willing to sacrifice the consistency of official rules for the more personal subtlety of negotiated settlements.

In many local runs, for example, some players routinely break one of the official rules of the game in almost every move they make. One player in my game has a devastating move to the basket in which he takes an extra step *every time*. But he has established that move as his own, and no one would think of making the call on him. They would need to make the same call every time he handled the ball, and that would surely lead to a confrontation. So the official rule is just negotiated away. Local games operate on unspoken precedents rather than abstract laws. We know that the official rule exists, and we do not hesitate to enforce it in other circumstances, but local custom has greater power than official regulation. Even the NBA has local exceptions to the official rules. Bill Russell, the great Celtics' center, reports that stars often get a "free foul" from the officials, in recognition of a personal style that has succeeded over the years, even if it falls outside of a strict construction of the rules.

The *unofficial* rules of the practice, the moral rules of thumb that I have just described, exist in a complicated relationship with local practice. Everyone knows about "Call the pick" and "Rest on defense" and all of the other generalizations that I have made about ethical play, but what matters are the negotiations of the moment, the interpersonal exchanges that the game requires. Was that a legitimate push, or was it excessive? Is that guy shooting too much, or is he making good shots? Are we going to play tough defense in this game, or are we just going to have fun? These and many other judgments about behavior aim to facilitate successful and pleasurable practice. It is a better game if we cooperate as a team, or if we control physical confrontations, or if the trash talk does not get too personal. Players internalize these norms throughout their history in the game, but in any given moment of play they encounter others who have a different set of norms, a different ethical style, and the negotiation goes on. The result is a complex ethical practice embodied in the players and emerging from their interactions.

One explanation of ethical behavior that therefore seems particularly inappropriate to pickup basketball is the argument that ethics are abstract principles that moral agents apply to specific cases. The virtue of an ethic, in this sense of the word, is its removal from the details of experience. In order to achieve justice we must have principles that transcend time and place, universal truths that will guide us in our murky, everyday lives. And these principles must align in a systematic, reasonable structure that can be grasped by the moral agent so that actions in the world can be morally informed. Angela Lumpkin, Sharon Kay Stall, and Jennifer M. Beller's book *Sports Ethics: Applications for Fair Play* invokes "universal guides or universal rules of conduct that govern our lives" (1985, 184) as the basis for ethics in sport. And we can see in Warren P. Fraleigh's (1984) work, *Right Actions in Sport: Ethics for Contestants,* the logical outcome of this approach. For Fraleigh sports are governed by a hierarchically ordered system of "guides and ends of right action," rules for moral behavior that can be applied consistently in local circumstances. For example, what Fraleigh calls "the guide of equal opportunity for optimal performance" is one of the fundamental principles that necessarily entails a more specific moral rule that he calls "the guide of expulsion," which requires that "Contest officials shall expel from the remainder of the contest any participant who, in their judgment, inappropriately attempts to decrease an opponent's performance effectiveness or to increase his/her own more than once in a contest" (1984, 153). In his system there is a manifest logic that proceeds from universal and rational principles to specific ethical applications. Reason is the key to the system, since Fraleigh sees it as the duty of the ethical participant and the official who must make judgment calls to resist the pressures of the emotional situation and to act in accordance with a universal justice. Fraleigh's work implies a transcultural, universal truth that can be discovered by human reason and that can apply as a basis for just action in all circumstances, across lines of history and culture.

Such universalist reasoning seems particularly out of place in the intensely local world of basketball. There are decidedly different ethics in play in my oldguygame, and in the student games at the campus rec center, and in the driveway of a suburban house, and in the games at the Rucker league in Harlem, and in the NBA game, and in the women's game, and in the game at a housing complex in Paris. The ethic is discernably different even in the two games in my gym, one game dominated by players a little younger than the other. These differences do not derive from metaphysical disputes but from the mix of personalities, playing skills, and social relations in all of these games. For example, taking an intentional foul after you have been beaten on defense is much less acceptable in the game I play in than in many other pickup games. And of course in the NBA such fouls do not even register on the ethical scale—they are just part of the game. No one in these games reasons through their position on this issue on the basis of their abstract notions of justice; rather, they feel their way toward an acceptable code of behavior, given the goals and expectations of their particular game.

The universalist-rationalist model also seems much too rigid for the improvisatory style of the game. Obviously no one could make such logical deductions in the midst of a game, but I cannot accept even the more convincing notion that instantaneous decisions put into play an abstract logic that can be articulated after the fact in a systematic fashion, even if the decision was made in a flash. Bourdieu has beautifully described the decision-making process of a player deeply engaged in the practice of a game:

> A player who is involved and caught up in the game adjusts not to what he sees but to what he fore-sees, sees in advance in the directly perceived present; he passes the ball not to the spot where his team-mate is but to the spot he will reach—before his opponent—a moment later, anticipating the anticipations of the others and, as when "selling a dummy," seeking to confound them. He decides in terms of objective probabilities, that is, in response to an overall, instantaneous assessment of the whole set of his team-mates, seen not as they are but in their impending positions. And he does so "on the spot," "in the twinkling of an eye," "in the heat of the moment," that is, in conditions which exclude distance, perspective, detachment and reflexion. He is launched into the impending future, present in the imminent moment, and, abdicating the possibility of suspending at every

moment the ecstasis that projects him into the probable, he
identifies himself with the imminent future of the world, pos-
tulating the continuity of time. (Bourdieu 1990, 81–82)

Or, to put it another way, players are *busy*! They are not abstracted,
they are engaged, and their ethic must emerge from their engagement, or
else it could not achieve its undeniably swift and almost instinctive immediacy. The practice of basketball suggests that ethics do not derive from
ontology, they derive from practice within a community. They are, therefore, local, historical, contingent, shifting, disputed—anything but abstract
and universal. They are not derived by reason; they arise from practice.
They are not top-down, but bottom-up. But they are no less in force for
lacking an ontological ground. Their force derives from their verification
in and through the practice itself.

Another approach to the ethic of sport that I find ultimately dissatis-
fying is ideological analysis. From this perspective the function of rules in
games is to teach players the importance of rules in everyday life, to teach
the virtue of obedience to legitimate authority. As John Hargreaves says,
sport can be seen as an integral part of "the training of a docile labor
force . . . inculcating an acceptance of the kind of work discipline demanded
in the modern production process, and encouraging a positive orientation to
hard work as such" (Hargreaves 1992, 41). More generally, sport can be seen
as "inculcating and expressing the quintessential ideology in capitalist society: egoistic, aggressive individualism, ruthless competition, the myth of
equality of opportunity, together with authoritarianism, elitism, chauvinism,
sexism, militarism and imperialism" (1992, 41–42). Rigauer (1981), in *Sport
and Work*, sees athletes subordinating themselves to bureaucratic controls
that regulate and rationally organize competition, just as workers must subject themselves to the rules of work set by owners and managers. The rules
of games, especially in the spectacle of media sport, are vivid justifications
of the rules we come to accept as necessary in all social interactions.

The limits of ideology critique in this context seem to me to be
threefold. First, ideological analysis seems to assume that the ethic of the
game transfers directly into behavior outside of the game, and, as I will
argue later, that assumption is highly questionable in a culture in which all
subjects engage in *many* practices. Second, reducing the ethic of the game
to a form of brainwashing overestimates the extent to which the meaning
of the game is controlled by power elites. Sports, especially for adults, are
voluntary associations, sustained by the agency of the people who choose
the game. They bring to the game their own agendas, their own moral
beliefs and political orientations. Each derives from the experience of the
game lessons that are not fully controlled by the dominant, institutional

"meaning" of the game. Basketball and other team games may be put to the task of teaching compliant teamwork in the workplace, but there is no guarantee that the message will be passively received. Players and spectators are moral and intellectual agents who make their own meanings out of the experience of play. Third, ideological analysis underestimates the importance of pleasure in the game, or depicts pleasure simply as the sugar that helps the ideological medicine go down. My conviction is that the ethic of basketball arises out of the pleasure of the game itself. The selflessness at the heart of this ethic is not a good in itself or a good for the world of work, it is a good *in the game*. It maximizes pleasure for all of the players. The ethic of selflessness matters only because the good of the game demands a principle to affirm practices that increase pleasure. "The team" is important in the ethic of basketball not because it reinforces what are defined as desirable economic traits—which it may well do—but because the pleasure of the game is undeniably greater when the players are playing together.

This ideological critique of sports seems particularly limited when it comes to pickup basketball, in which the rules that matter most are generated by the players themselves. Rigauer says that "the less the form of athletic action is rule-bound and subordinated to the value of achievement, the more likely that action is to disintegrate the behavioral patterns of industrial society" (1981, 103). Organized sport may strive to produce a docile workforce, but if the players themselves engage in a rough moral democracy, then their docility is not assured. Jean Paul Sartre has said that play is an exemplary instance of human freedom in that the individual "consents to play only according to the rules which he himself has established and defined" (1995, 110). In pickup ball the process of establishing the rules is more social than Sartre suggests—the players work in a loose, intersubjective process to define the local rules—but he is right to see in this process an expression of freedom and self-government rather than a docile acceptance of rules established by alien powers.

Much more satisfying to me is the concept of an ethic as the logic of a practice. In this context two associations of the word "practice" appeal to me—it speaks of institutions and social groups but also of spirituality and community. An ongoing basketball game generally requires an institution or a social group to maintain it. Basketball gets played by people who work together, or go to school or church together, or live in the same neighborhood. A fairly large number of people have to conspire to find time together, and they have to use a space that is usually controlled by some kind of organization. As a result, the practice of basketball almost always occurs within social and organizational networks. It is part of the complex fabric of social relations within a culture. Its ethic will therefore inevitably reflect the influence of its social context. But basketball also can be thought of as a spiritual "practice," such as yoga or tai-chi or dance, a physical regimen in which a spiritual dimension can be found. I hesitate to go into this point too deeply, thinking of my hardheaded and ironic friends in the game who are at this point rolling their eyes. But engaging in the practice of basketball over a long period of time leads players into a complex state of consciousness—totally concentrated on the moment, highly aware of bodies in motion in a complex space, improvising movement within a knowledge so deep that it can hardly be articulated, collaborating in ways that sometimes seem psychic. In such a heightened state of awareness, evoked powerfully in Phil Jackson's (1995) *Sacred Hoops*, a socialized ethic can become a personal code, a way of being in the world. Thinking about the ethic of basketball as the logic of a practice therefore seems to have great explanatory power.

Here is Alasdair MacIntyre's definition of the term, from his book *After Virtue*:

> By a "practice" I am going to mean any coherent and complex form of socially established cooperative human activity through which goods internal to that form of activity are realized in the course of trying to achieve those standards of excellence which are appropriate to, and partially definitive of, that form of activity, with the result that human powers to achieve excellence, and human conceptions of the ends and goods involved, are systematically extended. (1994, 187)

MacIntyre explicitly includes sports among his examples, largely because they are so frequently pursued for the sheer joy of the "goods internal to that form of activity." Of course people play basketball for external goods such as money or a college scholarship, but the vast majority of pickup players—think of those 35 million—play because the game itself is deeply satisfying to them, more deeply so as they develop in the practice. For MacIntyre the ethic of a practice affirms the attitudes and behaviors that enhance excellence in the practice. Practices are important to MacIntyre because they are the sites in modern culture that impart to life a clear telos that makes sense of right actions. MacIntyre's analysis of modern moral judgment is that it has become incoherent because the culture lacks a shared sense of human nature and purpose that might ground a shared ethic. Practices are activities in which that telos is regained, at least in a socially specific form. The nature and purposes of human action are understandable at least within the sphere of the practice.

The ethic of basketball develops in players as they mature in the game. It does not exist as a systematized whole, but rather it emerges over time. Young players who already have it, such as Tim Duncan of the San Antonio Spurs of the NBA, for example, who seemed to embody the ethic of the game when he was a freshman in college, come to seem like spiritual marvels, wise before their years. But for most players the ethic is learned over years of practice, move after move, nuances always coming clearer. The "goods internal" to the game become clearer too. Foremost among those is the pleasure of collaborative improvisation—the "give and go"—and much of the ethic of the game flows from that pleasure. MacIntyre allows us to think of ethics not as a set of prohibitions against "evil" but as a set of beliefs that encourages behavior directed at joy. The ethic of basketball aims to produce joy; it seeks that heightened state of awareness and rewards the tiny behaviors that make it possible. In this sense the ethic of basketball seems to me to do good cultural work. It challenges our ordinary sense of ethics as censure wielded by power. The notion that the ethics of practices might be searches for particular forms of pleasure may explain some of our fascination with sport and may cast *play* as a counterforce to power.

Bourdieu's (1990) contribution to understanding the ethics of basketball is his emphasis on how deeply practices are incorporated. The ethic is immanent in the practice, in the attitudes, beliefs, and actions that it encourages. An outside analyst might be able to articulate the logic as a system, but the practitioner would experience it as a set of habits, attitudes, and procedures inherent in the practice. The practitioner is so caught up in the practice that its ethical logic seems self-evident. It therefore makes possible instantaneous ethical actions and judgments.

If the ethic of basketball is the logic of a practice in this sense, then the ethic can be put into play with speed and unself-consciousness. To a player in the moment of play, the ethic is obvious; it is right on the face of the game. But the player's grasp of the ethic is not unchangeable. It grows through each encounter with new players, with their own ethical histories, in every game played, each with its own ethical tone. At any moment in that developmental process, the ethic may seem to be beyond question. In the press of the game, the player just does not have time to reflect. "Call the pick, dammit" comes out as quick as an exhale, in the breath that gets knocked out of you. But outside the game, in locker room conversation, elements of the ethic get discussed and analyzed. "That guy shoots too much." "Yeah, but he makes them." "But he's no damn fun to play with." "Yeah, but he plays some D." No one takes on the ethic as a system and questions its ontological ground, but everyone talks about the

ethic with the expertise of the experienced practitioner. As an ethic growing out of a practice, it is an insider production, not easily translatable to
someone outside of the practice. Knowledge of the ethic is required for
membership in the practice, and membership in the practice is required for
knowledge of the ethic.

I argue, then, that the ethic of basketball comes from the experience
of playing it. It does not derive from a divine principle of order or from
universal rights but from people having fun playing the game. Could the
ethic of basketball then not make us wonder if ethics as such derive from
joy, from taking pleasure in a practice? Basketball coaches might tell you
that they need to drill the ethic of the game into the unwilling heads of
their players. Moralists might tell you that ethics must be enforced by
righteous and just social powers. But if MacIntyre is right, and modern
moral life occurs inside of practices, and practices are aimed at "the goods
internal to the practice," then maybe we have to reject our commonsense
connection of ethics and authority. Maybe, over time in a specific practice,
an ethic will emerge.

Feminist thinking about ethics also has emphasized its local rather
than abstract-universal character. Patriarchal ethical systems claim to be
based on universal truths of human rights and duties. They rely on a moral
calculus that depends on the notion of absolute truth and justice. Carol
Gilligan contrasts the "formal and abstract" systems of "rights and rules"
with more feminist/feminine emphasis on a sense of "responsibility and
relationship" that is "contextual and narrative" (1982, 19). Nel Noddings
defines abstract thinking as a belief in an intellectual space "where a person's
thinking can take place clearly and logically in isolation from the complicating factors of particular persons, places, and circumstances." And she
contrasts this patriarchal mode of thinking about ethics with a feminist
"concretization" that produces an ethic in which "feelings can be modified
by the introduction of acts, the feelings of others, and personal histories"
(1984, 36–37). Feminist accounts of ethics emphasize local circumstances,
personal identities, and social relationships as central factors in moral
judgment. I cannot quite claim that basketball is a feminist practice, but
I would claim that the feminist account of ethics is a more adequate explanation of the nature and function of the ethic of basketball. Its ethic is
profoundly concretized; it adapts to the people, relationships, and situations of any particular game. The implicit rules of my oldguygame, for
example, have developed over the years as a complex adaptation to the
skill levels, personalities, and feelings of the players involved. As I mentioned earlier, even poor shooters are encouraged to shoot if they are open,
because we realize that feeling *right* about taking that shot adds to the
pleasure of the game. We realize that in other circumstances that encour-

agement would be out of place, and the same player would have to gain pleasure by passing up the shot, moving the ball to a better shooter. But in our game, the open shooter feels right about taking the shot, even if the odds against success are long.

A similar set of particular and personal judgments governs our attitudes toward the full-court press. When the team on defense challenges the offensive team's possession of the ball as they try to move it upcourt, they put tremendous pressure on the offensive players. It is pretty widely accepted in basketball that you do not press when your team is safely ahead—there is no strategic reason to do so, and all you accomplish is the humiliation of the other team. In our game we do not usually press in any circumstances, mostly because the quality of the game can deteriorate fast if there are a lot of turnovers. But this "rule" is much more specific and personalized. Certain players *love* to press, and if they are matched up with players who do not mind the pressure, then the press is okay. But pressing a weak ball handler (such as myself) or pressing when your team is way ahead is considered bad form, and a player can say "back off" to stop the practice. We know the strengths and weaknesses of individual players, and we know the pain of athletic humiliation. And our game is too social, too tied up with long-term on-court friendships to allow strategies of humiliation. But in other games, where the aim is winning and the assumption is that all weaknesses will be exploited, pressing is not a moral issue at all. If strategy calls for a press, you press.

I have been fascinated to see the way the ethic of the press is deployed in some church-league games. I have seen church teams press all game long, even if the score is 50–20 with one minute left to play. What puzzles me is that their circumstances are similar to ours—they have known and will know each other for a long time. But even though the team getting killed is *very* unhappy about it, some church teams will press relentlessly, to the point of outright meanness. To me these decisions seem contrary to the spirit of the game, especially in the context of the churches' own ethic of Christian charity, but I lack knowledge of the personal and institutional relationships that make sense of their practice, in which, no doubt, the necessity of the press is perfectly obvious. The ethic of the press is always profoundly contextualized, as feminist ethical theory argues, taking into account the personal histories of the players and the specific context of play.

It therefore seems to me that the feminist take on ethics is more applicable to the ethic of basketball, and maybe to the ethics of practices in general. In our game we know each other well, and we adjust our decisions to the players involved. No one, for example, would take advantage of an injured player or take actions that would exacerbate the injury. Our local game rewards relatedness, an awareness of the needs of other players, and a selflessness that counters the self-centered, competitive male identity that so much of our culture reinforces. How many places in our society can men learn an ethic of selflessness, sharing, caring about the feelings of others, and connecting with others in a common endeavor? Basketball, for all of its associations with the supposedly hyper-macho world of sports, is a place where selflessness and relatedness are necessary to a satisfying experience of the practice.

Of course the ethic of basketball also can be imposed on players in a dictatorial style, especially in highly competitive, elite contexts. Authoritarian coaches are common in basketball, and they often do not care a damn about personal histories and feelings. For them, selflessness is a means to an end—victory and success—and the micro-ethical moves of the game must be drilled into players who are seen as naturally selfish. Perhaps the most vivid example of this authoritarian approach to ethics is the 1986 film *Hoosiers*, starring Gene Hackman as a high school coach who believes that his players can learn the ethic only if they submit to absolute obedience. Coach Dale takes over a team that knows nothing about the game as an ethical practice. He believes that the game must be played with perfect fundamental skills and with a total dedication to the team. His *great* player is reluctant to play because of family responsibilities, but the coach brings the player back to the team through the coach's dedication to the ethic of the game. The film makes clear that even the great player can thrive only if he and his teammates develop a total dedication to the team rather than to their egos. Unfortunately, that dedication is seen in the film necessarily to entail unquestioning, immediate obedience to the coach's rules. The moral centerpiece of the film is a beautiful montage of a practice in which no one shoots the ball. They run, they dribble, they pass, they defend. They learn the tiny fundamentals that the ethic requires—"*Pop* the ball," the coach yells as they practice the two-hand chest pass. And they learn the pleasures and beauties of that precision, along with the satisfaction of self-abnegation and obedient submission to righteous authority.

I think of this film as conservative ideology from the Reagan era. It is set in rural Indiana in the 1950s, before what the film sees as the moral catastrophe of the 1960s (the alcoholic father of one of the players is played by 1960s' icon Dennis Hopper, for goodness sake, and he too is saved by Coach Dale's stern ethic). The film counterposes to selfish "1960s" values a belief in moral absolutes validating absolute power. It claims that our culture needs such a power to right its moral compass. The ethic of basketball in this film is seen as a subset of an entire culture's ethical imperatives, and no deviation from the moral norm is permitted—obedience must be perfect.

Obviously I do not share this film's moral calculus, but certainly many basketball coaches, players, and fans *do*. The public persona of coaches such as Bobby Knight of Indiana and Pat Summit of Tennessee communicates this authoritarian ethic. Many fans agree with their disciplinary style and believe that only top-down discipline, imposed with authority, can save us from moral anarchy. I am not at all certain, as I will explain later, that ethics emerging from practice are a moral panacea, but I know in my gut that the authoritarian disciplines cannot save us. They may appeal to the masochist in some players, and they make for great ethical PR, but they alienate most players and delay their opportunity to become moral agents. In pickup ball there are no official authority figures, no top-down discipline, and yet an ethic emerges out of the negotiations of the players. On the local level, they develop and interiorize a sense of right practice, often similar to the one that Coach Dale wants to impose. In terms of the ethical culture of basketball, what matters is not so much the content of the ethic as the process that produces it. Pickup basketball is a game of physical, spatial, and cognitive negotiation, not authoritarian discipline, and its ethic should also arise out of negotiation, rather than from a discipline imposed from above.

I do not mean to suggest that there are no power relationships involved in the ethic of basketball. Even pickup ball, far from the eyes and influence of coaches, subtly enforces an ethic on its players. Or rather, the players enforce it on each other. Veteran players in a given game become the keepers of its ethic. New players have to pick up the nuances, learn the personalities and histories that shape behavior in this particular game. In pickup games where there is no stable group of players, such learning is of course more tentative and superficial, but even in the most casual game an ethic quickly emerges, through the cooperative learning of the players. Here is a quick example: My son-in-law and I were shooting baskets at a recreation center in a beach town where we were on vacation. An extended family of fortyish men and teenage boys was shooting at the other basket and asked us if we wanted to run full-court. An oldguy-youngguy game was arranged (my son-in-law was a bit chagrined to realize that he had become an oldguy), and we played pretty hard for about half an hour. The personal relationships and histories were complex, but everyone perceived them quickly. One of the older guys had not played in a long time, and one of the teenagers was too young and frail to compete, so those players got no pressure. No one tried to block their shots or steal the ball from them, though both were kept in the flow of the game. The more competitive players challenged each other and contested each play, but the situation ruled out seriously competitive attitudes. It was the summer, it was vacation, it was a chance to *play*, a family time. A very precise ethic emerged

within minutes, recognized and observed by all. Everyone tacitly understood the issues involved and helped create the ethical climate.

In ongoing games the interpersonal knowledge is deeper and the
ethical adjustments are subtler. Long-term players set the ethical tone and
pass it on to new players. Most frequently this process is unspoken and
even unconscious—it involves modeling and enacting ethical practice. But
at times it requires explicit teaching—we do not do things that way here.
Each game devises its own ethical culture, and as noted literary and cultural historian Stephen Greenblatt has said: "The ensemble of beliefs and
practices that form a given culture function as a pervasive technology of
control, a set of limits within which social behavior must be contained, a
repetoire of models to which individuals must conform" (1995, 225).
Greenblatt argues that these constraints are enforced through strategies of
praise and blame, or to use the literary words, "satire and panegyric."
Every time one of the players in our game says to a weak player as he is
taking an open shot that he will likely miss "Good shot," he is weaving the
ethical fabric of the game. And every time someone says "Call the damn
pick" the offending player learns a little more about the ethic. But basketball is a physical game, and sometimes the ethic is enforced by a strategic
deployment of the body. You "get in someone's face" or give a mostly
symbolic push to show your disapproval. Players yell and confront and
adopt what a zoologist would no doubt see as simian gestures of ritualized
violence, the aim of which is precisely to forestall real violence and to
define the limits established in the ongoing game. This is, of course, the
behavior that keeps me from calling basketball a feminist practice, but this
symbolic violence is relatively rare, and its goal is not to enforce a rigid
moral code but to create an atmosphere in which a physical game can
remain nonviolent and the joy of the game can emerge. It is important to
emphasize that Greenblatt sees cultural constraints not as merely negative
injunctions but as guarantors of "mobility" or "improvisation." The improvisatory flow of the game requires *some* limits, or else the ensemble of
possibilities available to a player at any given moment would have no discernible shape, and no appropriate decisions could be made. The ethic, I
would argue, makes the distinctive improvisatory joy of the game possible.

Over years of play, every player evolves a distinctive ethical style, and
it is difficult *not* to think that the ethic comes to transcend the practice
and to shape the player outside the confines of the game. I could name,
and almost everyone in my game could name, the players who bring a
strong and conscious ethical commitment to their play. And when I am
engaged in civic or institutional work, I tend to think of those players as
trusted allies and righteous opponents, people I want to deal with, no
matter what their views on a given issue. I expect them to operate with

honesty and respect, just as they do on the court. Those expectations usually have been fulfilled, though I recognize that my expectations shape my perceptions. When I hear someone speak ill of the politics or social behavior of a player I admire, I want to rush to his defense, but I also realize that ethical play does not *guarantee* ethical work or ethical relationships. Because the ethic is so closely tied to the practice, it is not necessarily portable. In these players' lives, the ethic of basketball intersects with the ethics of all the other practices they engage in, and there is no formula to describe how that intersection will shape out. But the ethic of basketball enters the mix, pushes the vectors of personal and social ethics in a distinctive direction. Selflessness, cooperation, improvisation, the ability to make fine ethical judgments on the run, realistic self-assessment, incorporating knowledge of other persons into moral decisions—these lessons of the game are applicable elsewhere, but only insofar as they encounter practices that reaffirm them. Basketball and other sports build character, but so do the arts, business and social practices, workplaces, educational methods, media experiences, church traditions, and so on. Ethical character in individuals is a function of their engagement with the distinct and extensive array of their practices. As a result, there is no guaranteed or predictable carryover from on-court ethical behavior into the other everyday activities of their lives.

Nevertheless, there is now a sizeable industry based on the idea that the ethic of basketball can be carried into other endeavors. Pat Riley, Rick Pitino, and many other coaches have a second career as motivational speakers for corporate and institutional clients. Basketball now has tremendous visibility in corporate culture, both because of the corporate presence at NBA and big-time college games and because of the usefulness of basketball in advertising and marketing. Some coaches have taken advantage of that visibility, selling the virtues of teamwork and commitment to competitive excellence. Pat Riley has been particularly successful in this field. His book, *The Winner Within: A Life Plan for Team Players*, argues that the behavior that basketball promotes is the behavior necessary for corporate and civic success. Teamwork is the key, and Magic Johnson is the prime example. Riley says, "Magic Johnson believed that if he helped everyone around him get what they wanted out of the game, then winning would always follow. And so would his own rewards, in their own time and of their own accord" (1993, 32). For Riley, Magic's attitude creates success in any field. The Magic Johnson of Riley's narrative has a great desire for personal success, as does any aspiring corporate careerist, but he sublimates that desire into group success, confident that he will be recognized as the invaluable catalyst, just as the corporate structure requires the hard charger to become the company man. Riley teaches that promoting teamwork and a commitment to excellence lessens the likelihood of strikes and other conflicts within the organization and creates an atmosphere of belonging in a tough era of inevitable corporate downsizing. The metaphor of teamwork is so common in corporate culture that basketball stands ready to hand as a moral drama in which the values of competition and teamwork play powerful roles. It is, of course, the highly competitive world of professional and semiprofessional (college) basketball that appeals to these corporations. Riley is not selling the subtler, more interpersonal virtues of the pickup game, where today's opponent is tomorrow's teammate, and where competition is tempered by the full complexity of personal relationships. Those virtues of the game that millions play are lost in the shadow of the hypercompetitive pro game, which is offered as a model for corporate behavior.

Of course the world of professional and college and even high school basketball is not known these days for ethical behavior. Popular journalism is full of revelations about the sleaze surrounding the game—shoe contracts for high school teams, street agents paid under the table, gun-toting NBA entourages, ticket prices so high that ordinary fans can only watch on TV, violence against coaches and officials, abusive and unethical coaches, greedy owners, greedy players, hype and self-promotion. How is it that the world of elite basketball seems so unaffected by the ethic of the game itself? Why does the ethic encouraged by the practice of the game not set a tone for the ethic of its practice as a business? The practice of the game itself, which may seem to be at the center of its organizational structure, is not in fact at the center. It is merely the commodity that the organization sells, and the organization's ethic is shaped more profoundly by the practices of business and marketing than by the ethic of the game. Within corporate practice the team is a means to personal success. Professional players are economic free agents, corporate entities with little loyalty to teams or other players. Many of them openly assert that they are larger than the game. "Shaquille O'Neal" is the name of a media figure rather than a basketball player. Kids see him more frequently as an action figure or a character in a video game or a celebrity in a commercial than as a player. In this economic environment the ethic of basketball as I have described it seems irrelevant, even childish. No player could survive in this corner of the entertainment business on the basis of an ethic of selflessness and relatedness. If an NBA player is in the last year of a contract, then he is very unlikely to play hurt for the good of the team. Self-centeredness is his only viable strategy. The ethic of the game gets pushed out of the way.

It also is a matter of public concern among basketball fans that the self-centered ethic of the corporate world has begun to affect the game itself, on the schoolyard as well as in the NBA. Allen Iverson is often offered as an example of a player whose game has been spoiled by the cult of celebrity and arrogant economic power surrounding big-time basketball. Iverson has a huge contract, a celebrity's entourage, and run-ins with the law that suggest he feels exempt. Of course this is a description of his media image—I know nothing of his real behavior. But many fans and journalists see a direct connection between his gangster image and his behavior on the court. Iverson began his career as a point guard, which is supposed to be the most unselfish position, the player who distributes the ball, who leads the team in assists and steals, not points. The point guard is the traditional keeper of the ethic, the coordinator of the team game. But Iverson often played as if he was the only player on his team. He put up shots against the triple team, launched three-point shots from anywhere, and looked for his own offense first. And his game therefore "worked" as a pop-cultural style that could be commodified for advertising. He has been packaged as a symbol of a street-tough youth—a style for which his shoes are the perfect accessory.

On talk radio and in the sports columns, Iverson often has been a symbol for the decay of the game, the loss of the team ethic with its beautiful, improvisatory interplay. More recently, it is interesting to note, Iverson's image has changed. Larry Brown, who coached the Sixers for several years, turned Iverson into a shooting guard, a position that encourages aggressive and "selfish" offensive play, for the good of the team, which needs one player to lead the offensive effort. Iverson has been recuperated in this new position as a team player, one who cares only about team success, not his own statistics. As a media figure, though, he maintains the images of the brash, selfish player who disdains the conventional rules of basketball behavior. Older fans and players often lament the loss of that ethic in younger players who have been influenced by media images of what constitutes basketball success. I think most observers of the pickup game would agree that young players are much less interested in selfless ball and much more interested in self-display. In fact, young players often see the team game, what I have called "ethical ball," as "old school," part of the oldguy game. And this change has clearly been affected by the power of media images, the ESPN highlight reels, the posters of astonishing dunks. The anti-Iversons in popular culture are teams like Princeton in the NCAA or Utah in the NBA, teams that succeed because of their devotion to the old-time virtues of teamwork and fundamentals. But their success is the exception that proves the rule—for many fans the ethic of the game seems clearly to be decaying, under the influence of the corporate world and celebrity culture.

This nostalgia for the lost ethic is complexly connected to issues of race. Since the 1970s professional basketball has been dominated by great black players, so it is tempting to some fans to read the decline in the ethic in racial terms. Fans and journalists speak explicitly about the fact that Princeton's team is usually *all* white, and that Utah plays more white players than the NBA norm. Too often within the game, among fans and players and in the media, the ethic of the game is identified as "white ball," and the selfish, flamboyant game is identified as "black ball." As I will argue more fully later in this book, those terms signify within basketball culture and within American culture all too clearly. They show up in broadcasting cliches. "White ball" is "heady," "blue collar," "fundamentally sound"; "Black ball" is "athletic," "gifted," "talented." "White ball" is a function of will and desire and dedication: "black ball" is based on sheer athletic talent beyond the will of the player, a pure gift from the gods of the body. "Black ball" is artistic and improvisational, like jazz and soul and rap. "White ball" is a product of coaching—drills on the fundamentals, set plays and gritty defense, the ethic of the workplace, the job well done. And the culture of basketball often defines ethical ball as "white ball."

Fortunately, this racial polarization is not the whole story. It is commonplace in fan conversations to recognize that there are black players of "white ball" and white players of "black ball." Tim Duncan of the San Antonio Spurs and Jason Williams of the Miami Heat come to mind, and every pickup ballplayer can cite local examples. Because of these and many other easy-to-come-by anomalies, the categories are seen by people within the basketball community to be artificial and oversimplified, even if they are still accepted as common cultural sense. Being a player or a fan of the game at least provides the opportunity to question these "commonsense" categories. The game is too subtle and various to be reduced to this simple dichotomy. Did Michael Jordan play "black ball" or "white ball"? He improvised in the air, he competed with steely calm, he shot technically perfect foul shots, he had the greatest hang time in the history of the game, he played fierce defense, he found the open shooter, he took on the triple team, he was a coach on the floor, he had a perfect body for basketball, his work habits were legendary, he studied with Dean Smith, his model was Doctor J, he played off of his emotions, especially his anger, he taunted the opposition, he loved the spotlight, he loved the team. His game made the question hard to answer. His ethical-athletic style was not just a hybrid, a mixture of "black" characteristics and "white" characteristics; rather, it was a distinct personal creation that overly simple race categories cannot accommodate. Michael Jordan's game—the great African American athlete and icon of the basketball ethic—provides a cultural opportunity to deconstruct a deeply held racial ideology.

This is not to say that the ideology disappears. It lives on in the unchallenged, unconscious racism of white journalists and coaches and fans. And the traditional, racialized discourse of basketball also plays a complex role in the writings of black cultural critics who see the game as an embodiment of African American culture. Nelson George, in his rich history of black basketball, *Elevating the Game*, sees contemporary basketball as an expression of "the black aesthetic" and of black, masculine folk culture. He contrasts the rigid, coach-controlled style of "classroom" basketball with the free-flowing, emotional, improvisatory "schoolyard" game epitomized for him in the Rucker league, a Harlem summer institution that values "individual forays" rather than geometric designs, where the fans see "gravity defied and good sense ignored" (1992, 74–76). George is an example, I think, of the many black players and fans who accept the conventional racialized dichotomy but reverse its valence. For him the value of the game is its ability to express authentic African American values and traditions—exuberance, intensity, physical force, creative innovation. George seems willing to cede what I have been calling the ethic of basketball to "white ball," and to characterize it as limiting and predictable.

More challenging to the conventional racial opposition are the insights of Todd Boyd, in his essay "True to the Game: Basketball as the Embodiment of Blackness in Contemporary Popular Culture." Boyd makes a familiar contrast of the "white" style of Larry Bird's Celtics with the "black" style of Magic Johnson's Lakers, but he also reminds us that the "blue-collar," defensive-minded Detroit Pistons' championship teams of the late 1980s and early 1990s were also powerful expressions of black traditions:

> The Detroit Pistons . . . became highly successful by playing in a style that had clearly evolved from the depths of Black culture. The game of basketball stands out for its emphasis on offense, yet the Pistons emphasized defense in their climb into the league's elite. With a style similar to that of gangsta rap, the Pistons brought a menacing and aggressive, hard-nosed, no-bend defense that many criticized for being too violent. The team (and its style) became known as the "Bad Boys," using the image of physical intimidation to dominate the league. (2000, 110)

Tough defense is a hallmark of the basketball ethic, and Boyd convicingly associates that "hard-nosed" commitment with black culture rather than with "white ball." Boyd reminds us that the traditions of black culture contribute to the flamboyant style of Doctor J *and* to the gritty, defensive genius of Bill Russell. His vision of "black ball" is more inclusive than the stereotypical opposition.

I do not want to deny the importance of black traditions and values in the culture of basketball, but I do not believe that the stereotyped dichotomy of "black ball"/"white ball" accounts for that importance. The ethics of basketball are diverse and complex, and they are not the sole possession of "white ball." Too often in the white imagination, African American culture is depicted as a site of immorality and ultraviolence, and therefore "black ball" is associated precisely with an absence of ethical premises. Ethical ball of course exists in all basketball games, whether it is inspired by the puritan ethic of dictatorial white coaches, by the communitarian ethic of the African American church, by the feminist ethic within a women's team, or by the tribal pride of Native American societies, where the game has gained enormous popularity. As Boyd points out, the ethic of the game has been profoundly shaped by its complex history within urban, African American cultures. The ethic of the game is not white property; it carries the marks of all of the contexts where the game is played.

If the ethic of the game is in decline, then surely the cause is not the domination of the game by black players but the takeover of the game by corporate and marketing forces that encourage the kind of fame that selfish and flamboyant play can bring. Basketball is now marketed as an aspect of youth culture, and the NBA, along with the shoe companies and the soft drink companies and the fast-food companies, has learned that what sells in youth culture is flamboyance, hypermasculinity, and the selfish drive for fame. Young players who want to get huge contracts and commercial endorsements have learned that leading the team in assists or steals will not make the headlines. Dunks for the highlight reel and displays of self-aggrandizing aggression are the hot commodities in basketball as a media spectacle. The subtler pleasures of the ethic of the game are harder to sell, so they play almost no role in the pop cultural image of the sport, the image that is passed down to younger players. Of course the ethic of the game is under attack—what products do its virtues sell?

The connection between corporate culture and the decline of basketball ethics is the theme of *New York Times* sportswriter Harvey Araton's book *Crashing the Borders: How Basketball Won the World and Lost Its Soul at Home.* Araton's thesis is that "while capitalism reigned, American basketball values warped, creating a system set up to benefit those who feed off the talent more than the talented themselves" (2005, 7). One of his prime examples is the notorious brawl that broke out at a 2005 Detroit Pistons-Indiana Pacers game at the Palace at Auburn Hills, the home court of the Pistons, a brawl that involved players on both sides as well as fans in the stands. Araton's analysis is that the fight was "a by-product of a regrettable marketing scheme to create an in-your-face product that was edgy enough to resonate with the young and rebellious, those who would buy the jerseys, play the video games, create the buzz" (2005, 27). Araton argues that basketball has come to "suffer from a sickness deep in its soul, from a cancerous greed" (2005, 107), and that the cancer has spread from the NBA to the college game (which he sees as simply minor league professional basketball), to the high school game, right down to the pickup game at the local rec center. The cancer is selfishness, a desire to make oneself visible to the scout who might change one's life, at the expense of learning the subtle skills of the game and the complex interactions of team play. Araton believes that this decline in the ethic of the game may be changing, under the influence of European and other world players who are bringing an "old-school," team-oriented ethic back into the professional game. But will that retro style work its way down to the playground? Will the negotiations that produce the ethics of pickup games enforce a new commitment to unselfish play? The answers to those questions will be forged in a million future conversations in tomorrow's pickup games.

The entanglement of the ethics of basketball in the racial and economic realities of our culture is a reminder that there is no philosophical purity for this ethic—and maybe for any ethic. It is caught up in the myriad moral practices of the culture—in racial logics, in corporate codes of conduct, in the ethical practices of the schools or churches or prisons or workplaces where basketball is played. The ethic of this practice, or of any practice, cannot be set up as the basis for a general ethic of human behavior. All of us engage in many practices, all with their own ethical patterns, and they do not cohere into one inclusive system. These practices collide and conflict as often as they blend and mutually reinforce. Behavior sanctioned by one practice may be condemned by another. The complex moral landscape of contemporary culture is in part a function of the stunning array of practices available to us. If practices shape character, then there are an incalculable number of shaping forces at work in our ethical culture, and no one practice can dominate the others.

But this is not to say that the ethic of basketball has no effects at all. Those who play the game can learn to connect pleasure with selflessness, joy with improvisation, satisfaction with heightened awareness. These lessons can be lost in the welter of other practices in which we engage. They can be forgotten in the harsh competition of the marketplace. But they still have their subtle effects; they still shape the "character" of the players who are open to the lessons of the game. As a teacher I am always passing the ball. As a father I am always setting picks for my kids. And I have not undercut anyone since I was a child, too young to see the wisdom of restraint and respect. I have learned from the game, and I take those lessons into the other practices of everyday life. That is all we can ask of an ethic in our time. It cannot give our lives a totalized coherence. It cannot order the behavior of the entire society. But it can exert a moral pressure on anyone connected to its practice.

Chapter 3

"Man to Man"

Basketball, Movement, and the Practice of Masculinity

Alonzo Mourning, the great center for the Miami Heat, was diagnosed in the Summer of 2000 with a rare kidney condition that threatened to end his career at age thirty. At a minimum he was advised to take off a year from the game in order to adjust to his medications. Instead, when play-off time came around in 2001, Mourning could not resist the urge to return, and so he sped up his rehabilitation process and played in the last twenty games of the regular season, along with the play-offs. When he was asked by a reporter why he decided to take the risk, Mourning talked the usual sports-media cliches about his dedication to winning and to the good of the team, but he also said with great energy that he missed the physical contact in the game, what he called "the traffic." Mourning's game is very physical. He is best known as a fierce defender, patrolling the lane, contesting every opponent's shot, fighting for every rebound. He scowls in menace and roars in triumph, and his body language communicates rage and violence kept barely in check. But when he described what he missed about the game, movement and contact in close quarters with other players, he did not seem violent at all. He evoked an atmosphere of friendly, competitive physical contact, and he seemed to miss it like an addict.

Mourning's term *traffic* articulates one of the chief pleasures of playing basketball—forceful and complex movement in contested space. Players move at high speed through a limited, articulated space, all of them at every moment making movement decisions that alter others' movements, creating together an impromptu dance. Their decisions are informed by the rules and objectives of the game, so their movements are neither random nor natural. They are shaped by the culture of the game, which is itself connected to larger cultural formations. For its players and fans, basketball is an important cultural practice precisely because it operates on the body, teaching kinetic and perceptual habits specific to the game. Players learn how to negotiate a spatial field occupied by many other agents, all with their own interests and goals, and the unspoken rules of that physical negotiation are part of the cultural payoff of the practice.

Because it is so deeply embodied, basketball affects the physical and emotional lives of players. Pickup basketball creates a loose, subcultural community whose members recognize each other through their subtle embodiment of the lessons of the game. And since that community is mostly male, those lessons play a role in the development of their identity as men. Those lessons are very much a part of my own life, my way of being in the world. Playing basketball has been central to my experience of being a man and of being in the company of men. I have occasionally played the game with women, but for the most part my regular practice has been with other men. In fact, it is the only regular practice in my life that is so exclusively male. Playing basketball provides men with the opportunity to move together and make physical contact in a nonviolent and nonsexual practice. It is one of the places where men learn to negotiate their masculinity, right down to the level of the body, movement, and emotion.

Sports have long been recognized as crucial cultural sites where masculinity is taught and learned. Muscular Christians at the turn of the twentieth century saw sports as necessary antidotes to the feminization of work and culture. Late-twentieth-century feminists have criticized sports as practices that teach and legitimate male power and the oppression of women. Young boys are taught to see sports as tests of their nascent manhood, and they recognize that the outcome can shape the rest of their lives as men. Coaches use the word "manhood" as a weapon to push players to risk injury and cause pain. Behind the belief that sport teaches masculinity is the assumption, acknowledged or not, that masculinity is not natural but cultural, a learned pattern of behavior and attitudes. Many of the coaches and moralists who believe that sport teaches masculinity would argue for a *natural* masculinity that modern culture denigrates and sports can recover, but their own practices suggest that if the lessons of sport must be repeated and drilled so frequently, then masculinity is an effect of their teaching—as one element in the vast gender-training mechanism of the culture—rather than a natural state.

But if it is true to say that sports teach masculinity, then it is also important to remember that this teaching is not simple or monolithic. There is no essential masculinity that sports teach; there are only various modes of masculinity, and different sports teach different modes. Golf is not football. Both are powerful teachers of stereotypical masculine behavior, but one teaches its players self-reliance and rational decision making, while the other teaches group loyalty and righteous violence. Adding to the complexity of this teaching is the fact that the men who learn these lessons are not blank slates. Men and boys who engage in sports are active participants in learning gender codes, and what they learn may well not be what sports are officially intended to teach. They learn the codes of masculinity from many sources, and they process that information in an active, critical manner. As a result of these diverse and often contradictory practices of teaching and learning, what sports teach about masculinity differs from sport to sport and player to player.

There are, of course, millions of women who play basketball avidly and with great skill. This fact clearly demonstrates that there is nothing inherently masculine about the game. But the practice of basketball is clearly *coded* masculine within our current cultural binaries. One day the growing number of women who play the game will change that coding, but for now they have to deal with the "masculinity" of basketball, just as male dancers have to deal with the "femininity" of dance. The question of how women negotiate that deal would have to be the subject of an essay in itself, and I am not the person to write this. But as a man who has played and watched the game for over forty years, and who has learned his own modes of masculinity at least in part on the court, I am positioned to make use of my own experience in the daily practice of the game in order to reflect on basketball as a teacher of some particular modes of masculinity. The question is whether they are the modes of a "hegemonic masculinity" to oppress women and institutionalize homophobia, as many analysts of the cultural role of sport have argued. Eric Dunning characterizes team sports as "mock battle," and Varda Burstyn argues that sport should be thought of as a "protomilitary ritual practice" that encourages "the cult of the warrior." But Burstyn also sees a "liberatory potential" in unsupervised sport, played more for pleasure than for victory. My conviction is that pickup basketball should not be dismissed as a mechanism for the teaching of oppressive masculinity, though it can be and often is just that; rather, I will argue that the game engages men in a movement system and a way of occupying space that provide a rich aesthetic and emotional experience more complex than the stereotypes of traditional masculinity.

SPACE

Basketball occurs in a variety of environments, but the space of the game is always carefully demarcated. Perhaps we first think of huge arenas sponsored by municipal, corporate, or academic institutions, where a brightly lit court is surrounded by thousands of spectators assembled for a theatrical display of elite athletic skill. But the vast majority of basketball games are not spectacles at all. In the game that millions of people play each year, there are no spectators except for the players waiting for the next game. And the locations of courts are extremely various. Basketball is played in school gyms, church halls, schoolyards, rec centers, driveways, backyards, playgrounds, anywhere a basket can be hung. Some of these spaces are official courts with foul lines, three-point arcs, half-court lines, and out-of-bounds markers. But others are so informal that the space must be defined by the negotiation and consensus of the players.

In a street game the boundaries might be the car on the left and the truck on the right. And even on official courts, players in pickup games negotiate the use of the space. In my game, for example, there are three point arcs, but we do not count three-point shots. Our court is a little short, so we do not follow the "backcourt" rule. Similar negotiations of ground rules occur throughout pickup basketball. The definition of the space for the purpose of these games is a local social construct rather than a product of official rules. In organized ball, of course, the official rules are in place, and the men who play there learn to accept and follow the rules of a bureaucratic, top-down discipline. But in the informal game, rules do not matter as much as local customs and often unspoken community values, and men who play *there* are less constrained by arbitrary discipline and more able to engage in a peaceful and cooperative negotiation of the spatial rules.

But no matter how informal the game, players construct or accept territorial rules and boundaries. Philosopher Johan Huizinga sees such boundaries as essential to the nature of play. In his classic study *Homo Ludens* he argues that play must have its own separate space: "All play moves and has its being within a play-ground marked off beforehand either materially or ideally, deliberately or as a matter of course." Such spaces are "forbidden spots, isolated, hedged round, hallowed, within which special rules obtain. All are temporary worlds within the ordinary world, dedicated to the performance of an act apart" (1950, 2). While I will argue later that the "apartness" of the play space and game is far from absolute, basketball clearly exists within an arbitrary, delineated space and enforces its boundaries with precision. In organized ball, if even the tip of a toe of a player with the ball touches the out-of-bounds line, then the ball goes over to the other team. If the offensive team does not get the ball past half-court within ten seconds, then it loses the ball. An offensive player can spend only three seconds within "the paint," the space directly in front of the basket. In pickup ball these rules may be amended or ignored, but even in the most informal game the space of basketball is demarcated, and players accept and enjoy the feeling of moving within a complex but defined space that at least seems to exist apart from the space of ordinary experience.

Here is a story about the emotional charge that these arbitrary boundaries can create. They define not only where the players can go but also where those who are not players cannot go. The oldguygame at my university gym runs on Mondays, Wednesdays, and Fridays at noon. Some semesters there is a class in this space beginning at one. Students often arrive early and hang around the edge of the court. One day some of the students were milling around, chatting, getting gear out of storage. And they were getting on to our court, in the periphery of our way. They didn't think twice about it. Teen basketball culture tolerates sideliners edging onto the court. Oldguy basketball culture *does not*. We felt pinched and distracted. Serious players get into a Zen state, which is the whole point of the exercise and therefore precious. And the students were disrupting that state. They did not intend to, but that did not matter. I and others said, "Get off the court please. Somebody's gonna get hurt." No response. "Get off the court." Raised voices, sharper tone. "Get off the damn court." Testosterone and adrenaline, space and limits, contest and anger. Some of the guys on the sideline did not like it, bristled, thinking who are you to talk to us? But the answer to that question was—old guys who, because we were older, felt the right to tell young guys to give us space. "Heads up," we were saying without saying, "the rest of the world exists. We're playing a game here. This is our space and time. Twelve to one. Sideline to sideline, baseline to baseline. We play our game within these limits for this moment. Respect that. Back off." And they did. One football player would have liked to kill us, as we probably deserved. But he backed off too, then quickly forgot about us.

This is a story, of course, about *men* and space. Any woman of our time is likely to roll her eyes at it, lamenting the stupidity and the simian predictability of men. Contesting spatial boundaries often is seen as a basic element of biological masculinity. Our testosterone makes us territorial, so the argument runs, willing to fight to defend the space of the clan, willing to kill and die in wars that expand the space we can define as our own. On the contrary, women are seen to inhabit and domesticate space, make it a surrounding, an extension of the body. Men conquer and defend space, making it a commodity, a sign of wealth, a symbol of masculine power. But my story suggests that this particular example of the desire for boundaries is not so much a biological imperative as it is a profound habit learned in the game itself. It is one of the key lessons of basketball that boundaries matter, and there would be no need for the lesson if the desire for boundaries was simply in our testosterone. As Shirley Ardener says in *Women and Space: Ground Rules and Social Maps*, "Space defines the people in it. At the same time, however, the presence of individuals in space in turn determines its nature" (1993, 3). The "ground rules," or definitions of boundaries in space, are dialectically related to "social maps," the definitions that produce social groups and hierarchies. Space is defined by social process, and spatial rules in turn shape the people who inhabit the space. Basketball teaches—among other things—that play is made possible by limits, and that the play space is worthy of defense. In this lesson basketball is clearly a conservative force, teaching a traditional male value, but as we will see, not all of its lessons are so traditional.

Within and because of these boundaries, basketball is played in a highly *oriented* space. The baskets and backboards at either end of the court are the most obvious orientation points. Because the goal of the game is to put the ball into the basket, the game flows from end to end, and the players operate within a clear, understandable, and reassuringly rectilinear space. The basketball court is far more defined than a baseball field, with its wide-open outfield spaces, and it is smaller than the rectangles of a football or soccer field, so its orientation markers are closer and more powerful. But within this simple grid, more complex orientation points exist in endless movement. The most obvious is the ball itself, which as it moves orients all of the players' movements. Offensive players move in relation to the placement and direction of the ball, and defensive players react to the offensive players' movements and to the likely direction that the ball will take. Players also know the points on the court where strategic moves are best performed, so they orient to those points as well. "The post" is a spot from which a strong player can get an easy shot, so it is often an orientation point and a contested location. Players push and jostle for control of that space, and some of the most physical play in the game occurs there. Defensive players learn over time where an offensive player likes to take a shot, so those spaces also are orientation points. Or a player might set a pick for one of his teammates, blocking the teammate's defensive player so that an open shot is created—another point of orientation. Unlike the basket, these points are constantly shifting and require adjustment and expectation. Players do not know where they will occur until the flow of the game creates them. But once they are created, they shape the movement of the players and provide points of visual interest for fans. Albert Mehrabian's (1976) *Public Places and Private Spaces: The Psychology of Work, Play, and Living Environments* provides a useful scheme for describing spatial arrangements. He assesses the "information load" of spaces. The continuum between "high-load" and "low-load" environments is a function of their location within the following qualitative oppositions:

Uncertain-certain
Varied-redundant
Complex-simple
Novel-familiar
Large scale-small scale
Contrasting-similar
Dense-sparse
Intermittent-continuous
Surprising-usual
Heterogeneous-homogeneous
Crowded-uncrowded
Asymmetrical-symmetrical
Immediate-distant
Moving-still
Rare-common
Random-patterned
Improbable-probable (Mehrabian 1976, 12–13)

On most of these scales, the highly kinetic basketball environment is closer to the left than the right term of these oppositions, creating a "high-load" information space. Basketball occurs in a complex space that requires a high degree of attention and mental process. What tames the complexity of the space is its symmetry and familiarity to the practiced player. Over time, the shifting, complex space of the court becomes more manageable and more pleasurable as a movement environment. And as players move together on the court again and again, the points of orientation that their cooperative movements create become clearer and more available for strategic use.

The result for players is a rich, engaging environment within an arbitrary but comforting set of boundaries and points of orientation. The character of this space might explain in part why basketball and other sports are so popular in contemporary culture. Fredric Jameson (1991) has characterized the spatial environment of postmodern culture as disoriented and confusing, like Mehrabian's left-hand column:

. . . this latest mutation in space—postmodern hyperspace—has finally succeeded in transcending the capacities of the individual human body to locate itself, to organize its immediate surrounding perceptually, and cognitively to map its position in a mappable external world. It may now be suggested that this alarming disjunction point between the body and its built environment . . . can itself stand as the symbol and analogon of that even sharper dilemma which is the incapacity of our minds, at least at present, to map the great global multinational and decentered communicational network in which we find ourselves caught as individual subjects. (1991, 44)

The spaces of most sports, in particular basketball, could therefore be thought of as anti-postmodern, in that they provide a comforting experience of orientation and belonging within a complex but comprehensible environment.

Doreen Massey makes a similar point in her book *Space, Place, and Gender*, when she describes a gendered contrast between "space" and "place." She argues that our culture connects "space" and its connotations of openness, freedom of movement, and disorientation with traditional definitions of masculinity, and that we associate "place" and its connotations of limits, belonging, and community with traditional femininity. But Massey wants to undo this opposition and rethink "place" as a node in larger spatial systems. She characterizes the desire for place in the traditional sense as a nostalgic, romantic need to get our bearings in a disorienting postmodern world (1994, 162), and she demonstrates clearly that even the most tightly knit, community-oriented "places," such as villagelike neighborhoods in cities, are in fact connected to larger spatial environments through the economic and communicational apparatuses that Jameson evokes. Following Massey, one could therefore argue that, in Huizinga's terms, there is no such thing as the "place apart" that he believes play requires. The "place" of the basketball court, for all of its boundaries and orientation points, is in fact part of, say, a university space, which is part of a municipal space, and so on out. Basketball does not exist in an "other" place, cut off from the wider geographical and social world. But the fact that it *feels like* it does is clearly part of its appeal.

If playing basketball gives pleasure in part because it occurs in what seems like a comfortable, enclosed place, then I would argue that part of what it teaches in terms of gender definitions is not so traditionally masculine. For all of their connections to macho style, basketball and other sports could be seen as enacting traditionally feminine desires for a defined and comforting place. Massey's analysis suggests that this desire for a "feminine" space cannot finally be sustained, but it is a desire that men replay almost daily in their consumption of and participation in sport. The notion that sport expresses a doomed masculine desire for a "feminine" place flies in the face of conventional cultural assumptions, and it suggests that men may be less comfortable in their traditional masculine roles than we assume. It also suggests that easy oppositions between masculine and feminine cannot account for the complexity of gendered experience. Perhaps the fact that sport is defined by our culture as a hypermasculine pursuit provides an effective cover for an exploration of traditionally feminine spatial values.

MOVEMENT

A similar argument can be constructed with regard to the movement that occurs within the spatial boundaries of the court. Of course all sports involve movement, but each sport encourages different movement patterns with different aesthetic styles. Think of the precise and constrained movement of the golfer putting, the flamboyant and courageous leap of a wide receiver in football, or the dancing feet of a soccer midfielder. And even within a particular sport, movement patterns vary. Professional basketball, for example, went through a period in the 1990s when the game stagnated, becoming much less fluid than it was in the 1970s and 1980s, returning to a faster tempo only in the last couple of years. Different teams feature characteristic movement patterns, from the precision motion and passing of the "Princeton offense" to the wide-open athleticism of recent Duke teams. In pickup basketball there is a similar, even wider variety, depending on the space in which the game is played and the personalities of the players. In some pickup games the player with the ball and the defender covering him are the only players moving, while the rest of the players stand around and watch, but in other games all the players move in perfect concert. Movement styles also differ from player to player. Some are balletic and light-footed; some are muscle-bound and bullish. Some are angular, some are fluid. Part of the fascination of the game for fans is the idiosyncratic movement styles of great players, from the transcendent grace and power of Michael Jordan to the darting speed of Alan Iverson to the sheer strength of Shaquille O'Neal. Basketball is a kinetic experience for fans and players, and part of the appeal of the game is the simple pleasure of movement for its own sake.

Despite the variety of movement styles in the game, it is possible to describe the characteristic movement qualities of basketball, which I believe explain its appeal to men and its effects on their gendered identities. "Movement for its own sake" is not of course the official function of movement in sport. Sport *uses* movement for goal-oriented purposes. In basketball, players leap in order to rise above the defender for the shot;

they run in order to get to a strategic spot first. But we need not constrain our analysis of athletic movement to its overt, official purpose. There is an aesthetic, kinesthetic appeal to sport, almost independent of its competitive goals. The competitive and utilitarian function of movement in sport is part of its traditional masculinity, but that function does not explain all of the appeal of athletic movement.

One of the first films ever made, out of the studio of the Lumiere brothers in France over 100 years ago, focuses the camera for about fifty seconds on a soccer exhibition. The players are all congregated in one quarter of the field, so they can all be seen in the shot. The cinematographer, apparently an apprentice, still learning the principles of composition, leaves the player with the ball out of the frame. We see all of the players reacting to the movement of the ball, but we never see the object that orients and makes competitive sense of their movements. Bertrand Tavernier, the suave narrator of a recent collection of Lumiere films, notes that their movement is therefore abstracted from its game context, so that the players appear to be engaged in dance rather than sport. Basketball also can be thought of as improvised dance, even if the players do not have aesthetic purposes in mind. What if the ball is just an excuse for men to dance together? Maybe the competitiveness of sport is an excuse for joyful movement and bodily contact, a way of minimizing homophobia while still enjoying the "feminine" pleasures of exuberant movement, friendly bodily contact, and complicated cooperation in space. Noel Dych and Eduardo P. Archetti, in the introduction to their collection of essays in *Sport, Dance, and Embodied Identities*, argue that sport and dance are "techniques of the body" with "a vital capacity to express and reformulate identities and meanings . . . powerful means for celebrating existing social arrangements and cultural ideas or for imagining and advocating new ones" (2003, 1–2). The movement habits of pickup basketball, I will argue, have the potential to achieve both of those outcomes simultaneously.

Once the analogy between basketball and dance is admitted, some of the similarities are striking. Drawing on the vocabulary of ballet, think of the layup as a *grand jete*. Think of the defensive shuffle as a *chasse*, the defensive stance as second position. Think of spin moves as *chaines* turns. Some of the players we remember most vividly have this dancelike quality. Michael Jordan and Michail Baryshnikov are the great artists of the air in my memory. Both of them created the illusion that they could leap, pause in midair, and then go higher. Clyde ("The Glide") Drexler got his nickname from his smooth but powerful movement style. Jerry West's jump shot had a beautiful and precise delicacy in the extended fingers of the follow-through, the pointed toes of the jump. Even in pickup games a casual observer can notice the *beautiful* player, the one with extension, lift, balance, and balletic grace.

Of course basketball need not explicitly resemble dance in order to be aesthetically pleasing. There is an aesthetic quality to the ordinary movements of the game: running, jumping, gliding through complex traffic, spinning off opponents, dribbling with extreme dexterity. Kareem Abdul-Jabbar made beauty out of the simple basketball move of pivoting and taking a hook shot. Players develop a repertoire of individual moves, practicing them endlessly in solitary practice sessions. As skill increases, the beauty of the movement increases. The aesthetic move is usually an effective move. How much of the pleasure of those individual practice sessions has to do with the pleasure of aesthetically pleasing movement? Little kids (and not so little) shooting in the driveway at a basket above the garage door are engaged in a complex practice. Bill Bradley (1998), in his book *Values of the Game*, astutely lists "imagination" as one of those values. That kid is often thinking to himself "three, two, one, he shoots, he scores!," playing out endgame heroics, grace under pressure. But is he not also enjoying the pleasure of graceful bodily motion, lifting off the court in a leap that is a good in itself, even if the shot misses? This pleasure in beautiful movement is underappreciated in the analysis of sport, perhaps because it does not fit our assumptions about what constitutes manly pleasure. To be traditionally masculine is to ignore the aesthetic and to deny the more delicate pleasures of the body. But basketball gives players and spectators an experience of aesthetic enjoyment and thereby quietly extends the range of "masculine" pleasures.

The dancelike pleasures of the game become even more intense when we turn from the individual player to teams moving in concert. Especially in informal games of basketball, the game flows without interruption across the full-court. No foul shots or time-outs interrupt the action. Players must move together at high speed without benefit of pre-exiting paths. They improvise, opponents together with teammates, without choreographed plays, making up the game on the run. They race for those shifting points of orientation, and their movement creates other races on the court as the ball moves and as the advantage shifts from team to team. Sometimes players crash into each other in those races, sometimes in the air, so there is an element of risk in the movement of the game; people can get hurt banging knees or getting poked in the eye or getting elbowed. But much of the movement in the game is an attempt to *avoid* contact, running around screens, avoiding picks, eluding contact with defenders who want to block the way. As a result, among experienced players, almost all contact is intentional, almost none accidental. Given the constraints of space on the court, making strategic contact and avoiding accidents require spatial awareness and grace. Like dancers on a stage, players have to share space while engaged in vigorous movement, and the pleasure of the game comes from the improvisatory process of group creation.

Group movement in basketball is a shifting and subtle process, usually learned through years of practice, or sometimes miraculously grasped in an intuitive flash by even the youngest of players. Skilled offensive players watch for shifts of weight in a defender's stance in order to make a move that takes advantage. A good player will cast his eyes in one direction and pass the ball in the other. Passers notice the precise angle of advantage that a teammate has on his defender and deliver the ball at the strategic moment and at the right angle so he can receive the pass and make his move, which is sometimes another split-second pass, sometimes a drive to the hoop, sometimes a quick shot, sometimes a dribble and hesitation, and so on, depending on how defenders react, how teammates move in response, how confident you are in the moves available to you, how well you know and how much you trust your teammates, and how they can best use your move to their advantage. The understanding that leads to those decisions would be very difficult to lay out in a logical system. It develops through testing and observation, experiments in movement in real time. Players take pleasure in this group movement experiment, and informed fans take pleasure in the resulting kinetic patterns.

Enhancing the parallel to dance is the fact that man-to-man defensive play is, in dance terms, a form of partnering. Wherever the offensive player leads, the defender will follow, or if possible try to anticipate and arrive at the orientation point first, forcing the offensive player to revise his plan and make a countermove. If the offensive player fakes right and moves left, then the defender will move as an exact mirror image. Matched-up players will move in this responsive way throughout the game, sometimes initiating the move on offense, sometimes replying on defense. Simultaneously, both players must be aware of the other pairs on the court, and the pairs interweave in complicated and nonrepeatable patterns. If a team is playing a zone defense, then the movement pattern changes, but it still resembles dance. In a zone defense each player defends an area of the court rather than an individual opponent, so as the offensive team moves the ball, looking for open areas in the zone, the defensive players must move as a team to cover the areas threatened by the opponent's moves. A good zone defense team moves as a coordinated unit, as an *ensemble*, a choreographer would say. The team shifts from side to side of the court, not all five with identical movements, but each player moving in support of all the others.

As a group improvisation, basketball resembles "contact improvisation," a movement practice developed in the 1970s that involves two or more dancers who improvise movement following the direction of energy created by the contact of their bodies. The point of contact energy moves, and the dancers' bodies follow it. The movements of each dancer produce the movements of the others. As Cynthia Novack, in her book on contact improvisation, *Sharing the Dance*, says, "Contact improvisation defines the self as the responsive body and also as the responsive body listening to another responsive body, the two together spontaneously creating a third force that directs the dance" (1990, 189). The goal is *not* to arrive at predetermined body shapes or movement patterns chosen for their aesthetic appeal but to move through a process of kinetic flow. Contact improvisation has appealed less to trained dancers than to alternative culture students of movement and the body. Its goals are spiritual as well as somatic; the aesthetic of the movement arises from the spiritual practice.

The movement of basketball, as in contact improvisation, is produced by the shared energies of the players in the game. My move makes your move possible and necessary. I spin off your body to follow the energy of the play to the right spot. And in basketball these moves are almost always improvised. In organized ball there are plays, but plays are only choreographed opportunities for structured improvisation. In pickup ball, there are no plays at all. No one knows what the next movement will be. Players have to know the possible moves, the likely strategies, given the situation and the players on the court. But they never *know* what will evolve in the improvisatory flow. Gina Caponi-Tabery, in her article on the connections between basketball, dance, and jump blues in the 1930s, says, "Basketball depends on a fluid interaction among a group of players whose roles are interchangeable. . . . No other sport so closely resembles the flow and flair of jazz and jazz dance" (2002, 52). In pickup ball, as in improvised jazz, the future is always open. In this uncertainty, players rely on imagination, anticipation, and adjustment. Surely the ball will go here, so I move here, but the ball goes *there*, so I shift my strategy and make a new move. All of these creative decisions are made possible by the choices of the other players, and this trading of energy, these movements in exquisite response, is shared by opponents as well as teammates. I react to my teammates' moves, but also to my opponents' moves. There are *ten* movers in the space, creating the energy that shapes the movement.

Of course this account of movement in basketball has so far neglected one crucial point—basketball is a competition, and its movements are *contested*. It is this fact above all others that characterizes basketball as a stereotypically masculine practice. Unlike contact improvisation or ballet or jazz dance, in basketball players fight for space and for control of orientation points. Many of the movements in the game are blocking tactics, attempts to get in the desired path of opponents, forcing them to change direction, denying them the moves they like best. Playing defense is an effort to create kinetic frustration, to take away options and dictate disadvantageous movement. Much of the contact in the game is antagonistic, shoving for position in the post, colliding in air on a layup, boxing out for a rebound. Players throw elbows and push with their back and hip and shoulder, and sometimes the competition turns violent. Players will get angry, and there is, on occasion, shouting, shoving, and even an ineffectual punch. So it is certainly not true that all of the movement in basketball is cooperative and shared in the manner I have been describing. The goal of the game is not—at least not consciously—to share the energy of movement. It is to gain spatial advantage and to impose one's will on the opponent. But the cooperative flow of the movement arises precisely out of its antagonistic structure. Defense not only stifles offense, it creates offense. When Michael Jordan beats his defender off the dribble, another defender shows up to help, and some of Michael's most memorable moves were his reactions in midair to that second—or third—defender. That is when he seems to leap, pause, and soar again, or somehow manage to turn in midair. Still, if we are to understand the gender lessons that basketball teaches, we cannot forget the sometimes fierce competitive spirit of its players. Novack explains the difference between sport and contact improvisation in just these terms: In contact improvisation, she says, "the realization of the individual is placed within the context of cooperation and group activity rather than in the context of competition and personal achievement" (1990, 190). And though I will later question this simple opposition of competition and cooperation, it is important to acknowledge the fact that basketball is an agonistic game, that in its battles for territory it is a form of ritualized, civilized violence, and that as such it is a central element in stereotypical masculine culture.

Feminist critics of sport have used the words "force" ("the irresistible occupation of space") and "skill" ("the ability to operate on the objects within that space, including other humans") to describe the aspects of power that sport teaches (Connell, quoted in Kidd 1987, 259). Bruce Kidd has connected these forms of power to a dehumanizing, instrumentalist mind-set that encourages athletes "to treat each other as enemies to be intimidated and brutalized" (ibid.). Kidd and many other feminists see this mind-set as a central element in patriarchal power over women (1987, 250). David Whitson argues in "Sport in the Social Construction of Masculinity" that the mastery of force and skill gained in sport encourages boys "to experience their bodies, and therefore themselves, in forceful, space-occupying, even dominating ways" (1990, 23). Sport therefore contributes to male "assertiveness and confidence," and the traditional exclusion of girls from sport encourages their acceptance of male domination (1990, 24). Whitson also notes that the experience of skillful force in the flow of a game is one of the great pleasures of sport, even if it has dire social consequences. Certainly basketball teaches force and skill, and it therefore contributes to patriarchal ideology, but I would argue that force and skill are not *necessarily* patriarchal, and that they need not lead to the dehumanization of opponents. On the contrary, they can lead to strong affective bonds with other players engaged in the struggle, opponents as well as teammates. Force and skill may in fact be elements of patriarchal power, but they *need not* be, and basketball places force and skill within a peaceful context that limits their aggressive, dominating function.

One of the attractions of basketball for me is that it is a contact sport. When I think about getting too old for the game, I cannot think of any of the individual sports—such as tennis, golf, bowling, aerobics, or weight training—that will provide the same pleasure of physical contest. One easy explanation for this pleasure is that it provides an outlet for stress and repressed aggression. Working in a sedentary, intellectual profession, I and others in my game certainly enjoy the chance to blow off some steam. But the pleasure is more positive. The bumping and pushing for strategic advantage are a satisfying experience of force and skill, and they are constrained enough by the rules and ethics of the game that they very rarely turn to outright violence. Physical contact in basketball is strategic and specific, as in the contest for position under the basket, getting exactly the right angle for receiving a pass or blocking a path. This contest requires not just force but insider knowledge of the precise patterns and possibilities available in the game situation, and the combination of physical struggle and intellectual strategy constitutes the unique pleasure of the game.

The pleasure of the game also derives from the skills it requires. Players take pleasure in repeated practice at shooting the ball, for example. A simple jump shot requires skilled attention to precise body movement, from elegantly extended fingers in the release to the pointed toes of the jump, along with hand-eye coordination and an ability to judge angle and distance that can only be gained by long practice. The skill of putting the ball in the basket, from within a contested space, with opponents trying to deny the shot, is one of the attractions of the game. There also is the skill of delivering the perfect pass at the perfect angle, manipulating spatial arrangements to one's advantage. Or the skill of anticipating the shooter's move and blocking the shot, or the skill of blocking out an opponent in the struggle for a rebound. "Skill" and "force" are apt words for describing the pleasure of the game, for the player as well as the spectator. And the fact that they are connected to patriarchal practices should not blind us to their pleasures, for women as well as for men. They are especially attractive for men who do not use physical force and skill in their professional lives, which would include most men these days.

Historians and sociologists of sport, working from a feminist standpoint, have shown that sport developed as an institution in the late nineteenth century and became a dominant cultural force in the twentieth century because of its complex ties to masculine identities in a time of crisis. What we now think of as sport has not always existed, and feminist historians make a strong case that it developed within a culture and an economy that devalued the physical strength of men and thus created a need for a ritualized space in which physical force could be displayed as a symbol of male political and cultural dominance, even in a world in which men's physical power was no longer needed. The institution of modern sport originated in late-nineteenth-century British and then American culture, in the elite schools of the upper classes. As demonstrated in Michael Kimmel's (1996) *Manhood in America: A Cultural History,* texts from this period make it clear that educators and moralists saw sport as a replacement for the physical labor and adventure that early industrial economy and American westward expansion had required. The worry was that men would become feminized by their more sedentary work, and sport was seen explicitly as the manly antidote. Eric Lott, in an interesting article on the styles of masculinity of Elvis impersonators, sees a similar need to assert masculinity in the context of "a massive shift in political economy. . . a shift from 'Fordism' to 'post-Fordism,' from an industrial regime of mass assembly-line production to a halting and low-wage service economy in which, moreover, the sexual division of labor was blurred" (1997, 196). This historical analysis explains particularly well the rise of televised sport as a fantasy repossession of lost physical power. As Kimmel says, "If manhood could no longer be directly experienced, then perhaps it could be vicariously enjoyed by appropriating the symbols and props that signified earlier forms of power and excitement" (1996, 118).

Sport also contributes in quite direct ways to the culture of violence against women and homosexuals. Many commentators have noted the vile misogyny and homophobia of the adolescent locker room, and statistics show clearly that college athletes are disproportionately responsible for rape and other crimes of violence against women on campus. Sport is often presented in the media as a hypermasculine practice, focusing on its fierce competitiveness and its displays of masculine dominance. Think of the extremely photogenic high fives, chest bumps, and sexualized dances of victory that seem inevitable in any televised sports event. More generally, the popularity of sport can be seen as an aspect of hypermasculine popular culture, a panicked symbolic reaction to the ebbing real power of men in our culture and economy. Considering these historical and cultural realities, I agree that sport must be seen as an institution that reinforces patriarchy and heterosexual power.

But I do not think that is the whole story. To say that sport as an institution reinforces patriarchy is not to say something unique about sport. The same critique could be and has been raised against all of the important institutions of our culture. Religion, education, media, medicine, law, the arts, science—all have rightly been identified as sites for the teaching of patriarchal values. This thoroughgoing critique suggests a simple fact—that we live in a patriarchal culture, and that its values prevail in all of our most powerful institutions. So once the critique has been made, the question becomes, how do we engage in cultural practices in ways that question and challenge their patriarchal values, and how can we rethink those institutions and practices to uncover the qualities in them that have antipatriarchal potential? My argument is that basketball possesses such qualities, especially in the habits of movement and occupying space that it allows for the men who play the game. Given the feminist critique, which elements in the game can be thought through freshly as opportunities for men to operate outside of the patriarchal mind-set?

We could begin by questioning the assumption that competition is the soul of the game, or of sport in general. Perhaps we overestimate the importance of competition because so many of us experience sport through mass media rather than through personal involvement. On television, basketball seems extremely competitive. Players who make it to the top of the game are the most gifted, the most dedicated, and the most competitive. We see and vicariously enjoy their fierceness, especially if we live in places where fierceness is not useful or tolerated. Elite-level basketball is extremely physical; it has become almost a dogma in pro basketball that no player should be allowed a layup without getting fouled, and players such as Michael Jordan have become global icons of single-minded, fierce determination. But even within elite basketball there are features of the game that could attract more media attention, which almost always fixates on the competition. The beauty of the game is rarely mentioned, nor are the moments of kindness and even tenderness that occur routinely in the flow of the game. Players show respect and concern for their rivals, sympathize with injuries, even ones that lead to a competitive advantage, and show signs of personal relationships outside of team identifications. But for the media, basketball is a ritual of competition, often explicitly connected to masculine competition in the economic sphere.

But when one focuses on the huge world of basketball outside of this elite circle, competition must be understood in a much more nuanced way. Some pickup games are intensely competitive, even more violent than in the pros, while others are very casual, with players investing almost nothing in the outcome of the game. Think of a couple of kids shooting baskets in a driveway, or a game at a family picnic, or a single person shooting around, just for the pure pleasure of movement and skill. In some of these situations the competitive factor is near zero. And who is to say that the more competitive games are closer to the essence of sport? In some pickup games players lose track of the score and could not care less who is winning or losing. Their concern is, is the flow good, are we "getting a good run?" My own game is pretty competitive. We do keep score (in part because we take a needed break every total of seven baskets), and we feel better when we are ahead or when the game is close. We do not like losing big. But half an hour after the game, I would be hard pressed to remember who won. What I remember are plays that were satisfying or frustrating, moments of pleasure and shared spirit. I engage in the game as a contest for space, but I do not feel vindictive about opposing players. They are my friends, and the next game might be my teammates. I want to play well, and I want the game to go well. I want us to play in a way that honors the game, and excessive competition and brutal play are outside of its spirit. Some pickup games, of course, are much less friendly, and there are routinely vicious players. But that is just my point: It is difficult to generalize about the competitiveness of the game, and it is a mistake to assume that competition is the soul of the experience for most players.

Even George Orwell, in his ascerbic essay "The Sporting Spirit," makes a strong distinction between organized sport, which he calls "an unfailing source of ill-will," and informal games, which he evokes with pastoral nostalgia:

> On the village green, where you pick up sides and no feeling of local patriotism is involved, it is possible to play simply for the fun and exercise: but as soon as the question of prestige arises, as soon as you feel that you and some larger unit will be disgraced if you lose, the most savage combative instincts are aroused. Anyone who has played even in a school football match knows this. At the international level sport is frankly mimic warfare. (1958, 160)

Orwell is writing in 1945 on the occasion of the visit to England of the Soviet soccer team Dynamo for games against the English national team. This visit, touted as an opportunity for "goodwill between the nations," evokes in Orwell memories of the Nazi Olympics of 1936, an occasion in which sports became "orgies of hatred." Sports for Orwell are hyper-competitive spectacles at which fans "work themselves into furies over these absurd contests," dividing the peoples of the world along nationalist lines, rather than drawing them together in sentimental fellow feeling. Henning Eichberg (1998), in *Body Cultures: Essays on Sport, Space, and Identity*, makes a similar point, connecting the territoriality of team sports such as soccer and basketball to the nationalistic projects in which they often are involved. At the elite level, basketball can and does evoke the partisan passions that Orwell describes, inspiring bitter feelings between players and fans, on the assumption that the dignity of their nation or city or neighborhood or school is at stake. But pickup ball is played on Orwell's "village green," often with nothing at stake except the feelings of the players, and sometimes with no sense of competition at all.

I also doubt the easy connection that some analysts claim between the competitiveness of the game and a habit of domination by players in their lives outside of the game. My self-observation suggests that I leave a lot of my competitive drive out on the court. I do not think of myself as a highly competitive person, nor have I observed this trait in my many friends who have played the game for years. Perhaps sport can serve as a cathartic experience for players rather than reinforce competitive drives. The players I know are gentle and nonviolent men who *do not* seem to have learned domination from their playing experience. Obviously I am not making empirical claims about psychological causation here. I am relying on years of casual observation rather than experimental verification. And on the structural level it is important to remember that individual men may be gentle and nonviolent without disturbing the domination that men enjoy in our society. So I am not claiming that sport does not teach and reinforce male domination. But I would claim that there is a wide spectrum of competition within basketball games, and a wide variety of masculine practices that derive from the experience of playing.

Returning to the analogy to dance, especially with contact improvisation, I think it is more accurate to think of the competition in basketball within a framework of group cooperation. The energy that directs movement within the game is produced by *all* of the players, not just teammates. And that energy creates a bond among the players and an agreement as to the limits and nature of the contest in which they will engage. Each player is trying to outdo the other, but the very existence of the contest requires a cooperative act as its premise. We agree to accept the spatial and ethical limits of the game, and we agree to share a communal expertise, a mutual awareness of possible moves and countermoves that can exist only within a community of shared knowledge and expectation. We have much more in common, even on opposing teams, than we would perceive if we thought only in terms of a competition model. The pleasure of the game derives in great part from being a part of that community, no matter what the "sides" are at a given moment. We gather to play together, and that sense of belonging is much more important than our play at opposition. Anyone who dehumanizes or thinks of the other team as the enemy is either an adolescent or an idiot or a victim of excessive coaching. I believe that the relationships among players are much more complex, much warmer, than we would observe if we thought of competition as the sole purpose of the activity.

Competition in basketball also operates within a strict ethical code, as I argued in "The Ethics of Basketball." The game allows much less violent competition than football or rugby or ice hockey, for example. The fierceness of hitting in those games is just not present in basketball, where players accept more severe restraints on the "force" they may bring to bear in the effort to impose their will on the objects in the game-space. On defense, I want to take the ball away from the offensive player, but it would not occur to me simply to knock him down and take it away. I have to work my will within the limits of the practice. Eric Dunning (1986), in "Sport as a Male Preserve," sees these ethical limits as the essence of the "civilizing" role of sport. Dunning, influenced by the figurationist sociology of Norbert Elias, sees one element of civilization as the process of constraining violence, particularly among men, by legal institutions and shared ethical norms. His history of sport is a narrative about how the unmitigated violence of premodern folk sport comes under the control of game-specific rules monitored by governing athletic institutions. Dunning makes clear that sport serves patriarchal ends by allowing men to exclude women from their activities and to worship a cult of physical strength, one of the grounds of their power over women. But he also argues that the "civilizing" of sport in the nineteenth century may have contributed to an environment that fostered the development of feminism, in that it restrained male violence at a time of female challenge. Modern sport placed "a complex of internal and external restraints on the expression of aggressiveness by men, for example via the code of 'gentlemanly behaviour,' thus restricting their opportunities for using one of their principal power advantages relative to women—their physical strength and superiority as fighters" (1986, 273). Dunning's analysis seems to me to overstate the role of modern sport in the history of feminism, but I mention his work because he emphasizes the *restraints on violence* in sports rather than on their promotion of violence, and he suggests that those restraints may have positive effects on male behavior outside of the sports arena. I believe that athletes accept these restraints not because they are seeking to become better people but because the restraints make the pleasure of the game possible. Nevertheless, it is just as logical to argue that these restraints on violence cross over to social behavior as it is to claim that violence itself crosses from the game to life in society. Competition in basketball is part of the pleasure of the game, because players can trust that the competition will remain within safe limits, limits that allow players to trust each other, even if they are on opposite sides in the struggle.

THE BODY AND EMOTION

Within this atmosphere of trust, strong emotional ties can develop among the men in the game. Competition and friendship interact in complicated ways within communities of players. Michael Messner, a sociologist who has interviewed many male athletes on the subject of friendship, found that the close ties between teammates were compromised by their competitive drives. They saw teammates as potential threats to their status within the group, and they could not share weakness or vulnerability because they could not risk giving another player a competitive advantage. Messner's subjects were elite-level athletes who had experienced a substantial career in sport, and I believe that his choice of subjects skews his results. My observation of lifelong athletes who never had an elite career or who left it behind long ago is that such perceptions of threat are less common. As a result, strong emotional bonds can develop. Messner tends to generalize his findings from elite athletes to all men in sport. His explanation for these comparatively superficial friendships derives not from an analysis of the specific situations of elite athletes but from his sense of the general configuration of masculinity in our culture. Messner argues—as many psychologists do—that men tend to have less intimate and intense same-sex friendships than women. He says: "An interesting consensus has emerged among those who have studied gender and friendship in the United States: Women have deep, intimate, meaningful, and lasting friendships, while men have a number of shallow, superficial, and unsatisfying 'acquaintances' " (1992, 91). Women tend to share the intimate details of their lives, while men tend to bond around a shared activity, forming "external" relationships that allow them to maintain their ego boundaries and avoid homophobic suspicions. In sports, then,

> the hierarchical and rule-bound pattern of athletic careers, and especially of "antagonistic cooperation" on the team, dovetails with men's ambivalent need to develop "closeness without intimacy" with other men. In short, competitive activities such as sport mediate men's relationships with each other in ways that allow them to develop a powerful bond while at the same time preventing the development of intimacy. (Messner 1992, 91)

Messner and others have relied for their understanding of male friendship on Nancy Chodorow's analysis of child-rearing practices. Chodorow analyzes male emotional life as a reaction to early nurturing by the mother that requires a rejection of femininity in order to establish the young male's identity as a function of his differentiation from the mother. Men thus create selfhood based on difference from others, while women create selfhood through connection to others. Men have stronger ego boundaries and strong fears of their own femininity, which become expressed in misogyny and homophobia. The result for male friendship is emotional impoverishment and a failure of intimacy. Following this theory, Messner, in my opinion, underestimates the depth of emotional ties among men who play a sport together. I believe that we must rethink the definition of intimacy if we are to understand bonds among male players.

I would report from my own game that strong bonds among players have developed over time, though I would agree that they are not intimate bonds in the terms that Messner uses. That is, they do not involve explicit, verbal sharing of personal information and emotion. But I feel a strong affection for the men with whom I play basketball, even the ones whose playing style and spirit I do not particularly like. I do not know much about their lives off of the court, and we do not tend to socialize, even though we live in a small community. In some cases, I do not even know the last names of the men with whom I have played for many years. But I would maintain that I know these players intimately—as players. I know that one player cannot go left, that another will always pass on the fast break, and that another will back off if the game gets too physical. To someone outside of the game, such knowledge might sound superficial, but within the game, this embodied knowledge (multiplied by 1,000) is both strategically useful and emotionally satisfying. It plays a role in the calculations I make about improvisatory choices, and so it may seem instrumental rather than intimate. But this personal knowledge, built up over time in the game, is also central to the familiarity and comfort of the experience. Knowing other players as I do means that we can move together in predictable and nonviolent ways, because of our familiarity with each other's kinetic habits. And I would argue that such knowledge is rich and significant, not emotionally impoverished and shallow. If I know that another player is more likely to make a shot if he shoots quickly rather than if he has plenty of time to calculate and get set, then what do I know about him? Can I judge that, outside of the game, he is likely to be mercurial rather than deliberate in his decisions and actions? That is not my goal. My interest is in the game itself, in the knowledge of players as players, where men reveal deep truths about themselves. I believe that such knowledge is extremely intimate, though nonverbal and in a sense impersonal. And it leads to strong bonds of affection. Because we share the energy of improvised movement and deep interpersonal knowledge, we have what I consider an emotionally fulfilling friendship, based on the experience of the body in movement, underneath what seems to be a stereotypically male bond.

Basketball also involves an intimacy of physical presence and touch. Players spend a lot of time in the personal space of other players. Defenders "get in the face of" the players they are covering. Rebounders command space by bumping and pushing and leaning into one another. And this physical closeness is on the move, reacting to the changing strategies of the game. Maintaining close contact on the run requires physical cooperation between these "opposing" players, or else the game would be nothing but collisions and falls to the hardwood floor. Defenders study offensive players' moves, trying to anticipate direction and speed, relying on an intimate knowledge of others' movement patterns. Their ostensible goal is to frustrate the offensive players' strategies, but players also rely on this knowledge to keep the game free of pointless, accidental contact that can lead to injury and needless friction. Of course some players also enter this personal space just to *bother* the opposing player, to demonstrate who has control of the space on the court, even the space the others believe is their own. Personal space in the game is at once contested and shared, so that much of a player's time in the game is spent in close proximity to other players.

Let me take us back to the post. An offensive player gets the ball close to the basket, at a 45-degree angle, with his back to the goal. The defensive player is usually directly behind him, mirroring his position, denying the path to an easy shot. Students of proxemics say that in our culture each person is surrounded by a personal space equal to the size of his or her body in all directions (Scheflen and Ashcraft 1976, 40). A really good post player can take advantage of that personal space. If the defender enters the personal space on his right, then the player can spin left, and vice versa. But if the defender stays out of those side spaces and remains directly behind the offensive player, he can step back and take an easy shot over the top. Post players are therefore constantly jockeying for position within that personal space, and taking account of others who might enter it, to set a pick or make a steal. As a result, players spend a lot of time in each other's personal, intimate space.

And of course they touch in that space, making powerful and aggressive contact. They push for advantage in the post or for rebounding position. They set picks. They foul. But this contact takes place within a context of ethical restraint and good feeling. Players enjoy the contact, and they feel safe within shared constraints. One of the attractions of basketball is the physical contact that the game requires/allows. A "good run" in basketball is a fluid game in which the movement of the ball and the players is constant, and the contact between players is intense but intrinsic to the game, not accidental or intentionally injurious.

Spatial proximity and contact are elements of the intimate knowledge of others that basketball encourages. Players not only know the histories and tendencies of other players, they know each other's bodies—physical strengths and weaknesses, shifts of weight and force that can be anticipated and countered. They not only share the energy of improvisatory movement in a limited space, they share the energy of bodies in strong contact. They sweat together in their cooperative and contested work. If playing basketball together is an example of an "external" male friendship, one based on a shared activity rather than a verbal sharing of intimate personal experiences, then it still has an interpersonal, physical intimacy of its own and leads to strong, affective bonds.

The dismissive take on such relationships is that they are examples of a repressed homosexual desire that simultaneously produces homophobia—"male bonding." Same-sex desire needs the cover of competition, and the violence of the game expresses a loathing for the object of desire and for the desiring self. Under this rubric, which is usually delivered with a dismissive attitude, the complexity of life in the body is ignored. *Of course* the contact has a somatic charge, an erotic charge, but it does not anticipate or stand in the place of sexual contact. It is a good in itself, the object of desire, not a symbol of some other desire. Too often men in our culture are taught, and sport certainly is one of the places that they learn it, that touch can be used to dominate and oppress others. And they learn that same-sex erotic touch is to be despised in others and repressed in the self. Men learn to be suspicious of all touch insofar as it reminds them of this despised erotic touch. It is not surprising in this cultural context that male touch requires elaborate legitimation. And if athletics serve that function, then they do good psychological and cultural work for the men who play the game and for the culture with which they connect. Along with the competition and homophobia that sports undeniably teach, they at the same time provide an opportunity for physical contact with others in a context of play rather than violence. Basketball particularly, I would argue, with its limits on violence and its energetic movement flow, provides players with an experience of kinetic pleasure that is missing from the rest of their lives and from the lives of most men. Women in our culture are allowed much more nonsexual touching, and it contributes to their emotional health and their nonviolence. Could the touching that sport makes possible do the same for men? If we thought of sport less as competition and more as *play*, could men find in games such as basketball a way past homophobia in an acceptance of their desire for physical contact?

Despite this utopian reading, I do not deny that sports teach homophobia. Messner is certainly right to emphasize the role of sport in teaching normative heterosexuality. "Heterosexual masculinity is collectively constructed through the denigration of homosexuality and femininity as 'not-male' " (1992, 97), and sport plays a central role in the denigration of homosexuality. Homophobic locker room jokes are a staple of the high school experience, and they do not completely disappear in adulthood. And as I said earlier, coaches and players can use the phrase "be a man" as a call to violence, an implied questioning of the player's sexuality aimed at manipulating an angry response that might be useful in the game. I would only claim that sports *need not* teach homophobia. Or at least *only* homophobia. They can teach—they have taught—me and many others modes of movement and touch that are nonviolent, friendly, nonsexual, and humanly affirmative.

Varda Burstyn is one of the cultural critics who sees organized sports as a practice that encourages homophobia, as a compensation for the physical intimacy that sport encourages. Because sport is an experience of "intense physical engagement," it creates "erotic effects" that men must disavow by a show of hypermasculinity. But Burstyn also sees a more affirmative possibility in sport: "Delight in sensual and sexual experience is part of the human constitution, and men's delight in each other could conceivably be a force for bonding and solidarity" (1999, 101). Unfortunately, that delight has been mobilized to oppress women, stigmatize homosexuality, and militarize sport and the culture for which it is such a central spectacle. Pickup ball, which is not a media spectacle, is less available for that ideological mobilization. It can devolve into macho violence and irrational competition, but it also can be an occasion for the "delight" that Burstyn describes.

What basketball teaches men, in its ways of defining and occupying space, in its modes of movement, in its mix of competition and cooperation, in its promotion of friendly, nonsexual touch, is a complex mix of traditional and emergent modes of masculinity. About ten years ago a friend asked me if I wanted to join a men's group. He had in mind a group that would *talk about* how their lives had been changed by the changes in women's lives, and how men could learn to contribute to these positive developments. I knew instantly that I did not want to be a part of the group, in part because I felt that I was already in one. I made the joke at the time that I was a member of a men's improvisational movement group—the basketball group. And now I offer the joke as a serious proposition, that the regular players in the game are in fact *working out* and *embodying* new modes of masculinity, in a new world in which the patriarchal order cannot be taken for granted. I believe that we are playing this old and traditional game in new ways, finding in it more than competition and facile male bonding. Basketball has the potential to teach men how to move with grace, in complex cooperation with others, sharing the energy of movement, the excitement of improvisation, and the pleasure of close, nonviolent physical contact. These are not the lessons of a "hegemonic masculinity." Of course basketball also teaches force, domination, competition, and homophobia. As a powerful, traditionally male practice in a patriarchal culture, it cannot avoid those destructive lessons. But like many practices, basketball conveys contradictory messages simultaneously, thus making it possible for men to learn lessons that they never expected from a game that most people think of as nothing more than exercise and recreation.

I do not offer these lessons in movement and spatial behavior as a panacea for men moving beyond patriarchy. Basketball will not save us. But the somatic lessons it teaches have their effects on the everyday lives of players. So much of men's lives is spent in a physical isolation that results from the homophobia they have been taught and from the belief that they are engaged in the economic war of all against all. Men in our culture are taught in many of their practices that life itself is competitive, that they cannot trust anyone who might one day be a rival for power, and that they cannot make contact with others except in sex or domination. A movement experience that teaches cooperation and movement *with* others must be healthy for men caught in the fortress of the competitive ego. Basketball teaches tenderness and peace. It teaches respect for physical limits and restraint. It teaches the joy of play. It teaches men much more than the stereotyped virtues of the traditional athlete. Michael Messner, in "Men Studying Masculinity," warns against the tendency of postfeminist thinkers to glorify "men's homosocial retreats from women's emotional control and from the general feminization of social life" (1990, 141). But I do not think of basketball as a retreat; rather, I believe it is an affirmative practice that provides men an opportunity to engage with new ways of social being, new modes of masculinity.

Chapter 4

Basketball, Decision Making, and Postindustrial Culture

The previous chapter emphasized the physical practices of the game, but basketball also makes complex cognitive demands on its players. The discipline of basketball moves the players' bodies through space, but it also moves their minds through a complex and fast-paced process of observation, awareness, decision making, and assessment. Coaches and game analysts recognize these mental requirements: They will say of a player, "He makes good decisions," or "She has good court awareness." All sports make cognitive demands, of course, each requiring a unique set of strategies and mental processes. In basketball, decision making is the most pressing intellectual challenge. Particularly in its purest cognitive form, in the uncoached pickup game, basketball encourages *group, real-time, improvised decision making*. In Bourdieu's terms, this decision style is the cognitive element in the habitus of the practice, operating in an embodied, often unconscious mode. And one of the factors that explains the current popularity of basketball is the fact that *group, real-time, improvised decision making* is encouraged in many practices throughout contemporary culture, particularly in corporate and institutional work environments. Thus basketball might be understood as a distinctive game of our time, mirroring and shaping broader social formations.

One of the cognitive challenges of basketball is that players are faced with decisions at high frequency. Because the game is played on the run, and because it involves ten people moving in a restricted area, players must make decisions at almost every moment: Do I cut left or right, do I pass or shoot, do I challenge the player with the ball, or do I back off? And since all of the players are moving and making frequent choices, the situation in which individual decisions are made is constantly shifting, requiring new decisions and revisions of strategy. A sharp contrast to basketball can be seen in golf, in which the decision frequency is much lower. A golfer must make subtle and complex decisions about which club to play, or how to judge the wind, or how to read the line of a putt, but then he or she walks or rides to the new location of the ball, and decisions are delayed until the next shot is addressed. Basketball requires high-speed decision making in a fast-moving, often unpredictable environment. Mark Edmundson, a longtime veteran of faculty basketball, says in an article in *The American Scholar* that "basketball, which can look like a game of raw instincts, is a game of second-splitting judgments," made possible by what he calls "educated instinct." For him, the speed of the mental game is one of its great attractions, allowing players to "live in the pure present" (2006, 67–69).

This cognitive style is most fully developed in pickup ball, rather than in basketball played as an official, organized sport. In organized ball it is precisely the role of the coach to limit the decisions players must make. Some coaches devise elaborate set offenses and disciplined zone defenses that control players' movements very specifically. Other coaches ask players to make frequent, creative decisions, but within a general strategic framework set by the coach. In pickup games all of the decisions are made by the players, within a general strategic framework that emerges from the players' collective perceptions of the situations that arise in the flow of the game. Even the most elaborate coaches' schemes do not eliminate player decisions—set plays only provide strict structures inside which players must still make their own decisions—but it is in the pickup game that we can see most clearly the *group, real-time, improvised* nature of these decisions. Let me briefly unpack that phrase.

First, basketball requires *group* decisions. Ten independent agents scan the situation, interpret cues from other players, and make decisions that immediately affect the decisions of all the others. A simple example would be the "backdoor play." A player moves from a position near the basket out toward a spot where he can receive a pass from the player with the ball. A good defensive player will want to move between the offensive player and the ball so that he can discourage or steal the pass. But if the defensive player moves impetuously, too soon and too far, then both offensive players might see an opening: the player without the ball will cut "backdoor" toward the basket, and the player with the ball will pass to him for an easy, open shot. In pickup ball, no coach will have structured and planned this play; it will occur when two decision makers take advantage of an opportunity made possible by their common perception. Of course this example is not "simple" at all, if only because of the large number of players whose decisions affect the outcome of the play. The defensive player covering the player with the ball might see the opportunity for the backdoor play and move back into the passing lane. Or one of the other defensive players might see the play coming and move over to block the shot. Or the offensive player without the ball might *fake* the backdoor play, cut back out away from the goal again, thus fooling his own teammate, who might then throw the pass clear out of bounds, in the direction he thought the other player was going. There are many other possible variations. In such a complex decision environment, with many independent agents assessing situations and making decisions, it seems almost miraculous that coordinated plays develop, especially in an uncoached game. And yet coordinated decisions occur routinely, and some games attain a flow that feels magical, as though all of the players were sharing a single, complex consciousness. The group decision process in basketball does not lead to a consensus or to a deliberative vote on a common choice, yet decisions cohere routinely in collaborative play.

This coordination is especially striking in *real-time* decisions. In some decision situations it is possible to devise a general strategy or decision rule that can simply be applied by all of the parties in particular circumstances. Because of the speed and complexity of basketball, only the most general decision rules apply—a short shot is better than a long shot, find the open player, and so on. These shared heuristics do play an important role in group coordination, but almost all decisions are made by individual players in the moment, without forethought, in the midst of hectic action, as a response to stimuli that exist only for a matter of seconds. Decisions are therefore made at full speed, and in pickup ball they are made without an authoritative general strategy to guide them. Decision theorists tend to think of speed as a prime enemy of rational decisions, but speed is an inescapable condition of decision making in basketball, and remarkably, these full-speed decisions are often "rational" in that they mesh with the decisions of other players and lead to success. Doc Rivers, a great NBA player who is now a television commentator, has described the mental work of great jump shooters: "They watched one guy moving that way, and saw where this other guy's path would intersect this third guy, and how that would create a little pocket of space right *here*, just about now . . . and the ball would come and *koosh*, two points." "So tell me," he argues, "how did they always figure it out if they weren't some kind of engineers. It was physics: motion, time, space . . . it was spontaneous physics, it was calculated on the spot" (1993, 91). The speed of these calculations seems to argue against a linear, rational model for understanding decisions. Rather, *real-time* decisions suggest a less conscious, more intuitive and embodied logic, one that can adapt to new circumstances and operate without sequential reasoning. In basketball, decisions cannot be preprogrammed or subjected to a linear logic, but the regular "success" of those decisions demonstrates that a powerful form of logic is present.

Decisions in basketball are *improvised* by the group in real time. The game often has been compared to jazz, in which the musicians must make creative decisions as a response to the play of others and to their own feel for the moment. Earl "The Pearl" Monroe, a great Philadelphia player who went on to star with the New York Knicks, once famously said, "The thing is, I don't know what I'm going to do with the ball, and if I don't know, I'm quite sure the guy guarding me doesn't know either." That unpredictability, that openness to the moment, is a quality shared by many great players. And if the defender does not know how Earl is going to shake and bake, then neither do his teammates, who must react to his decisions in the moment with their own creative choices. A basketball game is created by all of the players, teammates and opponents, in the real time of the game. In fact, "creative" is the word used in basketball culture to describe the best decision makers. Basketball requires players to use imagination in their practice and in their play. Almost all basketball players love to shoot around by themselves on an empty court, in part to sharpen their ball handling and shooting skills, but also to imagine themselves in game situations. Those sessions then translate into an ability to anticipate the action in real game situations, to imagine where the action might go, and to make decisions that foster that imagined future. Passes go to the spot where a player *will be soon*, not where he is now. Improvisation requires that players imagine the possibilities deriving from a present situation, and "creative" players see more possibilities and often act on ones that almost no one else would perceive.

We can see the complexity of this *group, real-time, improvised decision making* by looking at an extended example, the post play. A player who is "posting up" is taking a position diagonally in front of the basket, five feet or so away, back to the basket, in order to be in position to take a pass from the outside and spin toward the goal in either direction. When the ball goes into the post, the post player is faced with many possible alternatives that he must assess on the basis of many factors. If the defender covering him is smaller or weaker, then he will simply turn to the basket for an easy shot. But as he spins, another defender might come to help on defense, in which case the post player will usually look for the teammate that the help defender has left open. The help defender might be anyone on the other team, so the post player's job is to "read" the court, see who has come to help, and find the right teammate. Sometimes, if the defenders are very good, they will "help the help"; that is, a defender will see that one of his teammates has gone to help the post player, so he will rush to pick up the offensive player left unattended. The post player might then decide instantaneously that the play just is not going to work, so he will pass the ball back outside, in effect starting the offense over again.

While the post player is reading and deciding, other players on offense and defense are moving and making decisions. The player who passed the ball to the post player has to decide whether to stay on the outside and wait for a possible pass back out, or to cut around the post player and head for the basket, or to move away from the post player in order to give him room for maneuvering, or some in-between combination of these alternatives. Defensive players have their eyes on the ball in the post, and their eyes on the player they are covering, trying to anticipate the strategy the post player will choose, watching which options are open to the other offensive players, and deciding on the best defensive move. As the post player turns, in that split second, the players must not only make an assessment of where the other players are and where they are going but also *who* they are, what their tendencies and skills are. If a defender comes to help, and the offensive player he has left alone has no shooting skills or has shown a tendency not to take the open shot, then passing to that player makes no sense, even if he is in the right position. All of these subtle, interpretive decisions happen in an instant, in a time much too brief for deliberation, and they are only pertinent for one moment, which will quickly be followed by other moments of decision.

Many coaches feel compelled to control the decision situations that their players face. In fact, all coaches have at least some set plays that control the players' movements and prescribe picks and cuts and passes. The most controlling coaches call a play every time their team has the ball, on the conviction that decisions are best kept in their own hands. Others, more friendly to the skills of the pickup game, set up a general strategic framework and leave the instantaneous decisions to the players. Dean Smith, in his influential book *Basketball: Multiple Offense and Defense*, advocates a "free-lance passing game" that relies on the ability of his players to "read the defense" within a general set of decision rules. The result of this system, he says, is that "the more our men play the free-lance passing game, the better they like it. The initiative exercised at finding their own ways to counter all possible defenses probably accounts for much of the satisfaction" (1999, 39). Mike Krzyzewski, coach of University of North Carolina's (UNC) archrival Duke, advocates a "running motion offense," in which "each time down the court, we evaluate the situation." "No one," he says, "should be slave to their plan" (2004, 55). Phil Jackson, who has made famous use of Tex Winters' "triangle offense" in Chicago and Los Angeles, sees this system as one that encourages creativity and real-time group interplay. In *Sacred Hoops* Jackson describes the game as requiring from its players a Zen state of "awareness," an ability to "live in the moment" and be open to the opportunities that the defense provides. Jackson says, "Basketball is a complex dance that requires shifting from one objective to another at lightning speed. To excel, you need to act with a clear mind and be totally focused on what *everyone* on the floor is doing. Some athletes describe this quality of mind as a 'cocoon of concentration.' But that implies shutting out the world when what you really need to do is become more acutely aware of what's happening right now, *this very moment*" (1995, 115). The triangle offense provides a structure, but Jackson encourages his players' creative decision making, a skill that they have gained from years of scrimmaging and running in unsupervised pickup games, where there is no structure except what the players create. Coaches may try to discipline this freewheeling creativity, but players and fans know that the game is at its most beautiful when all ten players are reacting to the events that unfold.

The cognitive practices of basketball can be illuminated by the discipline of decision theory, an effort by logicians, mathematicians, psychologists, sociologists, and experts in management and marketing to understand the ways that people do make and should make decisions. Scholars are interested in decisions for a variety of reasons. Mathematicians and logicians attempt to describe the rules by which a perfectly rational decision would proceed. Psychologists investigate the behavior displayed by actual decision makers. Business consultants devise processes that will improve decision making within organizations (see Bell, Raiffa, and Tversky 1988, ix.). My interest in decision making in basketball is in this sense behavioral. I want to describe some of the actual decision situations that players face and the decision strategies that they employ.

I contend that basketball players *are not* the perfectly rational decision makers that the logicians sometimes assume—the game just will not let them. Irving L. Janis and Leon Mann, in *Decision Making: A Psychological Analysis of Conflict, Choice, and Commitment,* sum up the ideal process of the rational decision maker in the following terms:

> The decision maker, to the best of his ability and within his information processing capabilities
>
> 1. Thoroughly canvasses a wide range of alternative courses of action;
>
> 2. Surveys the full range of objectives to be fulfilled and the values implicated by the choice;

3. Carefully weighs whatever he knows about the costs and risks of negative consequences, as well as the positive consequences, that could flow from each alternative;

4. Intensively searches for new information relevant to further evaluation of the alternatives;

5. Correctly assimilates and takes account of any new information or expert judgment to which he is exposed, even when the information or judgment does not support the course of action he initially prefers;

6. Reexamines the positive and negative consequences of all known alternatives, including those originally regarded as unacceptable, before making a final choice;

7. Makes detailed provisions for implementing or executing the chosen course of action, with special attention to contingency plans that might be required if various known risks were to materialize. (1977, 11; see also Wheeler and Janis 1980, 6–9; Carroll and Johnson 1990, 15)

I quote this entire passage precisely because of its length and elaboration. Keeping in mind the speed of the most ordinary decisions in the game, such a specific and demanding protocol seems wildly inappropriate. Real-time, improvised decisions cannot be so linear and so deliberate. Of course decision theorists realize that the ideal process is only an ideal, and that many decision makers do not and should not follow such a process. The logical rules of rational decision making lead to an "optimizing" decision, which aims to choose the alternative that best accomplishes the most important goals of the decision maker (see March 1994, 9). Because of the factor of speed, basketball players have to settle for "sufficing" decisions, ones that lead to acceptable outcomes in the given circumstances. They proceed not by a purely rational process but by "heuristics," rules of thumb, generalizations that can be applied flexibly in shifting situations.

I am not arguing that decision making in basketball does not have a logic, only that it does not have a linear, step-by-step logic. It is tempting to speak of the game in terms of pure intuition or instinctive response, but the experience of playing basketball argues that there must be an *embodied, implicit* logic, including many of the functions that Janis and Mann delineate, that can operate effectively at high speed, even if players are not aware of or able to articulate that logic. I am at best an ordinary basketball player, but when I am dribbling downcourt on a fast break, I can see my teammate cutting to the basket, and without conscious intention or reflection, deliver a bounce pass that goes inches under the hand of the defender and then arrives in the right hand of my running teammate. That action requires me to make calculations of geometry and momentum on the run at the same time I engage in considerations of interpersonal knowledge and strategy: Is my teammate likely to finish the play successfully? Do we want to push the ball to the basket or back the ball out and slow the game down? All of those simultaneous calculations of the mind and body cannot proceed by a linear logic, but they require a logic nevertheless, or else the coordination of teammates thinking together would not be possible.

What is the source of this shared, embodied logic? If it does not arise from linear rationality and logical reflection, then what accounts for its success? The answer, in a word, is *practice*. Decisions made at full speed in real time require a *software*, a flexible decision program that can be put to almost automatic use in any given circumstance, without reflection, "instinctively," as athletes say. And in basketball, *the practice is the software for the decision*. As players engage in the practice of the game, repeatedly, over years, they develop a set of heuristics that guides their decisions, and they share many of those decision strategies with other players they encounter. Some of these heuristics are the cliches of the game, the coaches' bromides: find the open man, fight through the pick. Some of them are so subtle and momentary as to be almost inarticulable: if you have the ball at the top of the key, read your defender's body—if he comes forward too assertively, trying to deny you an outside shot, drive past him to attack the basket, unless you know that he is quick enough to recover and block your shot. Such heuristics take years of practice to develop, though they feel instantaneous. The speed of the decision is precisely a function of the years of practice.

By *practice* I mean playing the game, of course, but also watching as a fan and being a part of the community of players, hanging around the game. Watching the elite game on TV or at an arena provides players with an expanded repertoire of possible moves, even if they cannot accomplish the moves with the power and flair of the great players. And "hanging around the game," listening to players talk, watching good players move and carry themselves, leads to a subtle knowledge of players' skills and strengths. Experienced players will tell you that they can spot a good player almost instantly, just by watching him or her hold the ball or oc-cupy space on the court. As Lars Anderson and Chad Millman say in *Pickup Artists: Street Basketball in America*, "You can always tell a basketball player by the first touch of the ball. . . . It's the way a player corrals a pass, grabs a rebound or just picks a ball up off the ground like it's the most natural thing in the world. . . . The player controls the ball with grace, spinning it in the palms, leisurely hoisting shots or dribbling with nonchalance. Such moves say, 'I've done this before and I've done it well' " (1998, 188). This subtle knowledge of bodies is the basis for players' ability to read cues from others in the midst of the game. Regular players become immersed in the game and its culture, internalizing the practice. It becomes embodied in their brains and their synapses, so that decisions come fast and without reflection.

Some of these heuristics derive directly from the official and unofficial rules of the game. Basketball is a global institution held together in part by the written rules, which figure into players' decisions, and also by unwritten rules, guides to good practice, shared by almost everyone who plays the game. The written rules are the parameters inside which play occurs; they are the constraints that make creative decisions possible. The "three-second" rule keeps the tallest players from simply standing under the basket for the whole game—it forces them to be mobile and creative. The "walking" rule limits how far a player can go without dribbling, and it opens up multiple alternatives out of sheer necessity—trick dribbles, quick passes. Players learn the rules explicitly in organized games, they watch and listen to TV games for interpretations of the rules, and they argue over the rules on the pickup court. In the practice of the game players also learn how the rules can be bent, how much pushing is allowed, and how to finesse the lane so that "three seconds" is not called. They also must estimate how tightly the rules will be applied in a given game. Are the referees calling the game very closely? How much "finessing" of the rules will the pickup players in a given game allow? The "official" rules of the game are always negotiated in a given play situation, but once negotiated they provide a platform for creative decisions. And since all of the players accept roughly the same official rules, creative decisions can be shared within the group.

I have already mentioned some of the *unwritten* decision rules, and there are many more: passing the ball is faster than dribbling the ball, move after you pass, clear out for a good offensive teammate so he can have room to maneuver, keep your eye on the ball and on your man, and so on. These heuristics become part of the mind-set that players bring to the game, the software they run as they play. They also bring to the game the micro-knowledge, the insider wisdom that they have picked up in the games of which they are part. They constantly observe players and their tendencies, looking for advantages, fine-tuning the decision program—engaging in what Edmundson calls, using the language of literary criticism, "a good close reading" (2006, 64). One of my local heuristics for my own game is that Michael will *always* try to pass the ball to a player closer to the basket. For Michael a pass back to a player on the outside is an admission of defeat, a grudging last resort, so as a defensive player I make decisions on the basis of that rule of thumb, just by recognizing that Michael has the ball. Rules of thumb and local knowledge derive from an ongoing practice that makes decisions at speed possible. I would argue that the role of *practice* in decision making has not been adequately understood within decision theory, and that *local practice* is an especially important part of real-life decisions in many circumstances. Rationality, with its implications of linearity, consciousness, and exhaustive comparison and assessment, is not as successful a description of behavior as a model that stresses the embodiment, the automaticity of decisions within a practice based on internalized and shared heuristics.

Decisions in basketball are a function of *situation awareness*, a term used by analysts and trainers in such areas as military strategy and air traffic control. The term refers to the ability to understand the relationships among many sources of data within a complex information environment. Think of the air traffic controller, who must monitor the positions and directions of many aircraft within a given space, and then make decisions about the right course of action for each participant in the situation, working with pilots and other controllers. Similarly, basketball players must keep multiple sets of information in mind as they make their decisions. "Situation awareness" is a fuzzy and subjective concept compared to "decision making," which seems to refer to discreet and objective actions. "Situation awareness" includes predecision perception and screening as well as postdecision assessment. Players must keep track of all of the bodies in motion around them, all of the tendencies and skills of the other players, all of the official rules of the game, all of the unwritten rules that serve as decision heuristics, and all of the local micro-knowleges that they have gained from experience in local practice. A player with good "situation awareness" perceives the court through the lenses provided by these heuristics, and as a result he or she processes the perceptual data from the game more efficiently, seeing meaningful patterns and "chunks" of data rather than a swarm of bodies in chaotic motion.

Players also must observe and analyze the results of their decisions. Was that player capable of catching that pass? Can he make that outside shot I allowed him to take, fearing that he could beat me off the dribble? These postdecision assessments are also "fuzzy." They do not proceed with mathematical certainty; rather, they are filtered through the subjective hopes and perceptions of the players. An offensive player may not make the shot, but he may *look like* a good shooter, so a defender will still have to respect the outside shot. A pass may not work out as intended, but players might recognize it as a "good look" worthy of another try in similar situations. All of this assessment data then become part of the mind-set that the player brings to the game as the framework for the next moment of "situation awareness." This fuzziness and subjectivity again suggest that decision making in basketball—and maybe decision making in many practices—cannot be reduced to a mathematical or linear logic.

In fact, "irrational" elements are routinely part of decision making in the game. Decision theorists tend to see emotional and purely personal responses as enemies of rational decision making, but in basketball these "irrational" elements can contribute to "rational" decisions. For example, when two friends come to a new pickup game with players they do not know, they will often look for each other on the court, making passes to one another instead of to a teammate they do not know, even if that player is in a more advantageous position. In a fluid and complex environment, people are attracted to the familiar, the predictable, even if they must ignore the strict concerns of strategy to find it. The results of this irrational choice often are positive. Because the friends have played together and move in coordination, a pass to a friend might be more successful than a pass to a more rational but unpredictable alternative. But these friends *are not* making the decision on the basis of this subtle rationality. They are making decisions based on loyalty and emotional connection. Any rational outcome is a bonus. Their goal is to produce a certain feeling in their experience of the game, one that affirms their friendship, yet they often succeed within the competitive structure as well. Players also make decisions on the basis of factors irrelevant to performance such as appearance, clothing, personal style, race, gender, age, and subcultural affiliation. A short and scrawny player is unlikely to get the ball until he establishes that his game is better than his body would predict. An older player will get the same treatment in some games, as will a white player in some games, a woman coming into a predominantly male game, or even a player dressed in inappropriate or unstylish clothes. Sometimes it really *is* the shoes, at least in the eyes of the other players. These irrational factors sometimes lead to successful decisions, sometimes to unsuccessful, but they are undeniably part of the decision process. They also operate as rules of thumb that make decisions possible. These rules of thumb are not always reliable, of course. By their very nature they are incomplete, and as we use them we must also be open to the possibilities they do not predict. But in a complex decision environment, they are the usable forms of rationality.

The complexity of basketball derives from the fact that this intense process of situation awareness, decision, and assessment, with all of its interpretive subjectivity, is multiplied by ten at every moment in the game. Every player in the game makes decisions, and no matter how rigid a structure a coach can construct, each of those players brings to every decision a different set of heuristics, based on idiosyncratic histories in the game, different styles of responding to cues, different perceptual habits, different goals, and different psychological profiles. Although there are general decision rules in basketball, there is no certainty that all of the players in the game share those rules. They bring to any given moment in the game the set of heuristics that they have picked up in their personal history in the practice. For example, players who grew up playing a lot of half-court ball are more likely to understand the nuances of the pick and roll than players who have been brought up in a freewheeling full-court game. Part of the process of adjustment that occurs in any game is the unspoken negotiation of heuristics. I was once playing in a full-court game with a much more experienced player, at a time when most of my experience was with half-court. On a fast break, he passed the ball quite pointedly to the spot where I *should have been*, just to let me know how he saw the future unfolding. Players also read perceptual cues from other players in distinctive and personal ways. Someone once told me to keep my eyes on the torso of the player I am guarding when he has the ball, since no one can fake with the trunk of his body, as he can with his eyes or head or with a shift of weight in the lower body. But I am not sure that anyone else I play with has that same habit; as a result, we do not just differ on how we read cues in the game, we are not even reading the same cues. Further, all of the players in the game make decisions based on different goals, even though all might loosely agree that they are playing to win. In some pickup games, some of the players may be motivated by intense competitiveness, while others just want a good run, and others might care more about outplaying the guy they are matched up with than about winning as a team. Such personal habits shape interpretation in any decision situation, but when it involves ten independent interpreters in close proximity at high speed, the decision situation is so complex that the sheer existence of effective group decisions suggests a powerful matrix of forces moving independent decisions toward correlation. Otherwise there would be interpretive and even physical chaos.

Decision theorists have addressed the unique demands of group decision making, speaking of "shared mental models" and "shared situation awareness." The ten independent operators playing the game certainly do bring with them their individual and unique experience, but they also bring *shared* experiences and understandings. Janis A. Cannon-Bowers, Eduardo Salas, and Sharolyn Converse (1993) have reflected on the difficulties of group cognition in their article "Shared Mental Models in Expert Team Decision Making." Coming from a background in military and emergency team training, they are interested in the cognitive mechanisms that make effective group decisions possible, especially in teams that involve experts from different disciplines who must work together under intense time pressure, often with lives dependent on their decisions. Such teams *must* be able to overcome their differences in perspective in order to make coherent decisions. The authors argue that what coordinates their decisions are "shared mental models," common understandings of decision goals and workable strategies. A mental model is a "mechanism whereby humans generate descriptions of system purpose and form, explanations of system functioning and observed system states, and predictions of future system states" (quoting Rouse and Morris 1986, 226). These models "provide a heuristic function by allowing information about situations, objects, and environments to be classified and retrieved in terms of their most salient and important features. This is particularly useful when rapid comprehension and response are required" (ibid.). The authors make clear that effective teams do not need to share *identical* mental models; in fact, such unanimity would limit the unique contribution each expert on the team could make, and it would work against creativity. Rather, the team must share some basic *expectations*, some sense of likely scenarios and appropriate responses.

Similarly, basketball teams must respect the unique contributions that all team members bring to the game, but they must at the same time develop some shared expectations so that the rapid events of the game do not result in interpretive chaos. They must know, for example, what a backdoor play is, what options it makes possible, what the current state of the play is, and where the players are likely to go in the immediate future, sharing as they do a frame of knowledge and expectations. Players acquire these shared models from their involvement in the practice, and players who have played together for a long time as members of a local game can develop an almost preternatural ability to foresee the future of the system and act in concert. These moments of shared understanding contribute significantly to the pleasure of the game. Shared cognition leads to shared pleasure and to the emotions that bring the players into community.

This understanding of mental models and situation awareness relies on the premise that such constructs and processes are precisely *not* exclusively "mental." Rather, their speed and automaticity suggest that game logic is *embodied*, a matter of the nervous system and the senses as well as the brain. The mental work of basketball does not only involve strategic decisions; it also requires players to make physical and perceptual calculations on the run. What is the mental work of such a simple fundamental of the game as dribbling the ball? Can a player be said to *decide* to dribble the ball farther in front of the body as running speed increases? Does a player *decide* on the correct angle for a bank shot? Tasks such as shooting, passing, catching, and jumping to block a shot require precise spatial and geometric calculations, all of which must proceed unconsciously so that such "higher-order" decisions as strategy and interpretation can occur. You cannot make a creative play if you are not scanning the court, and you can't scan the court unless you can dribble on the move without looking at the ball, and you can't dribble without looking unless you practice regularly and acquire a dexterity that requires no conscious thought. All of these micro-decisions require an intelligent body, trained in game-specific cognitive processes. Coaches recognize the necessity for endless task repetition in order to master physical and perceptual skills so that the player is free to make real-time strategy decisions (see Pruden 1987). Serious players often just want to have the ball in their hands in the midst of their life outside of the game, bouncing it against the wall, dribbling around the furniture, learning to handle the ball as if the skill were second nature. We return here again to the theme of *practice*. Higher-level decisions are made possible by the player's immersion in the practice. It provides both the heuristics and the trained body that produce cognitive speed.

Richard Widick's essay, "Flesh and the Free Market," makes a similar point about embodied practices in a very different decision environment. Widick uses Bourdieu's notion of practice to study the work of commodities traders in the San Francisco exchange. These traders must work so quickly that they cannot rely on linear calculations; rather, they must call upon the body's "deep-seated and socially trained cognitive structures, its inculcated classifications, perceptual schemata, and categorized dispositions" (2004, 197). They must develop a "sense of the game" that will allow "the spontaneous logic of practical action" (2004, 199). "The efficient trader," he argues, "has absorbed the logic of the pits and thus appears to *know* them *intuitively*, displaying for observers an obvious 'feel for the trading game' " (2004, 214). Widick's analysis of these practices suggests that the decision style of basketball, with its embodied speed, its ability to make intelligent decisions in a hectic environment, has a resonance outside of the game, in many decision environments in contemporary culture.

As a team sport, basketball requires group cognition, and we live at a cultural and an economic moment in which the word "team" plays a central role. Students at all levels of education learn in teams; workers in many organizations operate in project teams; corporations construct cross-functional teams. It is in fact part of the mission of many schools to give students team-learning experiences precisely in order to prepare them for their work future as team members, and of course coaches claim that their teams are the ones on which all others are modeled. Many management theorists believe that our work culture has been radically changed by the emergence of project teams rather than functional departments as the basic unit of workplace organization. They see the growth of workplace teams as a function of macroeconomic changes that require institutional speed, efficiency, and expertise for business survival. And the teams they describe and imagine sound a lot like pickup basketball teams. These workplace teams also require *group, real-time, improvised decision making*. Frontline workers are asked to make creative decisions in the flux of changing business situations, and they must cooperate with other workers who have different training histories and who will see situations differently. Clearly one of the functions that team sports—and especially basketball—play in our popular culture is to provide a visible model of teamwork. Because the rhetoric of teamwork can be put to malign political and economic uses, the cultural connections between sports teams and work organizations must be subjected to political critique. But I would argue that basketball can and does serve the affirmative function of providing an enhanced, even a utopian, vision of what cooperative work can be.

Evidence of the ideological connection between elite basketball and corporate work is available to the eye. Look up in the stands—corporate America loves basketball. The NBA and big-time college games have an audience of prosperous white men, many of them with tickets paid for by the firm. One of the reasons they are present is that the players are engaged in an economic and social practice structured very much like the fans' own corporate practice. That is, the players are independent economic agents seeking their own professional success but working in a complex team relationship with others in their enterprise. Both groups must negotiate team goals and individual goals; both must devise strategy on the run in a shifting decision environment that involves group cognitive interaction. And of course it is not only the corporate operators in the luxury suites that can identify with the decision situations in the game. At home watching on TV are the masses of contemporary middle-class economic life—office workers, bureaucrats, knowledge workers, organization men—all coping with the complexities of institutional life. We can all see ourselves in the game, even if we do not attend consciously to the analogy. Basketball attracts our attention because in our work lives we too move strategically through complex and shifting spaces. But the special appeal of the game is that basketball players do so literally, not just metaphorically. Their strategic decisions are *embodied*, made visible and beautiful, available to the gaze of a spectator whose work is precisely *disembodied*, caught up exclusively in symbolic exchange and knowledge manipulation. On the one hand, this spectator experience clearly reinforces current corporate and institutional work structures and thus serves a politically conservative function, but it also provides the basketball audience with a more affirmative vision of the pleasure and spontaneity of group practices. As Gina Caponi-Tabery says, basketball has always modeled "a way of group interaction that has become more important as large-scale industrial models of management have given way to postindustrial theories focusing on small groups and encouraging individual solutions" (2002, 63). The game raises the question, can the kind of authentic interpersonal connection required by basketball happen in a work environment that often cynically promotes a "team" culture that masks top-down corporate power and individual ambition?

The rhetorical connection between basketball teams and corporate "teams" also can be seen in the success of basketball coaches as motivational speakers. Pat Riley, Rick Pittino, and many others have spoken to corporate audiences about the need for team play, providing predictable cliches about selflessness and team spirit. Riley's prime example of the perfect team player, as I mentioned in an earlier chapter, is Magic Johnson, who created his own individual success out of a selfless style of play, out of his ability to "make the players around him better." Johnson is offered as a model for corporate behavior—he is a team player, but he looks out for his own economic interests, which are furthered by his skillful interaction with others on the team. This paradox of corporate team life is addressed in Andrew J. DuBrin's motivational book *The Breakthrough Team Player: Becoming the MVP on Your Workplace Team*, published by the American Management Association. DuBrin's advice to corporate team players is aimed at creating the Magic Johnson effect—how to be a team player and advance one's own career at the same time—and he uses the sports analogy explicitly: "In team sports such as basketball, baseball, football, and hockey, team play is essential. Yet the standout players are often paid ten times as much as the team players who do not distinguish themselves" (1995, xiii). DuBrin provides specific advice about how to "squeeze individual recognition" out of team situations: "An effective team player by definition uses group decision making rather than individual decision making. Yet people are often promoted because they are imaginative and bold decision makers. Again, you have to walk the tightrope to become a breakthrough team player. You have to know when the time is right to make a decision by yourself and when to involve one or more team members" (1995, 12–13). In this scenario, the team environment just happens to be a fact of corporate life, but individual ambition is clearly still the point of work. Teams must be manipulated in the battle of each against all.

"Team" rhetoric in the workplace is often politically and economically misleading. It is no coincidence that the rhetoric of team has gained currency at a time of corporate downsizing and cold "human resources" strategy. Employees, businesses say, are members of a team and so should feel a strong connection, a loyalty to their fellow workers and to the corporate "family." Meanwhile we reserve the right to terminate you at any time, subject you to drug tests, scrutinize your out-of-work life, replace you with outsourced workers, increase productivity demands, damage your family life, and so on. Team metaphors can simply be a cover-up, a feel-good diversion. However, I also am convinced that, for good or ill, team practices have in fact permeated the daily operation of our institutions. The literature of management experts and economists is convincing on this point. Cross-functional teams, project teams, and customer service teams are more and more the norm, to the point that we can characterize the postmodern economy as "post-Fordist," even "posthierarchical," at least in the everyday operation of many enterprises. Such arrangements are still in fact supported by a severe hierarchical structure, but its power is more subtle, less visible in the daily work practice. Basketball is open to appropriation by those who want to infuse their enterprise with a spurious team spirit, but it also serves as a model for the actual team practices that are increasingly important elements in contemporary work environments.

Maureen O'Brien is a basketball coach turned management expert who makes the team metaphor more specific and functional in her book *Who's Got the Ball? (And Other Nagging Questions about Team Life): A Player's Guide for Work Teams*. Dissatisfied with the vagueness of the team metaphor, she urges managers to think about their work situation more specifically. She asks *what kind of team* do you have? Some work situations, she argues, are like *football teams*: A strong manager at the top of a hierarchy sets the procedures (the plays) that workers put into practice following strict, preset guidelines. The job of the manager in such task environments is to define the procedures carefully and to discipline the workforce in order to ensure quality control. In *baseball team* workplaces, such as law firms and medical practices, the key work is done by skilled individuals working on their own initiative. The manager's most important job is therefore to hire individual stars and support their individual efforts. The *basketball team*, she argues, is the proper analogy for workplaces—like those of the air traffic controllers or emergency medical team members I have mentioned—in which real-time collaboration is required. In basketball, she says, "the players must be very flexible, responding to each other in a spontaneous and reciprocally cooperative manner" (1994, 7). She quotes the great Bill Russell, that "each player has to predict where a pattern of action will lead, and then act to change that pattern to the advantage of his team." In such an environment the job of the manager is to foster supportive and creative group interaction so that the team can make effective decisions without the manager's surveillance or intervention. Many management experts would argue in these terms that the football team has been the metaphor of the industrial era, while the basketball team should become the metaphor for the knowledge economy, which requires a workforce skilled in *group, real-time, improvised decision making*.

The embodied skills of the game provide a vivid visual representation of the disembodied skills of the knowledge work organization.

Basketball is not declared as the analogy in Lee Tom Perry, Randall G. Stott, and W. Norman Smallwood's (1993) *Real-Time Strategy: Improvising Team-Based Planning for a Fast-Changing World*—the authors prefer the jazz combo as their conceit—but even the title of the book touches on many of the words that I have used to describe decision making in the game. *Real-Time Strategy* is an argument against the effectiveness of long-range planning, which sets up a structure long in advance that members of the organization follow in particular situations. Rather, the authors propose that strategy should be improvised *in the decision situation* by the team doing the work. This decision strategy, so similar to a pickup basketball game, depends on "the theory of the small win." That is, real-time, improvised strategy produces "high-frequency, low-impact" decisions, rather than the "low frequency, high impact" decisions entailed by long-range planning. Improvised strategies can fail without creating catastrophes, because they can be quickly amended in the fluid situation. Therefore, frontline workers can be authorized to make strategy decisions rather than relying on upper management. These workers are closest to the emerging situation and are therefore best suited to make creative and effective decisions, not just to apply a principle constructed by a distant authority figure. One of the authors' examples is a fast food crew that huddles up in order to make strategy when they are faced with a tour bus full of customers in the midst of an already hectic lunchtime situation. Those workers must improvise adjustments to the process of making and serving the food in order to satisfy customers and increase profits. Of course there are general strategic guidelines set for the workers, but their moment-to-moment decisions are like those of a basketball team—improvised as a reaction to changes and opportunities perceived by the team.

The most frequently mentioned virtue of cross-functional teams is *speed*. If the group working on the problem has the authority to make decisions on the spot, then the organization saves bureaucratic time and cost. Central offices can be smaller and more efficient as decision power is moved to the front line. Cross-functional teams allow all of the disciplines in the organization to be present in the decision situation, applying their diverse analyses and skills to the problem, without delays of communication and logistics. Teams can take on complex tasks, analyze and solve problems, and learn from their experience (see Parker 1994; Mohrman, Cohen, and Mohrman 1995). In basketball, pickup teams operate exactly in this fashion. Each player is an independent agent, responsible not just for a given set of skills but for a creative understanding of the entire game, in the absence of direct supervision, cooperating with other independent decision makers in an ongoing cognitive process. Complex, real-time decisions require this kind of creative team that can see many aspects of a problem and communicate instantaneously. In group decision processes such as air traffic control and military strategy, speed is so important that decision teams routinely interact with cybernetic systems that can analyze data at hyperspeed, making effective, human, real-time decisions possible. Where once committees were seen as inevitable sources of delay, cross-functional teams are now seen as strategic sources of speed.

The speed of contemporary business also is cited frequently as one of the *macroeconomic* factors that have led to the emergence of the team model. In his book *The Horizontal Organization: What the Organization of the Future Looks Like and How It Delivers Value to Customers,* Frank Ostroff cites the "cross-functional organization" as a logical response to "a radically different business climate defined by new technology, intense global competition, a constantly changing marketplace, and the expanded aspirations of workers who are demanding increased participation and greater responsibility" (1999, 6). He argues:

> The collapse of borders, the wiring of the world, the need to tailor products to accommodate a diverse marketplace, and a clamor among available workers for more responsibility and job satisfaction—all this came together to make stability and predictability nothing more than a fond memory of a bygone era. With inconstancy becoming the rule, a bureaucracy weighted down by supervisory layer upon supervisory layer and its clumsy inability to coordinate efforts proved incapable of reacting with the speed needed to meet the varied and unrelenting demands of global markets and customers. (1999, 8)

Tom Peters (1992) strikes a similar note in *Liberation Management: Necessary Disorganization for the Nanosecond Nineties.* His argument is that in an "ephemeral" marketplace, one ruled by customer whim and transient fashion, businesses must reorganize toward flexibility, toward "adhocracies," teams assembled for an ephemeral purpose, teams empowered to make instant decisions.

Workplace teams, then, exist because of a powerful economic logic. A fast-moving marketplace requires a fast-moving organization, and teams make decision speed possible. Macroeconomic trends produce new workplace structures, and by a similarly powerful economic logic, new workplace structures produce new cultural forms that support and reflect the new forms of work. There is a strong realization in management theory that teams cannot just be constructed; they must be maintained and supported by changing the corporate culture of the organization. Teams must be valued and rewarded, and workers must learn the pleasures of working cooperatively. In such an environment, it is not surprising that our culture of recreation is dominated by team sports. The structures of the workplace are repeated and reaffirmed quite specifically in the structures of our popular games. Playing basketball or attending a game or watching on TV is an opportunity for knowledge team workers to *see* and *feel* the structures of their work acted out in the spectacle of the game. Basketball naturalizes their work experience; it makes it feel dramatic and important. In part because of the popularity of team sports, the emotional resonance of the word "team" is powerful: to be on a team is to feel that one belongs, that one is in on the newest innovation, that one's work has the energy and intensity of play. Team sports reinforce these new workplace innovations, giving the imprimatur of culture to the requirements of work. As I argued earlier, the team metaphor is often a cover-up for hierarchical corporate power, and it is always an effort at legitimization, a way of representing and selling a new corporate culture to the workforce.

But teams in the workplace have not only been a response to changes in the market. They also have addressed the emotional need of an educated workforce for more autonomy in decision making, more authority to control the conditions of work, more satisfaction in the day-to-day process. Educated workers with specialized analytical skills do not take well to authoritarian work structures—to football teams. They trust their own expertise, and they believe that they are in the right place, in the midst of the work rather than distant and detached in the home office, to make the important, moment-to-moment decisions. For many workers in the postmodern economy, workplace teams can be as empowering as the rhetoric claims. Teachers, medical personnel, high-technology production workers, committees creating a new product, and advertising teams designing a new campaign all benefit from the creative interplay and improvisational energy that teamwork creates. Despite the cloying rhetoric, working in groups really can produce pleasure in work, rather than the often lonely drudgery of the functional, one-dimensional processes fostered by the strictly hierarchical, industrial model. It would be foolish to forget that workplace teams still exist within nondemocratic institutions with powerful disciplinary structures, but it also would be a mistake to deny that *group, real-time, improvised decision making* can create great personal and social satisfaction.

Peter Senge says this in *The Fifth Discipline: The Art and Practice of the Learning Organization*:

> Most of us at one time or another have been part of a great "team," a group of people who functioned together in an ex-

traordinary way—who trusted one another, who complemented each others' strengths and compensated for each others' limitations, who had common goals that were larger than individual goals, and who produced extraordinary results. I have met many people who have experienced this sort of profound teamwork— in sports, or in the performing arts, or in business. Many say that they have spent much of their life looking for that experience again. (1990, 4)

Senge praises those organizations that are "dedicated to the well-being and growth of employees as well as to success" (1990, 15), and even mainstream management specialists realize that worker satisfaction and quality of life contribute to productivity. Working in teams contributes to that quality of life because of the complex human interactions—even the difficult ones—required. And when the members of the team are willing to work creatively together, in the moment, setting their own unwritten rules, negotiating their values, constructing their own decision style, then the experience can be as satisfying as Senge makes it sound.

Basketball fans get to see a team at play, creating shared accomplishments in the moment-to-moment flow of the game. In the enjoyment of the spectacle, the real economic struggles behind the game can be bracketed off, left to the gossip and speculation of the sports pages and ESPN. The beauty of group improvisation is plainly visible, powerfully embodied. I remember an NBA All Star game when for ten minutes or so Michael Jordan, Scotty Pippen, Grant Hill, and Penny Hardaway (along with Christian Laettner to rebound and make some outlet passes) got into a run that showcased their unmatched open-court games. They were down ten or so when they came in, and they put together about a ten-point lead before they left. They did not run a single set play. They just got the ball and ran, making the game up on the fly. It was a classic pickup run, a sequence in which energy, intensity, and the sheer joy of play come together, transforming a group of individual players into an entity that shares energy and consciousness, that makes decisions in perfect interplay. I remember that run as a model of human group interaction, the way work should be, a recovery of play in the midst of serious endeavor.

For me, getting to *play* the game as an adult has meant having the opportunity to experience group interplay at a high level. I have played with a shifting set of other players over the years, and we know each others' styles well, so that we make effective group decisions regularly. In these games I know the pleasure of improvising in the moment, of thinking on the run. I have particularly benefited from the fact that my game occurs in my work space, at one of the university's gyms. As a result, I do not sharply distinguish between work and play. Some of the people are the same, and because of my long immersion in the game, many of the interactions are the same. I have sought out team situations in which to work—team teaching, problem-oriented ad hoc committees—and I have made my own classes more playful, more improvisatory, more interactive. The pleasure of the game routinely washes over into the daily tasks of work. Basketball, the perfect team game, the perfect democratic game, can serve as a model for work in our culture. It articulates an ethic of team relationships, and it puts into play a cognitive style from which all kinds of teams can learn. *Group, real-time, improvised decision making* requires working without a script, without top-down leaders, and without a secure and predictable outcome. But the risks of this strategy are overbalanced by the pleasures: the opportunity to work in the moment, with respected peers, in a cooperative effort to create an unforeseeable future.

Chapter 5

Basketball as Community
of Practice

"Community" is a contested term in contemporary culture. On the one hand, its absence is often lamented, in the sense that America and other advanced societies are seen as radically individualistic, failing to provide people with meaningful connections, shared beliefs and values within a coherent tradition. On the other hand, the urge to create communities is often seen to result in essentialist groupings around race, gender, sexuality, ethnicity, religion, and nationality, imposing strict membership rules and creating conflict with what are defined as opposed communities. Either we live in a society in which we bowl alone, as Robert Putnam's influential and controversial book has it, or we live within Balkanized encampments, as Paul Gilroy has argued in his recent book *Against Race*.

Within the contemporary debate about community, I can discern four ways of understanding the term. For classical philosophical liberals, who are now mostly political conservatives, a community is an assemblage of individuals freely choosing association out of the desire to maximize each individual's goods. In fact, in this context "community" is a less apt term than "association" or, in the flattest sense, "society"—something external to the self, often a power to be defended against, hence the classic liberal emphasis on individual rights. From this perspective the most perfect communities are those that weigh the least, restricting individuals only to the extent necessary for safety and survival. Since individuals are self-created, self-suffecent, and self-governing, communities are connected not by shared identities or values but by mutual interests and benefits.

For communitarians, liberal or conservative, "community" is just the right term because of its emotional (classical liberals might say sentimental) connotations. It points to groups based on affective bonds, with shared ways of thinking and feeling about the world, along with a set of strongly held values. Individuals *find themselves* in these communities in the sense that they do not choose to become members but are born into communities or lead lives that connect them organically to others who share their experiences. They also *find themselves* in the sense that their identities are produced by the community and can only be discovered in that context. They also find in the community a moral order that derives from their shared way of life. For communitarians the perfect community is the heaviest, the deepest, the one that defines us most powerfully and connects us to others most profoundly.

For radical political activists, "community" is often used as a rallying cry for oppressed groups who need collective action in order to battle the effects of ignorance, stereotype, and hatred, as in terms such as "the black community," "the gay community," or "the differently abled community." In this sense a community is an action-oriented group, united by an agenda for change. Membership in these communities is not chosen—it is based on factors beyond an individual's control—but identity as an *active* member of such a community is consciously taken on as a political affiliation, a marginalized identity intent on gaining respect and power. In this usage "community" produces a heavy and deep identity, one that cannot be escaped, and demands to become the basis for action in the social world.

"Community" also is used in a less heated, more technical sense in the way that Stanley Fish thinks of "interpretive communities" or Etienne Wegner speaks of "communities of practice." For Fish, what defines an "interpretive community" is a set of assumptions and a shared discourse allowing members to interpret the world, to make sense of experience. Members of an interpretive community do not agree on everything, but they share enough cognitive and discursive habits that they can make common sense and even disagree with each other in a coherent way. Wegner uses "community of practice" to describe a group centered around a shared activity, a profession, or an avocation that provides a common set of experiences and therefore an identity. A community of practice develops tacit and informal ways of knowing that it passes on to new members in the daily process of engagement in the practice. What I like about Fish and Wegner as theorists of community is that they understand that individuals belong to *many* such communities. No one performs only one practice in the world, and no one interprets every experience in the same terms. In this sense they see community as a lighter, more mobile concept that provides connection but does not imprison the individual within an essential identity.

This is not to deny the existence or importance of deep community identities or the pressing politics that they generate. Despite the advancement of global economic and cultural systems, national communities still wield power and create strong affective ties. Despite modernist skepticism, religious communities still create strong identity affiliations for billions of people. And to turn to the themes of "identity politics," to be gay is to be connected to other gay people, both in shared oppression and in shared affirmations of gay identity. To be African American is to share a history and a social reality in America, no matter the politics and attitudes of the individual. Such identities are not freely chosen. They are inescapable, and they determine in part the life options available to individuals. As such, they are rightly the basis for political action, especially in societies in which these and other unchosen identities are despised and attacked. For me, classical liberalism fatally underestimates the social determinants of identity, indulging in a fantasy of self-creation, as though individuals lived in a cultural and historical vacuum, free to associate with whomever they please, unencumbered by group identities.

Nevertheless, I would argue that there *are* elective affinities, communities created by interest, aptitude, and choice. These are precisely "communities of practice," which bring individuals together in activities that they love, connecting them to one another in the values, beliefs, ways of thinking and feeling, ways of using the body, and ways of working with others that the practice fosters. Gardeners connect with gardeners, dentists with dentists, and bowlers with bowlers, even across the most fearsome identity divides. These connections may not be deep, and they do not eradicate the differences that deeper identities create, but they do suggest that no group identity is monolithic and no division is absolute. The danger of the communitarian and the radical political understandings of community is that they overstate the demands that the community places on individuals, setting up identity tests and demanding uncritical allegiance, and that they exaggerate group differences, as though there were no connections across divisions, rendering the other alien and unknowable. A comprehensive vision of communities of practice makes such monolithic notions of community and personal identity untenable. If, as Wegner argues, we all experience "multiple membership" in communities of practice—I am a teacher and belong to the community of teachers but also to the basketball community and the film fan community and the parenting community and the housework community and the charades community and the bodysurfing community and the writers' community and the modern dance community and so endlessly on—then our "deep" communities are not homogeneous and our identities are not simple and static. The concept of communities of practice creates a healthy complexity in a world that tends toward dangerous simplicities.

In order to analyze basketball as a community of practice, I will offer a nonce categorization system that I hope suggests the complexity of the phenomenon. I begin with a *game*, a single play event that I argue produces a momentary community of practice. I then move to the *run*, a slang basketball term for an ongoing community of players gathering to play at the same site on a regular schedule. And I conclude with the term *basketball* to suggest the huge, indeed global, community of players, fans, institutions, and media images that loosely organize themselves around the practice of the game.

THE COMMUNITY OF THE GAME

Three guys walk into a gym to shoot some hoops. They have been playing together since high school. They know each other's moves and strengths and weaknesses so well that they play together with preternatural understanding, making passes to places they do not yet know they are going. Two guys are shooting around at the other end of the gym. They just started getting together to shoot a few, once they found out they both played. The two groups stay separate, but they are aware of the others in their peripheral vison. Then a single player walks in, looking for a game. Six is the magic number, perfect for half-court, God's own game. Three on three, all the players you need to run all the possibilities of the game. So these three and that two and this one have to figure out how to become three on three, how to create a game. Typically the three will stay together. One of them will say to the two and the one, "Want to run?" "Three of us?" The two and the one will walk to the court of the three and begin to shoot around. All six will shoot the two balls, run down each others' rebounds, looking now from the outside like six members of the same team. But they are all keeping an eye out, evaluating the players they do not know. Maybe the one can *really* play, his grace and power visible to all in the second he picks up the ball. Maybe the other two are smart enough to see how they can play roles that will let his game operate, so they can counter the years of experience on the other side. After a few minutes someone will roll one of the balls off the court, and the formal negotiations will begin. There are decisions to be made, ground rules to be established, and, in the process, a small, ephemeral but real community to be created.

How long will the game be? Eleven baskets is a classic, or fifteen, or twenty-one. "Run to eleven?" "Win by two?" "Nah, let's go with one. I hate it when it drags on." Now they know they will play to eleven baskets, a good way to start, to experiment with the matchups. And they have decided that they will *not* follow a common half-court practice that requires one team to win by two baskets, a practice in which one team must win *decisively*—up 10–9 they have to finish off the other team, who knows they have to stop the play or lose the game. It is a highly competitive practice, typical of intense local games where you win or lose the court. Not necessary here. There is no one waiting, and at this point it seems like a friendly game. Besides, in a "win by two" game you can get into "advantage" situations, as in tennis, that can stretch out the conclusion indefinitely. Maybe the three come from that kind of local game, but maybe the two are less competitive, want to keep it simple.

The next point to be negotiated by this emerging community is specific to half-court ball. Since both teams are shooting at the same basket, there is not the inevitable end-to-end flow of teams taking shots alternatively. By convention, in half-court, two possibilities present themselves. Either the team that makes a shot gets to keep the ball—"make-it-take-it"—or the team that gets scored on gets the ball, as in full-court ball. "Make-it-take-it" is again the more competitive option, since a dominant team can run to eleven very fast, without its opponents seeing the ball much at all. So maybe the three say, "Okay, make-it-take-it?" but the others say no, so the game will go with alternate possessions. With each of these ground rule decisions, the specific character of this community is defined. In my hypothetical example, the decisions so far have created a friendly atmosphere, a community in which not much is at stake, but the decisions could easily have gone the other way, creating a community of intense contest, and all of the participants know the difference.

Other details remain to be negotiated, often in the midst of play. Someone will make a steal and take the ball right to the basket. But the other team might say "whoa, bring it back out," which means that any change of possession requires the team that takes over the ball on a defensive rebound or on a steal to take the ball out to the top of the key before its attacks the basket. And then there is the question of who calls fouls— offense or defense? The default setting is that offense calls, assuming that people can be trusted to make reasonable calls and not to take advantage. Once trust is established, though, defensive players will call obvious fouls on themselves, taking responsibility and relieving the offensive players of the need to make *every* call. "That's on me," they will say, or "Your ball." But who will call out-of-bounds plays? And who will decide how rough the contact under the basket will be? And who will settle disputes? Those issues will be negotiated when they come up, and the outcome will depend on the decisions of the players in the community of the game, conditioned by their histories, their personalities, and their shifting moods and feelings about the other players.

These negotiations can be instantaneous and easy, with all of the players willing to go along, to create the best game possible. Or they can be contentious and thus protracted, probably because the backgrounds of the players are too different, or because no one wants to give in to the other side, even in setting the parameters of the game. If the negotiations get too intense, someone will inevitably say "Let's just play ball," or even "Fucking lawyers," and questions will get settled so the game can get on. Or not, in which case no functional community has been established and the game will dissatisfy everyone.

These negotiations, or ones like them, happen every time a game begins. In pickup ball there are no rules and regulations, no preset patterns of operation to follow. Not only must players make the million in-game decisions that basketball requires, they also must decide on the rules and practices that will structure the game itself. It is these cooperative decisions, these complex negotiations, that create a community for the moment. Of course it is an ephemeral and extremely lightweight community. These six players may well never meet again, and the connections they make in and through the game do not have the heft of those shared within deep and abiding communities. But these lightweight communities, formed around a shared practice, serve important cultural functions. At a time when heavier communities often make rigid demands on the behavior of their members and set themselves violently over against other communities, these lighter communities, to which we all belong around all of the myriad practices of daily life, connect us to others without requiring us to disdain those who do not belong. These communities of practice place us within webs of connection, as many and various as the practices we engage in. If a cultural practice, to invoke the central term of this book, is an activity from which participants learn values and beliefs and ways of thinking and feeling, and if we all engage in *many* such practices, then we share vocabularies and cultural habits with *many* people, even those who may belong to sharply different "heavy" communities. Disabled lesbian gardeners can talk gardening with redneck straight guys who love their roses.

THE CULTURE OF THE RUN

Of course not all pickup basketball games create such ephemeral, ad hoc communities of practice. Many pickup games are played within an ongoing *run*. A run is a regularly but unofficially scheduled game at a given location attended by a loose but definable set of players. I know of a 6 a.m. run at a local Y that has existed for years, attracting the same set of businessmen who like to play before their workday begins. I played for over twenty years in a Monday-Wednesday-Friday noon run with faculty, staff, and community players. There is a Sunday morning run at a local school gym. There is a young guy run on summer evenings at the rec center. At the university's student exercise facility, there are several regular runs, based on ability level, friendship groups, and racial and gender affiliations. Across the country and indeed the world there are runs in prisons, in churches, and on military bases. According to Alexander Woolf (2002), in *Big Game Small World*, there is a run at the royal palace in Bhutan! There are lawyer runs and lesbian runs and coworker runs and seminary runs and congressional runs and Hollywood actor runs. At a local park there might be several runs: an oldguy run, a teenage run, a women's run, an elite player run. These enduring social formations, these informal but powerful communities, are the heart of basketball as a cultural practice. They are the places where players learn the game, refine their skills and understandings, and connect with other players on the deepest levels. A run also is the place where the magic of basketball is created, where the preternatural understandings of players who have played together for years come into existence. Any *game* should be understood as a function of the *run* in which it is situated, or in the case of a truly ad hoc game such as the one I described earlier, of the runs where the players learned the game. The run, therefore, is the fundamental social and cultural formation of basketball as a practice.

A basketball run is a local phenomenon. Just to know of its existence requires local connections. Interested players find out about the run from personal contacts with other players. They get a sense of who plays in the run, and thus the level and style of play. A run attracts players from a limited geographical or sociological set. A neighborhood game may get famous and begin to attract players from around the city, but day in, day out, the core of players is likely to be local. Church runs attract members of the church or their friends, usually from other churches. Oldguy runs at universities may attract a few players from the local community, but their regulars are typically faculty and staff. After all, how many nonacademics can find a couple of hours in the middle of the day to play basketball? As a result of this "localness," runs might appear fairly homogeneous. Lawyers play with lawyers, soldiers play with soldiers, convicts play with convicts, locals plays with locals. But within this apparent homogeneity, local runs are often for players an experience of encountering and negotiating social differences.

The difference is often one of status. At a university in North Carolina, there is an ongoing run between grad students and faculty within a large academic department. For all involved, differences of institutional status must be negotiated within the daily practices of the run. That is, a

person with high institutional status does not necessarily occupy a dominant position within the run, where status is fairly ruthlessly a function of
skill. A full professor with a lousy jump shot is not likely to be deferred
to by a grad student who is a great defender. And yet institutional status
is never not present. Think about the Department of Justice guys who
played with John Ashcroft, who apparently played for keeps. Those other
players can never forget with whom they are playing. In military games,
enlisted men may play with officers, setting picks and blocking out, but
they do not stop calling the officers "Sir." But although status differences
are not eradicated, they are up for negotiation. Differences become less
absolute, less natural. The boss may have power in the office, but on the
court maybe he is one of the role players, or one of the fools who thinks
he is better than he is. Once you have blocked the shot of your boss, the
relationship changes. Of course the question of *whether* to block the shot
of your boss must be addressed. Local knowledge and street smarts would
suggest that total domination would be a mistake, but every basketball
instinct would require at least enough effort to show that you respect his
game and *the* game enough to play it straight. Such negotiations of institutional difference are a subset of the range of interpersonal decisions
made within any game. As I pointed out in my discussion of basketball
ethics, the game requires instantaneous and ongoing decisions about how
to play with others, as a function of knowledge of their strengths and
weaknesses, their personalities and histories. Negotiation of difference is
fundamental to basketball, and within any given run those negotiations are
made possible by local knowledge developed over time.

As a result, play within a run serves the social function of fostering
personal connections across social dividing lines. At a local prison where
I have visited and observed the game, there used to be a regular run in
which both inmates and guards played. Guards were ordered by prison
administrators not to play in these games, not because there was a risk of
violence but because the run was encouraging friendships between inmates
and guards, and authorities feared that guards could be taken advantage of.
In my oldguy run, professors mix with administrators, maintenance staff,
coaches, and ROTC personnel. Universities, like most institutions, segre-
gate their workforce, and there are few opportunities for contact between
workers in different functional categories. The run is an informal community of practice that cuts across those categories. When inmates play with
guards, soldiers play with officers, and students play with faculty, the formal hierarchies become complicated by the rough-and-tumble of friendly
competition. Thus the local social texture takes on a richer interpersonal
coloring than the official institutional structure suggests.

A run also is a historical phenomenon. Unlike the communities created by individual games, the community of a run is relatively stable and leads to strong personal relationships that can only develop over time. My oldguy run has existed for over twenty years, and one university that I have visited has had a faculty-staff game for over *fifty* years. This historical depth produces rich and complex styles of play. Because players know each others' moves and tendencies, games become chess matches. Defenders know what to expect in given situations, and they adjust without conscious thought to the moves they know will come. Offensive players then counter their own tendencies, and defenses must in turn readjust, in ways that offenses can anticipate, and so on. In addition to this technical complexity, the history of the run also promotes interpersonal complexity. Grudges grow and sometimes produce outbursts of petty violence. Friendships develop out of respect for righteousness of play. Sensitivity to players coming back from injury or coping with life problems is enacted without conscious thought. If shared history is an element in all communities, then basketball as a community of practice stores its memories in the shared consciousness of the run.

That shared consciousness is made possible by the relative stability of the run, and it is kept fresh by the *shifting* nature of that stability. That is, on any given day, a set of players arrive for the run, but that set is never nearly as large as the total set of players who are regular members of the community. In my run, approximately twenty players are present for games, but there is a pool of at least fifty regular or occasional players. As a result, there is enough stability to allow the development of deep temporal knowledge, but there is always variability, always new combinations of players and new strategic challenges. In addition, players enter and leave the community. Old players leave traces of their legacy on the style of play, and new players must accommodate themselves to the style of the run but also contribute their unique style and history to the cultural mix. In fact, a run could be thought of as the dialectical outcome of all the past runs the players bring to the moment. My Philly-boy, gym-rat style mixes with Mark's highly schooled, coached style. The history of the run is a function of the sedimented histories of the players and their past experiences in other runs in other social contexts. In a given run, those histories combine into a predictable but creative community practice.

One of the most important functions of a run is precisely to establish the guidelines for the practice. All of the decisions that I described earlier being negotiated at the beginning of a hypothetical pickup game are decided in the long term by the members of the run. That is, when a run has been established, no one in a given game has to decide the length of the game or the ground rules for choosing teams or the protocol for calling fouls. All those decisions have already been made, deep in the history of the run. Typically, when new players come into a run, they watch, listen, and adapt to the local practices. But some newcomers, by force of personality and by the authority of their game, can challenge and change the practice. When my run began, we played a half-court game, under the assumption that we were old and incapable of running full-court. Then a new and great player came into the game and said "What's this half-court shit?" and we played full-court from that day on. Once runs become established and set in their ways, they are less liable to change radically, but they never settle into stasis. After all, the ground rules were established by local, personal decisions, not by executive fiat or by the official rules of the game, so they are open to challenge and revision.

The habit of negotiation runs deep in the game, so local practices are never finally settled. For example, in my run we take a very brief break after every seven baskets. This allows us to get a deep breath, and it is also the point at which we run in substitutes. If twelve players show up for a game, then we choose teams of six and rotate in a sub at those break points. In some runs the extra two would have the rights to the next game, and they would take three of the losers and play the winners. We decided that we would rather keep the game going, enjoying the continuity of teams throughout the hour or so of play. Our system also ensures that everyone who shows up gets to play an equal amount of time, since everyone is required to sit at some point as the substitutes rotate into the game. This system makes a lot of sense for oldguys who need a break and for players who believe that everyone deserves the right to a good workout. There is no hierarchy of skill in this system. The stars sit as well as the role players. However, younger players who come into the game are often baffled by this system, and they sometimes challenge it. They do not want to take a break or sit out for a while. They are not tired, and they cannot see the logic of sitting while some chump plays. They might be used to more competitive runs in which you have to "hold the court" by winning. If you lose, you sit. Their challenge has to be negotiated, usually by some older player with moral authority who makes it clear to the new guy that the "chump" is a longtime friend and respected member of the community. Maybe the accommodation is that the young blood will rotate out last, by which time someone may have left the game to go back to work, so no rotation will be necessary. But maybe the young blood will dislike the system so much that he will leave the run and find one that suits his game better. So be it. The collective consciousness of the run is open to challenge and change, but it is larger than any one player.

The consciousness of the run is most powerful in those elements of the game that are most open to negotiation. How much contact will be allowed? How competitive will the game be? What fouls will be called? The run builds up habits on these issues over time, and it thereby creates a distinctive personality for itself. But this process is not abstract or impersonal. The habitus of local practice is produced not by disembodied social forces but by the actions of social subjects within a historical process. The tone set for a run usually is produced by older or more established players, particularly those who play the game with conviction, with a dedication to ethical behavior and righteous effort. These community leaders are the ones who will call out transgressors, confront bullies, break up fights, and tell whiners to shut up and play. New players routinely defer to those authority figures, or else they move on to other runs. As a result, a run keeps a continuity of practice over time, adjusting to new players and changing circumstances but maintaining a recognizable personality.

A run creates community because the game itself requires constant contact and interchange among the players. As the various chapters of this book have described, basketball is created in every aspect by the cooperative actions of its players. Its ethics are locally negotiated, connecting all players at every moment of the game in a web of moral interdependence. Its cognitive style requires group improvisation in real time; players must literally think as one, reacting to others' decisions in a constant state of mutual awareness. Its movement patterns are made possible by an ongoing attention to the presence of all the other players in the game, each player choosing movements that play off the movements of others. These interactive practices promote strong affective ties and practice-specific friendships. Basketball players, especially in the pickup game, are not following a script or taking orders from an authority figure. They are creating the game in the moment of play, calling on all of these culturally charged acts of thinking, feeling, moving, and connecting. Taken together, they produce a dense and complex community of practice, sustained over time by the continuity of the run.

Perhaps most importantly, a run is an *informal* community of practice. Many runs are affiliated with institutions that operate on formal procedures and principles, but most runs are not directly sponsored or organized by the institutions themselves. Runs tend to use the facilities of the school or church or recreation center but not to require the institution for their operational principles. Church runs happen at times when the facility is not being used for any official function. Rec center runs are not organized by the staff but by the players themselves. School runs happen during off hours, with no supervision. Our local university run is made possible by the benign neglect of the institution. Key administrators have made sure that we have time in the gym, but they have not tried to turn us into an official program. In fact, there are times when we get into the gym without the official knowledge of any university personnel. Many of the runs with which I have been associated exist in this complex relationship with the institution that houses them. For me this is one of their great virtues. In institutions that usually require official sanction and control, runs exist at the margins, controlled by the players themselves. As a result, they create connections and community relationships in ways that the official operation of the institution cannot. In an official history of the institution, these informal communities of practice would probably go unnoted, working as they do under the official radar. But the history of the institution would therefore be radically incomplete, because it would fail to capture the informal but powerful connections that its members create in and through their unofficial institutional activities. In this, basketball is not unique. When I think of my own university, I can see the gardening community, the gun enthusiast community, the running community, the swimmers, the bridge players, the kayakers, the skiers, the film enthusiasts, the religious communities, and on and on. All of them connect on campus in informal and unofficial associations, creating webs of connection that make possible the operation of the institution. The formal and operational rely on the informal and affective in order to produce official institutional objectives. As the literature of institutional management shows, smart organizations know of these informal webs and stay out of their way, allowing them to do their work almost invisibly.

The run, then, is the local site for the cultural work of basketball as a practice. It makes sense of specific games and player behaviors, and in its historical dimension it provides the matrix inside which players make personal connections and develop insider knowledge. However, the run does not exist in isolation. It is connected to the institution that hosts it, to the social histories of its location, and to the personal histories of its players. And it is complexly related to the global practice of basketball and to the image streams that are produced by media ball. It may be local in its affiliations, but it cannot be understood outside of the larger institution of basketball itself.

GLOBAL BASKETBALL

I will use the term *basketball* to describe this third level of loose community organization. If a *game* creates a momentary community out of shared negotiation and play, and a *run* creates a stable and rich community out of long-term shared practice, then *basketball* describes the entirety of the community of practice, created out of the full range of its activities, including, of course, playing the game, but also watching it, reading about it, talking with friends about it, seeing video clips, belonging to fan organizations, calling radio programs, taking your children to youth group games, and so on. This vast, amorphous "community of interest" is loosely organized around the practice, to the extent that all of its members share the discourse and culture of the game and can therefore connect with all other members.

I also want to use the term *basketball* to describe the parameters of the practice, the outward circumference within which all local runs and all individual games—no matter how much they vary as local events—are recognizable as instances of the practice. The defining characteristics of this circumference, the forces that bring a loose unity to this global practice with its infinite local varieties, include the rules of the game, the official bodies that create the rules and sponsor organized competition, and the global image flows that are consumed by local players from Boston to Botswana. The global community of basketball has been in part created from the top down by televised images of NBA games. As Walter LaFeber (1999) has pointed out in *Michael Jordan and the New Global Capitalism*, the development of satellite communication systems, global markets, and the dissemination of American popular culture have created an international audience for elite basketball, which has in turn generated local, informal variants of the game. The official, elite forms of basketball are connected, on the one hand, to global movements of capital and to the circulation of American popular culture throughout the world and, on the other, to the indigenous local cultures of which basketball has become a part. The global corporate system has produced a global array of local practices. People in the Phillipines or Lebanon or Harlem may consume the same media images of elite basketball, but they also have created their own unique variants of the game in their own local *runs*. In discussing *basketball*, therefore, we encounter two images of globalization, one in which global culture is created by media and corporate elites and then imposed on local communities, and one in which local communities create cultural practices that connect through those media images and other webs of relationship to other local practices that, taken together, concatenate a global culture.

Ben Carrington, David L. Andrews, Steven J. Jackson, and Zbigniew Mazur's (2001) article "The Global Jordanscape" presents a vivid picture of the complex relationships between the global and the local. They agree with LaFeber that basketball has been circulated around the globe by powerful economic forces, but they are more interested in the local manipulation of global imagery. To demonstrate this process, they track the ways that the image of Michael Jordan has been adapted in New Zealand, Poland, and Great Britain. In New Zealand, they report, Jordan's effect has been complex. His success as an athlete-entrepreneur has created what they call "the Jordan generation" in New Zealand sports. In rugby, for example, players have demanded higher pay and greater media and marketing visibility. But his status as an *African* American athlete has inspired Maori athletes and young people to identify with him as a symbol of resistance to white power. In postcommunist Poland, on the other hand, Jordan is a straightforward symbol of American capitalist success. Stylish sneakers are called "jordanki," and his image is associated with the consumption of American products such as Nike, Coke, and McDonalds, which are in turn associated with transcending the limits of the failed communist regime. In Great Britain the authors see Jordan as a figure in "the sporting black Atlantic," one who has become, among many African, Caribbean, and American athletes, a symbol of "emancipated black masculinity" (2001, 205). This comparative analysis suggests that global basketball—even in its corporate form—adapts to local cultural circumstances.

The cultural studies connection to sport tends to focus on elite competition as it is represented in the global media. Members of the "community" created by consumption of those images are more properly described as market segments or demographic groups, made available by the media to global corporations. As a commodity in that global system, basketball has taken on an identity that facilitates the marketing: hypercompetitive, ultramasculine, promoting racial stereotypes, creating fantasies of easy wealth and willing women, providing global youth culture with a predictable and safe taste of ghetto cool (see Boyd 1997). Basketball has rightly been taken to task as an element in the complex process by which corporate and media elites have created a global culture in the service of market power operating at once in huge commercial networks and in the most intimate fantasies of individual consumers. From this perspective, basketball in specific and sports in general can rightly be seen as dangerous cultural influences, imposing consumerist cultural values on the world, as well as reinforcing racism, sexism, and homophobia.

But as a lover of the practice of basketball, my reaction to this critique has been ambivalent. To me the global media image is in a sense a betrayal of the practice, a simplistic, stereotyped misrepresentation of a complex, local, human-scale activity. Media images of elite basketball cannot capture the localness of pickup basketball, the ways it reflects and responds to the myriad cultural situations in which it finds itself. Basketball is played on farms in Indiana, in Mexican villages, in Philippine slums, in Sudanese neighborhoods of London, in church halls in Harlem, and so endlessly on. It is beyond the scope of this book to attempt to depict in ethnographic detail the variety of cultural negotiations practiced in all of those circumstances, but the sheer existence of that variety stands as a counterweight to the stereotype of the game disseminated in the global media.

Grant Farred's (2003) work on South African football suggests an alternative reading of the global significance of basketball. Farred's essay, " 'Theater of Dreams': Mimicry and Difference in Cape Flats Township Football," looks back at the role that English football played in apartheid South Africa. He focuses on local "coloured" teams that took the names and copied the styles of various English professional clubs, in spite of the fact that those famous teams were at the time all white. This mimicry, Farred argues, was a gesture of defiance against the predominantly Boer Nationalist Party and apartheid. What made the gesture possible was that football at the time was seen as a working-class sport, and so it translated into the colonial context as a practice that symbolically defied powerful elites and allowed local communities to assert their athletic skills and cultural independence. As Maurice Roche says in the introduction to *Sport, Popular Culture, and Identity,* "Sport has appeared to offer people in different genders, classes, and nations a cultural sphere in which, if only transiently, they could express embodied senses of freedom" (1998, 8). It is certainly true that basketball has become associated with American products and consumerism, but it also is a global export of *African American* culture, and so it is associated with resistance to power, with the assertion by an oppressed group of its ability to achieve and create a beautiful and an expressive culture of its own.

Michael Hardt and Antonio Negri's *Empire* (2000) teaches the lesson that in current economic and cultural conditions, the global and the local cannot be understood except by emphasizing their complex interaction. Hardt and Negri manage to think about global culture simultaneously as a technology of power by which a global empire works its will *and* as an unpredictable, energetic process engaged in by a globe full of desiring subjectivities, creating in collaboration an upsurging, dynamic culture, the very force that corporate global culture seeks to control. For me this conviction has meant thinking about how global media images of *basketball* affect—for better or for worse—the daily operation of *runs* and *games* in local schoolyards and church basements around the world, and simultaneously about how the global basketball community could be thought of as *the product of* all those local activities, as their complex, incalculable sum total.

In his discussion of communities of practice, Etienne Wegner is clearly most interested in the indigenous practices created by local groups, below the radar of official institutional management. But he also recognizes that communities of practice often create what he calls "reifications" of their own practice: official documents, mission statements, procedures, rules of operation, and institutionally sanctioned representations of the practice. These official products, Wegner says, "may seem disconnected, frozen into a text that does not capture the richness of lived experience" (1998, 61). Think of the disconnect between any organization's annual report and the actual events, relationships, failures, and successes of the year in question. The official version is by definition a fiction, a gross oversimplification of the real social process. Nevertheless, Wegner says, reification is necessary so that the practice has an image of itself, a way that diverse groups engaged in the practice can understand that their local activities are part of a larger operation, which can be discerned as a distinct cultural enterprise. In this sense, media images of basketball could be thought of as the "reification" of the endlessly variant local practices created by face-to-face basketball communities. Media ball provides the procedures, images, and official rules that give some global unity to the local diversity.

One positive function that global basketball provides for local players is to represent the full array of possible moves available in the practice. Images of elite performance lodge in the memory of players as they watch TV games. Without consciously imitating the move depicted, players incorporate into their neural habits images consumed in the media. When Larry Bird was playing, players realized the strategic advantages of driving left from the right wing, a move that required a strong left hand, which players acquired in part by watching Bird do the move with elite skill. In current pickup games you see step back jump shots and crossover dribbles learned from Michael Jordan and Alan Iverson. And the ranks of girls basketball are filled with kids playing with the courage and energy of Jackie Stiles. Kids often do this neural patterning explicitly, whispering to themselves "Latrell Sprewell" as they slash to the basket. I once worked to improve my rebounding by watching how Charles Barkley would *snatch* the ball out of the air, stretching his hand above the ball and windmilling it down. I could never recreate that windmill, but I did rebound with more force. The influence of media images is less conscious, more visible to others than to the player himself or herself. But if we could see a pickup game from the 1960s, we would see the influence of Oscar Robertson or Bill Bradley as we now see Jason Kidd and Tracy McGrady.

However, it is just as correct to think of this influence flowing in the opposite direction. Basketball at its most elite levels depends directly on the innovations that happen at the local level, outside of organized ball. Most directly, this influence occurs in the *runs* that elite players engage in when they are not playing with their organized teams. There they run into street players, neighborhood stars who create their reputation by innovating, by trying new shots and dribbles and passes that express their personal and local style. But more generally, new moves disseminate throughout the basketball community, even to the most elite levels of the game. That is, the images delivered through global communications systems are in part a function of innovation on the local level, even as they provide inspiration for that local practice. In *Saturday Night Fever* someone asks Tony if he made up a dance move. He replies, "Well . . . first I saw it on television, then I made it up." Creativity in basketball exists in that cycle of local and global, informal and formal practice.

On the other hand, global basketball does produce a rough uniformity in local practices. No matter how local the practice becomes, it always remains a local variant of *basketball*, an instance of a recognizable practice. Less complex than pickup ball, more fully coded as a cultural signifier, organized, elite-level basketball provides the public image of the practice, the shared repertoire that allows players from a local *run* to play with others from other local circumstances and to affiliate with a community of practice larger than their own. When American fans and players see a Brazilian team, for example, they do not process it as something totally alien, so peculiar to its own local situation that it cannot be understood by an outsider. The sense of "insiderness," of belonging to a community, thus extends past local boundaries that sometimes characterize the other as fundamentally other. Everyone who plays or follows basketball, no matter how different their cultural setting and their local version of the game, engages in a shared practice and belongs to a vast and diverse community.

Throughout that huge community of players, the fundamental moves of the game are fairly standard. Wherever you go, there are layups and jump shots and dunks and zones and mans and bounce passes and double teams. These moves are standardized (though infinitely variable) because coaches and players in the organized game have perfected the form necessary for successful play, and because those forms have become codified as visual images through endless media repetition, to the point that they become part of the neural equipment of every backyard player. These images provide not only a common standard for the game, so that basketball is always recognizable as basketball, but also a standard of excellence, a goal to be pursued throughout the practice. *Extend* on the layup, *follow through* on the jump shot. Part of the pleasure of a perfect pass on a fast break is that it recalls a perfect pass seen on TV or live at an elite-level game. I have heard guys say "Whoa, that looked like *basketball*" when a play works out perfectly.

Another standardizing factor provided by *basketball* for local *runs* and *games* is the very existence of the official rules of the game. Although ground rules are locally negotiated in the pickup game, there are official rules of *basketball* that provide the parameters for these negotiations. The rule for traveling, allowing no more than two steps before you must dribble the ball, is an interesting case in point. This rule is probably the most negotiable in the game. Even in the NBA and in college ball, where one would think the rules would apply most faithfully, traveling often is negotiated nearly out of existence. Many of the most spectacular plays, the ones that get repeated endlessly as highlights on *SportsCenter*, are made possible by a very liberal interpretation of the rules. Referees are clearly complicit in this transformation of the game for media purposes. And yet the call is sometimes made, and in living rooms and sports bars across the country some old guy will complain when it is not. That is, even when the rules are negotiated to the point almost of being ignored, they exist in the collective conscience of the basketball community. As a result, even in the wooliest pickup game, it is possible to call "steps" when someone takes gross advantage, especially if the move is less than beautiful. I have emphasized the "localness" of basketball throughout this book, but this is one of the moments when it is important to remember that some near-universal standards exist, and that they allow players to move comfortably from *run* to *run*, knowing that they can negotiate the different local practices they will encounter, because all local practices have access to the norm of the standard.

This standardization does not inhibit the creativity of local practice—in fact, it makes that creativity possible. Just as the rules of haiku or the sonnet have inspired poets to creativity precisely because of the restrictions they create, the rules and standards of *basketball* produce the necessary tension between restraint and freedom that creativity requires. Just a casual look at a local pickup game will include some local Jerry West, with a jump shot out of a coach's textbook, but it also will probably include a shooter with an odd idiosyncrasy, a foot that splays out or an elbow at an odd angle, one who still makes shot after shot because of a local adaptation that just works. That oddball player has the perfected image in his head, even as he pursues the refinement of his own style. Players who know each other's moves will make plays that are truly new, out of the particularities of the moment—the players involved, the precise angles of bodies, the spin of the ball—but they can do that not only because they are open to the present moment and rely on their own histories in the game, but because they know the possible variables, the codified alternatives, which are refined and displayed in the elite game, through the global reach of *basketball*.

Of course, not all of the effects of organized, televised ball on the local game are so positive. Some of the macho swagger and selfishness of televised ball has been replicated in pickup ball. Pickup games have always had dangerous players and cutthroat local runs, but many people who have played the game a long time have commented on the technical and emotional crudeness of current youngblood ball. One guy takes it to the basket while the others watch. The skill and athleticism level is very high, like the highlight shows, but there is little commitment to the game as total flow, with all ten players moving and thinking together. It is also easy to observe a coarse emotional tone, with lots of trash talk and pleasure in the humiliation of the opponent. Certainly televised ball has had its effects on this behavior.

However, the swaggering, stylized contemporary game cannot be explained merely as a local effect of global basketball media. It also derives from the daily lives of young players, especially style-setting young black players, learning to negotiate gender and personal identity in a coarse youth environment shaped by larger popular-cultural powers. In a popular and street culture that has returned to the simplest gender definitions, being a baller is a way of asserting masculine identity just safely within the limits of acceptable aggression. To be a baller is *not* to be a pimp or a gangster, but it is to be a man, skilled and competitive, confident in his own abilities, independent. The basketball played by guys in that youth culture is just not going to be the basketball played in *Hoosiers*. Television ball has its influence, but current youth ball also is a function of current youth cultures. Macho styles rise up out of the street, just as much as they emanate out into the street from the TV screen. Basketball culture is in part the product of media-produced images of elite ball, but *basketball* as a global practice is also the product of local innovations, responding to local conditions, transmitted to a global audience.

In *Hoop Roots* John Wideman expresses this ambivalence as he reports on a player he saw on a court at Houston Street and 6th Avenue in Manhattan. The guy has all of the crossover moves, all of the quick feet and body fakes of the contemporary style. Wideman's respect for his skill is grudging; he wants to dismiss it as a mere copy of the NBA style, disconnected from the game, focused only on the self and its histrionic display. But Wideman is always a self-aware observer, and he realizes that his own oldguy ego has made him too harsh, closed off to the carnivalesque pleasure of the guy's game. Wideman reminds himself "how sport is art and, like any other African American art form, expresses and preserves, if you teach yourself how to look, the deep structure, both physical (material) and metaphysical (immaterial), of a culture" (2001, 185). In fact it is the burden of Wideman's book to show how basketball emerges from the daily experience of African American culture and remains open to change generated in the pickup game.

Of course in a truly global practice those changes in *basketball* do not come only from African American culture. One recent instance of local innovation becoming standard *basketball* practice is the way that Eastern European players have affected the fast break. I can remember in the 1970s seeing Yugoslav teams take long jump shots off the fast break, at a time when the American game assumed that the wing player should always take the ball to the basket as strong as possible. To Americans at the time these looked simply like bad shots, even if they went in. With the establishment of the three-point line in American professional and college ball, however, this European style suddenly made sense, so that now the art of pitching the ball back out to the wing is highly prized in point guard play throughout basketball culture. And in recent years, as Harvey Araton argues in *Crashing the Borders: How Basketball Won the World and Lost Its Soul at Home,* European and other world players have revivified the NBA, bringing a renewed sense of team play and creativity to the league. Global *basketball* is dynamic, open to grassroots innovation, even as it produces a template for those varying local practices.

FAN CULTURE

One outcome of global media basketball has been the creation of huge communities of interest, fan groups that may never engage in the practice but only observe it and consume its mass media images. These communities of interest also are part of the basketball community, and they display the same dynamic of global and local that we have seen in the practice of the game itself.

The range and interconnectedness of this larger community focused around basketball as a practice can be illustrated by a game I attended recently. My university's women's team was playing a game that also was a fund-raiser for the local women's crisis center, which provides services for women who are victims of violence. The actual practice of basketball was of course the business of the members of the teams and their support staffs, coaches, trainers, advisors, and so on. But around the occasion of the game, the operation of the practice, a community was created that included the pep band, cheerleaders, dance team members, mascots, and several hundred fans. In addition, the athletic department that organized the game has institutional connections with local businesses that advertise in the arena and provide marketing materials, and on this occasion with a local social action group, which in turn has organizational connections to other local groups not obviously associated with the game. At halftime the women's group held an auction that featured items donated by a local manufacturer, a university-affiliated arts festival, and a local quilting guild. All of these individuals and groups were for this event connected to one another around the practice of basketball. Some were connected only for this one game, but others had long-term business and civic associations with the game, probably because key individuals in these organizations recognized the public relations power of the game in basketball-crazy North Carolina, or because they themselves were players or ex-players or fans. This one local event, seen as an instance of a worldwide practice, suggests the scope of the global community of practice and interest that surrounds the game.

The most fundamental form of this community of interest is the crowd at a live game. Like the players in an ad hoc pickup game, a basketball crowd is a momentary community. This combination of people has never before and will never again be in community together. But for the time of the event, they operate as an interpretive and emotive community. They bring to the event all of the peculiarities of their individual experiences and local affiliations, but they focus their attention on the practice unfolding before them, and in the process they take on a community identity, palpable to players and fans. Crowds have personalities: sometimes they are quiet and judgmental, waiting to be impressed; sometimes they are avid, wildly partisan, investing deep emotion in the outcome of the game. Fans in a crowd feel each others' presence, their moods and reactions, and they willingly commit themselves to the emotive community evolving around and within them. But a great basketball crowd also creates itself as an interpretive community, understanding this specific game together, making sense of it within a shared knowledge of basketball as a practice. Basketball crowds understand game situations, know when a key moment arrives, and feel changes in momentum. They anticipate plays and rev up their emotions as events unfold. They see a player streaking downcourt, they know that their team sees the same opportunity developing, and they roar their approval even before the pass is thrown. Crowds know when the game is at stake, they know when a mistake has been made, and they can anticipate a coach's strategy. That is, the crowd thinks together, acts as a cognitive community. Of course not all members of the crowd think in exactly the same way—some may be distracted or not knowledgeable enough to engage in the process fully, and two fans can certainly understand a game situation in different ways. But taken together, the crowd enjoys the emotional and intellectual experience of feeling and thinking along with many disparate others, of forming a momentary community.

Strong emotional communion provides the energy for crowds at basketball games. In this, of course, basketball is not unique. As Eric Dunning has said, the experience of being a sport fan makes possible the kind of powerful emotional expression that is routinely repressed in everyday social life. Dunning argues that we live in social structures that "impose on people a life of relatively even and unemotional routines, and which require a high degree and great constancy of emotional control in all spheres of life" (1999, 27). In this context, sports "perform a de-routinizing function . . . via the de-controlling of emotional controls" (1999,

30). They do this, of course, in a safe environment, without serious risk of social upheaval. In this sense, spectator sports have been criticized as "the opium of the people," distracting emotional energy and intelligence from the serious political and economic problems of our time. But as David Rowe says in *Sport, Culture, and the Media: The Unruly Trinity*, sports "help supply the meaning and commitment that rapid social change under late modernity or postmodernity have evacuated from many lives" (2004, 72). The emotional experience of crowds at sporting events creates a Dionysian loss of self, a sense of connecting with others, overcoming the boundaries that separate us as individuals from all others. And a basketball game, with its surging, dramatic physical energy, creates crowds willing to invest deep emotion in the unfolding narrative of the contest.

And just as for players a *game* cannot be understood outside of the *run* of which it is part, so no crowd can be understood outside of the long-standing fan communities that constitute it. Organized, elite-level games may be elements in the global structure of *basketball*, but most fan communities organize themselves at the local level and connect with multiple other local communities. They have a local history, with traditions and shared rituals, ways of thinking and feeling developed within an ongoing set of common experiences. They operate under the assumption that their team *represents* them, that it articulates in a public spectacle the lived experience of the local community. As Rowe says, spectator sports "tap into the affective power of territoriality as it applies to sections of cities, whole urban areas, regions, nations, even entire continents and hemispheres" (2004, 172). In professional basketball and elite college ball, with its players for hire, this assumption may be willful and imagined. Such players often feel absolutely no allegiance to the community they "represent" but only to their own careers. Nevertheless, fans commit their communal emotions to a team on the belief that they are playing by proxy, that they themselves have a stake in the outcome of the contest. There are, of course, organized teams that are truly local—high school teams in small towns or city neighborhoods, college teams that do not recruit nationally, teams with players known personally in the local community, and in such cases local fan loyalty requires no imagination. This allegiance to the team as an extension of the community does not entail an uncritical acceptance of the team's performance. Crowds and fan communities can be extremely critical of the team, and they can be divided in their opinions about issues surrounding play. In that sense fan communities are sites for *disagreement*, but they can produce varying and competing opinions precisely because they share enough knowledge and commitment to make meaningful disagreement possible. Like a *run*, a fan community is not homogeneous and it is not static, but it does develop over time a characteristic style of engagement, in the most part accepted by members of the community, even the dissenters.

I want now to discuss two fan communities that have been important in my own life as a basketball fan, first the Philadelphia basketball fan tradition, which I grew up in, and second the University of North Carolina (UNC) fan community, which I belong to peripherally and have observed for twenty-five years, and which all of my children belong to fanatically. What I hope to show is that both communities reflect local circumstances and histories, even though they are focused on media images that have made the teams and players they admire part of global basketball culture. There could hardly be two more global figures in basketball than Dr. J, who is part of Philly basketball culture, or Michael Jordan, who plays a complex role in UNC fan culture. But both fan communities reflect the economic and social histories of the larger communities to which they are connected, and each has a distinct local character. And on a personal note, both have shaped my own understanding of the game and its culture.

PHILLY FANS

I have been booed by the toughest basketball fans on earth. About ten years ago I was at a 76ers' game with my wife and oldest daughter, at the Spectrum in South Philadelphia. My seat number was chosen for a halftime contest— if you made a half-court shot, you won a trip for four to the Bahamas. Half-court shots are just dumb luck, but you need to heave the ball close enough to the rim so that dumb luck can even enter the equation. I did not. I threw up a dying quail that hooked weakly to the right, probably ten feet short. And so I was booed, as was right and proper. The fact that it was just a lame half-time promotion did not matter at all. These fans knew what a legit shot would look like, this was not it, and they said so. Fair enough. I took it as an honor. To be judged and executed by Philly fans was to enter in my very modest way into an elite group of basketball players. Philly fans have booed the greatest players the game has ever known—Wilt Chamberlain, Bill Russell, Michael Jordan, Charles Barkley, Julius Erving, Larry Bird. Whether they played for the home team or the opposition, if they did not play up to the standards of the fans, they heard about it.

Philly fans are tough because they know the game and they know what is at stake in the game. They can see when a player hustles back on the break or fails to block out, and they see in these successes and failures a moral and spiritual dimension, a respect or lack of respect for the game, a willingness or an unwillingness to sacrifice, to honor teammates and opponents by maximum effort, total dedication to quality, to the highest aspirations of the game. To Philly fans, you do not have to be a *great* player, but you had better be a *serious* player. In Philly this knowledge of the game has a long and rich local history. Along with New York, Philadelphia was one of the first big cities to pick up the game. In the 1920s the South Philadelphia Hebrew Association (SPHA) dominated the local game, and it was one of the best teams in the country. My father played against them with the Shanahan Athletic Association, a West Philadelphia Irish Catholic team. They played in a cage, in games so rough they needed a chain link fence to separate the players and the fans. Every school in the city had a gym and an outdoor court—the "city game," Pete Axthelm famously called it. Basketball still gets played in every neighborhood at local parks and churches and in streets and backyards. College ball has a great history in the Big Five. The NBA has been popular since the league began. It seems like everyone in the city knows the game. Out of that intense historical mix comes a style of player and a style of fan, both widely recognized for their knowledge of the game. To be a Philly point guard, for example, is to be smart and tough, a coach on the floor, a great passer, a clutch player, a class act. To be a Philly fan is to want just that out of players, that knowledge, that passion.

The style of the Philly fan community has developed out of the working-class roots of the local game and of the city in general. Americans sometimes associate Philadelphia with old money, the Main Line, *The Philadelphia Story*, but Philadelphia is overwhelmingly a working-class city, and basketball has its roots there in city institutions and practices—in public and parochial schools, in rec centers, and in schoolyards and public parks. The city's basketball history is Jewish and Irish and Italian and then African American, reflecting the tough history of ethnic change in the city. Local teams represent neighborhoods, ethic groups, religious affiliations, and class loyalties. The game matters because it is connected to identities that matter in the city mix.

Robert Gregg's (2004) "Personal Calvaries: Sports in Philadelphia's African American Communities, 1920–1960" traces the development of sports in Philadelphia's black community as it connects to powerful local institutions such as YMCAs, settlement houses, churches, and local sporting clubs. Gregg sees sports during this era as an element in the struggle for racial uplift, an activity encouraged by striving, successful families, eager to send their children to play basketball for Lincoln University, where they could gain the education necessary to return to the community as professionals and civic leaders. Because they were in these ways tied into the familial and institutional fabric of the community, basketball and other sports elicited fierce local loyalties.

These loyalties are sometimes the source of conflict and violence as racial and ethnic groups vie for power. But beneath the divisions in the city there is a discernible Philly basketball style, forged out of those local loyalties, represented in those tough fans who want even jaded NBA players to honor the game. This is why Allen Iverson was a star in Philadelphia. He has great physical courage, a willingness to throw himself into the traffic of the game, to take his hits and finish the play. The city sees its own tough daily style in his demeanor on the court, and it honors him even when he fails. Players who do not *represent* the values of the fans will hear their disapproval. Of course Philadelphia is not unique in this combination of working-class ethos and gritty basketball values. A similar set of factors can be observed in New York, Detroit, and other rust belt cities. But Philly fans have earned their reputation as the toughest among NBA fans.

UNIVERSITY OF NORTH CAROLINA FANS

The Philadelphia fan community that I have described is in fact composed of many fan communities. To be a Philly fan is not to be loyal to the NBA 76ers, it is to know and value the game and to invest in one way or another in local basketball, whether in one of the local college teams or in high school ball or in the street ball scene. Being a Philly fan is a style of cultural engagement rather than an affiliation with a particular team or community. Members of the UNC fan community, on the other hand, are connected to one another by their shared loyalty to the UNC basketball program. They may be highly critical fans, like Philly fans, or they may be diehards who never think a negative thought about the program, but they belong to the same fan community because they share a passion for this one team. While Philly fans recognize each other around their particular interpretive style, UNC fans connect with each other and form a self-conscious community of interest.

Again, this loyalty does not make the UNC fan community unique. Many American college, high school, and even professional teams demand an equal amount of loyalty and stir similar communal passions. I am focusing on UNC because I have lived in North Carolina for over twenty-five years, moving from a knowledgeable outside observer of UNC fan culture to a peripheral member of the community. Also, I am taking advantage of the work on UNC fan culture done by Thad Williamson in his 2001 book *More Than a Game: Why North Carolina Basketball Means So Much To So Many.* Williamson's work and my own informal observations suggest that the UNC fan community does have its own unique flavor, one that I will argue reflects the social, economic, regional, and historical conditions that surround it.

I am writing just after a time of moral crisis within that community. Much of the loyalty generated by the UNC program has been based on the achievements and personal style of longtime coach Dean Smith. Smith retired in 1997, and was replaced by his trusted assistant Bill Guthridge, who retired three years later, to be replaced by Matt Doherty, a UNC player in the early 1980s and a relatively untested head coach. Doherty had mixed success, and rumors were rampant within the fan community that he had alienated his players to the point of mutiny. Such rumors were completely impossible during Smith's tenure, which was marked by the certainty that Smith always had the best interests of his players in mind and treated them with class and dignity. Doherty went through a probably inevitable process of critical evaluation within a fan community based on personal loyalty to a gone but not forgotten figure. Many UNC fans became convinced that Doherty could not live up to Smith's legacy, both in terms of success and personal style. Eventually, the tensions were unsustainable. Doherty was fired, and the university hired Roy Williams, who had coached under Smith and who had run a program at University of Kansas that mirrored Smith's success and his ethical tone. Williams resolved the crisis by renewing the ethos of Smith's program and by leading UNC to the national championship in 2005.

Williamson's research into UNC fans shows that their loyalty is based on *both* of those factors—success and integrity. *More Than a Game* comes at UNC fans from a number of interpretive perspectives. Williamson is a lifelong UNC fan himself, and he provides in the book an autobiography of his life as a fan. In addition, he asked fifteen avid fans to keep diaries of their experiences during the 2000–01 season. Through his connections to a UNC fan Web site, he also conducted a survey that tracked the responses to the team of 600 other intense members of the community. Because his respondents were self-selected, Williamson does not claim scientific validity for his findings, but they do provide a snapshot of the feelings generated by the team in these elite fans. What Williamson's research shows is that this basketball community is focused around a set of values, a strict basketball ethic. UNC fans expect success at the highest national level, but they also expect that the program will be conducted within the rules of the NCAA and that players and coaches will represent the school with integrity and class. If for a long time University of Nevada at Las Vegas fans connected with the renegade success of Jerry Tarkanian, who recruited—often outside of the rules—tough kids who almost never graduated and often consorted with shady Las Vegas characters, UNC fans connected with Smith and his team's rectitude on and off of the court. For the UNC fan community, the team serves as a moral example, proof that success does not require unethical behavior.

Dean Smith was the personal icon for this communal ethic. During his time as coach, he showed himself to be a basketball genius—he devised many of the offensive and defensive formations that today dominate the college game. But he also created a personal aura of integrity as an educator and a citizen. Smith expected his players to graduate, even if it required them to return to campus during the off-season after they turned professional, and he only recruited players who were capable of succeeding as students. He also expected his players to play selflessly, in a team effort, rather than to aspire to the nightly highlight reel. North Carolina teams have always been favorites of fans who ascribe to the ethical style of play that I described earlier in this book. Smith's teams passed the ball, they played great defense, and they played with intelligence and intensity. In fact, they played in a style that would have satisfied the toughest Philly fan. Williamson's research shows that UNC fans saw their teams as models for character development, on-court examples of ethical daily life. And Smith also developed a reputation for integrity outside of basketball. A forthright Southern liberal, Smith was famous for putting himself on the line during the civil rights era, accompanying a black man to a segregated restaurant, and recruiting black players during a time when many Southern university teams were still lily white. Smith also has given support to Democratic candidates and announced his opposition to the death penalty. Certainly many members of the UNC fan community are more conservative than Smith, but they have admired his willingness to commit himself, even if they do not share his commitments.

I believe that it *mattered* in North Carolina that Smith's classy, selfless teams included many great black players. North Carolina, after all, elected Jesse Helms to the Senate repeatedly, and its history of race relations is bloody. And yet North Carolina has always had its racial progressives, and Smith's program served as a model for how racial divides could be crossed. Even people brought up in a deep-seated racist culture could see that black and white UNC teammates could in their chosen sphere overcome racial differences, and the fact that almost all black UNC players disconfirmed racist stereotypes created positive cognitive dissonance. Those classy, selfless players and serious students were *black*, and fan loyalty was therefore required to cross the color line. It is now easy to recognize the contribution that black players have made to the game, but early in Smith's career it was risky to recruit black players to a Southern university. His plan succeeded, I think, because the presence of black players, many of whom came from outside of North Carolina, made UNC seem a *cosmopolitan* place, a contradiction to the hick image of the state in the American consciousness. As a logical result, racism could then appear to be part of the hick image that North Carolinians wanted to leave behind.

The other iconic figure in UNC basketball history is of course Michael Jordan. Jordan plays a special role because he is the local boy who made good. A native North Carolinian, Jordan rose from humble beginnings to become a global image of basketball and the wealth it can create. However, his role in UNC history is more complex. As a college player, Jordan was outstanding, playing on a team that won the national championship, but he did not transcend the team. He was a great player on a great *team*, and his play was always suited to the team-oriented style that Smith preached. It has become a common basketball joke to say that the only person who could hold Michael Jordan to less than twenty points per game was Dean Smith. I am convinced that it never crossed Jordan's mind to play college ball in a self-promoting way, and it has become clear over the span of his career that his success owes much to the ways that his superhuman athleticism was enhanced by the fundamental skills and team-oriented ethic he learned from Smith. Jordan was so much a team player that most UNC fans do not think of him as their greatest player ever; that position goes to Phil Ford, who as a point guard was able to be Dean Smith on the floor and who therefore embodied the UNC ethic more fully than Jordan. UNC fans take great pleasure, I think, from being able to consider the greatest player who ever lived as only *one of* their heroes. Jordan's success also confirms Smith's status as a *teacher*, one who was concerned about the future success of his players, who wanted to give them a foundation for ethical behavior as well as success. The Smith-Jordan story is central to the development of contemporary basketball. It is a story about how individual skill and selfless play can be combined. The ethical player often plays a supporting role on the court, but Jordan showed that Smith's lessons could be embodied by a great player and make him a greater player. This story also is one of the cornerstones of the UNC fan community, a confirmation of the values that unite them.

Just as the harsh, interpretive style of Philly fans is a function of the harsh, working-class lifestyle of the city, so the civic virtue of the UNC fan tradition reflects the middle-class identity of UNC fans. In his wonderful personal account of being a fanatical UNC fan, Will Blythe (2006) contrasts the middle-class atmosphere of UNC with the upper-class elitism of archrival Duke. The title of his book, *To Hate Like This Is to Be Happy Forever,* suggests the intensity of this class-based conflict. The UNC fans see their school as virtuously middle class, drawing excellent students from across the state, training them to be local community professionals and civic leaders. The University of North Carolina may be "the people's university," as Charles Kuralt intones in the university's promotional TV spots, but only in the sense that it seeks to integrate all of its students, even those from the working class, into reputable middle-class careers and civic commitments. In this context, the ethical character of UNC fan culture makes sense. Just as the university teaches its students appropriate middle-class values, its basketball team teaches uplifting character lessons. University of North Carolina basketball *stands for* values, for the very process of character formation. Philly fans, in contrast, may share the same basketball values but would be unlikely to identify with a program that intended to uplift them. They see their job as judging the game as it unfolds before them, not as deriving a civics lesson from a basketball program.

This is not to say that UNC fans are uncritical. As I said, the program often has been beset by fan criticism. Doherty was seen by many as a coach who berated players, who used profanity, and who failed to comport himself with the innate dignity of Dean Smith. The intensity of these criticisms, Williamson argues, is in part a function of the recent development of Internet fan sites, where fans can express their dissatisfaction in the often harsh style of virtual communications. But there has always been a critical element in UNC fan culture—Smith himself was once hanged in effigy—especially when players did not seem to be living up to the competitive standards or the lifestyle standards of the program. That is, UNC fans are often critical of individuals, but they do not generally question the values of the program itself. No one in the community, for example, even after repeated losses to Duke, would suggest that UNC should begin to recruit players who cannot compete as students or to run the program in defiance of NCAA rules. However, it is interesting to note that only 13 percent of Williamson's survey said they would lose their loyalty to the program if it lost its sense of values. Obviously, winning matters to UNC fans, as a confirmation of the values of the program, and more primally as a satisfying experience in itself. If Doherty's teams had consistently been in the top ten, then there would certainly have been more tolerance for his acerbic style.

UNC fan culture can be understood as the product of an educated, Southern elite's aspiration to think of itself as loyal to its local traditions but open to a more cosmopolitan culture. Beginning in the 1950s, UNC has recruited heavily in the Northeast, especially in the New York area, for basketball players and for out-of-state students. The success of the basketball team has contributed to the national prominence of the university, and its fans enjoy that national recognition. They see it as a confirmation of their own civic values, rooted in class and regional interests, but successful on the national stage. This is a community held together by shared values, embodied in the on-court styles of the players and the off-court practices of the program. They offer their values to the national community and see themselves as the repository of ethical basketball, in the midst of a culture that seems to have rejected ethics and character development. To be a UNC fan is to believe that Dean Smith got it right, that success and integrity are compatible, and to believe that all of basketball culture, in fact all of American culture, needs to hear that message.

Basketball fan communities or communities of interest take many forms, and their variety is a testament to the extent and complexity of the community-building force of basketball. My two examples so far, the Philly fan tradition and the UNC fan community, are huge and diverse. Philly fans do not even share a single team as the center of their attention; they focus on the game in its many varieties, from high school to professional to pickup ball, but with a recognizable interpretive and critical style. The UNC fans are somewhat more homogeneous, in that they share devotion to a team and its values, but they are a diverse group in terms of geography (UNC has a national fan base), income, race, gender, religion, and so on. Fan communities range from intimate, local communities that follow the fate of the local team to loose, lightly connected communities that share little but an interest in the game.

BASKETBALL AND SOCIAL CAPITAL

In *Bowling Alone*, Robert Putnam makes use of the term *social capital* to describe the value created by "connections among individuals—social networks and the norms of reciprocity and trustworthiness that arise from them" (2000, 19), interconnections that he believes have been lost in contemporary American culture. He distinguishes between two kinds of social capital, both necessary for vital societies: the groups created by *bonding* social capital are "inward looking and tend to reinforce exclusive identities and homogeneous groups. Examples of bonding social capital include ethnic fraternal organizations, church-based women's reading groups, and fashionable country clubs," while groups created by *bridging* social capital are "outward looking and encompass people across diverse social cleavages. Examples of bridging social capital include the civil rights movement, many youth service groups, and ecumenical religious organizations" (2000, 22). Putnam also describes this difference in terms of the "strong" social ties created by bonding social capital and the "weak" ties created by bridging social capital. Both kinds of ties are necessary for socially healthy individuals: We need intimate connections to create our own identity, and we need diverse connections so that we do not trap ourselves in that identity. Basketball fan communities can be located all along this continuum, and their cultural function is in part a result of the kind of social capital they create.

There are many basketball fan communities that definitely produce *bonding* social capital. I am thinking of the inner-city high school that identifies itself with its basketball team, or the small town that fills the school gym every Friday night. The film *Hoosiers* presents a vivid image of the bonding social capital created by small-town basketball. In that film the local team, composed of the sons and brothers of the community, brings the town together, overcoming personal and social differences. These tight-knit fan communities, based on complex, local connections, produce much of the passion that energizes basketball culture. They are great live crowds, investing their shared local identity and sense of self-worth in the success of the team. They react as one to foul calls, scoring surges, and personal achievements by each of the players. They rightly see themselves *represented* by the team, which is an organic part of the local community. They have the sense that their community values account for the success of the team, and that their identity as a community is strengthened by the team's efforts.

The dark side of these tightly bonded communities, as Putnam acknowledges, is that they can define themselves *over against* some other community, which becomes the enemy, even to the point of violence. Some of the fan violence that surrounds basketball is produced by these excessive local loyalties, which require that I test my manhood against yours, simply because we go to different high schools. *Hoosiers* does not have the courage to depict the ways that Hickory High School fans defined themselves in part by being the *white* school, battling the intimidating black school, standing up for small town—read white—values. For Putnam, certainly the benefits of such connections outweigh the dangers, but they must be balanced by the moderating experience of creating social ties outside of the immediate community, by encountering difference in a civil setting. I believe that we can see both results in the tight fan communities of basketball.

NATIVE AMERICAN FAN COMMUNITIES

One of the most interesting networks of fan communities in America has developed among Native American basketball fans. Basketball is a phenomenon on America's native reservations, from Arizona to Alaska. Reservation high schools throughout the West regularly win state championships, boys and girls, and the teams are supported by rabid fans, in some cases virtually the entire local community. As in *Hoosiers*, reservation teams are the sons and daughters of the community. The team in fact does represent its fans, unlike in the NBA or in big-time college basketball, where the connections between fans and players are almost purely imaginary. Many Native American basketball fans see their culture represented in their teams' styles of play. Spokane writer Sherman Alexie hears in the percussion of the ball on the hardwood floor echoes of tribal drums, summoning the spirits. Many Native American fans have connected the current popularity of basketball in tribal cultures to the ancient Meso-American ball game that was played throughout Central America, Mexico, and the American Southwest in the precolonial period. There is ample archeological scholarship showing that a game played on a horizontal court with goals at either end was a staple of Mayan culture and religion (see, for example, Scarborough and Wilcox 1991), enough to suggest to many Native American fans that James Naismith's claim to have invented basketball comes about a thousand years too late. For these fans the bonds created by their shared interest in the local basketball team only deepen the ones created by their shared history and social conditions. And fans of successful teams clearly derive additional pride and satisfaction from the belief that their team truly represents their community.

Rick Derby's 2002 documentary *Rocks with Wings* examines the cultural complexity of Native American basketball by following two seasons of the highly successful Shiprock High School girl's team, which won the state championship and brought great pride to the Navajo reservation that they represented. Part of the cultural complexity in this situation was that the success of the team was created in great part by an outsider, an African American coach who challenged the girls to succeed and to develop a confidence and competitiveness that they had lacked. Jerry Richardson, the coach, often appeared to the girls to be too demanding, too mean, but they eventually accepted his teaching, and after losing in the finals one year, the team won the state championship the following year. In a shot that echoes *Hoosiers*, we see almost the entire reservation emptying the town in order to follow the team on the road, and in this real-life story the girls, like the boys from Hickory High, overcome the odds and bring pride to their community. In that sense, the film tells a conventional story about community bonds deepened by a shared interest in a truly local basketball team.

But the film has a more complex and controversial point to make about Native American basketball culture. The film is less interested in the fact that the team won the championship than in its loss the previous year in the state finals, which it felt it had the talent and skill to win. Derby sees in the loss a side of Navajo culture that does not fit with the traditional uplifting sports narrative. Throughout the film Derby intercuts the coverage of the team with interviews with Navajo artists, particularly weavers, who believe that it is necessary to leave their designs imperfect, to include in the work of art what seems like an error in design but is in fact a "spirit line" that leads the eye outside the work of art and connects it to the spirit world, allowing the divine energy to enter the work. Derby more than suggests that the girls failed because they had internalized this belief and therefore could not finally allow themselves to succeed, to seek the perfection of the championship. And when they do win, their success seems the result of internalizing the mainstream athletic values represented by their outsider coach. It is interesting to note that no one within the community that the film documents makes that cultural analogy—it is created by the filmmaker's own perspective, embodied in editing decisions and imagery. I cannot judge the accuracy of Derby's perspective, but he does show that the culture of basketball in Native American communities is anything but simple. Though these fans may evoke the image of the Mayan game, modern basketball was introduced to Native American culture by white missionaries and educators and therefore stands in a complex position within reservation life. Players and fans may feel that the game expresses their tribal identity in some way, but they also know that it is part of their colonized history, both an outside intervention and an authentic representation of local cultures.

In *True Tales from Another Mexico,* Sam Quinones (2001) examines the cultural dynamic in the basketball community created by Oaxacan immigrants in Los Angeles. In the Mexican province of Oaxaca, most villages have basketball courts, pickup games, organized teams, and tournaments. Though the game was introduced by U.S. missionaries and teachers, it struck a chord with the indigenous culture of the local Indian communities, as though it connected them to the ancient ball game. And when Oaxacans migrated to Los Angeles, they brought their own basketball culture with them, which now exists in the mix of basketball cultures in the city. There are hundreds of Oaxacan players, dozens of teams, and regular tournaments, often organized as part of neighborhood religious and cultural festivals. Oaxacan players in Los Angeles see their style of play, rooted in their regional identities, as one of the ways they negotiate their difference from white and black Los Angeles players as well as from other Mexican players. Their fans identify with the teams as representatives of their culture, inflecting this mainstream American game in ways that assert their own indigenous distinction.

In all of these fan communities there is a complex mix of the global and the local. After all, the games around which these communities are constructed are often official contests, not pickup games. They are played by organized teams within sanctioned leagues playing by standardized, international rules, in many cases broadcast by network television, covered by national and international journalism, injected into global media flows. And yet these fan communities have a local flavor, create social bonds, and interact in complex ways with other local practices. As in my university's women's game, the local basketball community is connected to other local communities of practice—businesses, community outreach programs, craft guilds, and so on. Even in these cases of *bonding* social capital, members of the community are connected not just within their community but outside of it, even in paths of connection that they never think about.

COMMUNITIES OF PRACTICE AND IDENTITY COMMUNITIES

These connections out to other communities and individuals, which Putnam (2000) terms *bridging* social capital or *weak* bonds, also are created by interest in the practice of basketball. Many of the communities of interest produced by basketball are as ephemeral as the connections made in a pickup game. Maybe someone is reading the sports page in a restaurant, and a passerby says, "Great game last night." Or two coworkers who have almost nothing else in common maintain an ongoing casual conversation about the local college team. The connections between these members of the basketball community do not depend on their membership in any other communities. They share no deep history or direct involvement. All they ever do is talk around the water cooler or over a beer after work. They may be different races, sexes, classes, sexual orientations, religions, and nationalities. Their only point of contact may be the common language they share through their interest in the practice. So what is the weight and importance of these casual ties?

Taken singly, they may count for little. Certainly the mere fact that a manager and a custodian talk on occasion about basketball does not dissolve the hierarchical differences between them. Real social differences, whether of status or race or other axes of identity, have real consequences and cannot be abolished by casual, even if friendly, contact. But taken together, all of the communities of practice and interest to which we belong do create complex ties outside of our heavy, deep communities. They connect us in multiple directions to multiple individuals. Basketball fans have something to talk about, and the practice that demands their interest brings along with it a serious set of values, beliefs, and ways of thinking and feeling that give their casual connection some cultural power. If each of us engages in many practices, and therefore experiences what Etienne Wegner calls "multimembership," then we are all connected in very complex cultural webs, sharing from each of those practices a cultural set to which anyone else associated with the practice can connect. The cultural practices of everyday life bring all of us out of our "heavy" communities into what ethnologist Mary Louise Pratt calls "the contact zone": "social spaces where cultures meet, clash, and grapple with each other, often in contexts of highly asymmetrical relations of power." The function of communities of practice in the contact zone is to make that grappling less simplistic, less diametrical, since members of "opposing" identity communities might be members of the same communities of practice. Thinking about cultural practices increases our sense of the complexity of individual identity. It forces us to take into account the *many* communities to which we belong, and it therefore provides points of relatively easy contact as we go about the difficult process of negotiating difference in a cultural situation often characterized by hierarchy and violence.

Within each of those communities of practice and interest, a rich conversation is always ongoing. It is precisely this constant talking that *constitutes* the community of interest, that creates Putnam's "weak bonds" so necessary to the social health of individuals. As William M. Sullivan says, "Living in institutions is thus always in part centered in language. It is a conversation, sometimes an argument, about who and what we and our shared form of life are" (1995, 176). Those who actually play basketball have their direct experience to connect them to others in the community, but fans create community only by engaging in the conversation, making some utterance that calls for a response. In this sense the basketball community should be thought of as a *discursive* community, held together by a shared language, an insider's access to the official terminology of the game, the current community slang, the informal jargon of coaches and analysts, and the conceptual apparatus that goes along with this complex language system. In the basketball community, everyone knows what an official term such as *free throw* means, but they also know slang phrases such as "fight through a pick" or "get in his face." Sociolinguists know that group affiliation is produced by shared language, in the simple sense that no outsider can even comprehend an insider conversation. "He didn't switch because he knew the guy would go left and the help was there to take the charge" either makes perfect sense or it makes no sense, and those to whom it makes perfect sense are by that simple fact members of the community.

Access to this discourse comes through two major forces—interaction with peers and consumption of media. Learning the language of the game is in one way an organic process. Newcomers learn from experienced members of the community, in the process of playing or observing the game, without either person thinking much about the teaching or learning process. They are unself-consciously engaged with the practice, and the language comes naturally. But the influence of media in this process cannot be ignored. One of the functions of the global media within the community is to construct a near-universal language for the game, which is then in turn used in local circumstances, in casual conversations. Televised basketball, with its narrators and analysts, can be thought of as an ongoing seminar on basketball, through which a discourse and a style of interpretation are disseminated. This discourse is open to local adaptation and creativity, as in the creation of new slang, but it also has a homogenizing effect, making the accepted discourse of the game available to all local communities. Unless a practice generates a relatively stable discourse—what Wegner would call a "reified" discourse—the conversations that create social capital cannot take place.

These informal conversations produce what Stanley Fish calls an *interpretive community*, a group of people trying to make sense of experience from within a loosely shared set of assumptions about exactly how to make that sense. They agree tacitly on how to define the truth, what counts as evidence, what are acceptable argumentative strategies, and how to decide between competing claims. The basketball community, then, not only shares a common object of perception it also shares a cognitive apparatus for understanding the game. There are still endless disagreements within the community, as any conversation in a sports bar will attest, but the arguments focus on shared questions that are meaningful to everyone in the interpretive community. Why did they call time-out? Should they go into a zone? What is keeping them from playing up to the level of their talent? How did they lose their confidence? Why is that player so selfish with the ball? How did the momentum shift? Who has the strongest schedule? Who deserves to get into the tournament? To be a fan is to share a set of questions open for debate and to engage in that debate. Fan culture is a culture of rhetoric, an ongoing argument that serves paradoxically to unite the community rather than divide it. Wegner emphasizes that "Peace, happiness, and harmony are . . . not necessary properties of a community of practice" because "disagreements can be viewed as a productive part of the enterprise" (1998, 77–78). Or, as philosopher Michael Walzer puts it, "Arguments bear witness to the connections, not the disconnections, of their protagonists" (1995, 61). Members of the community share a sense of what can be argued about and how the argument should proceed. Just as the game involves a group thinking and responding together though in competition, fan culture finds its unity in the process of friendly rhetorical contest.

These conversations occur in many different venues. There are Internet chat rooms and call-in shows on television and especially on radio, where sports talk has become one of the most popular formats in the medium. These public venues provide members of the community with an opportunity to intervene in the operation of the practice itself. Coaches and athletic directors cannot simply disregard Internet and radio fan conversations when they express a pervasive negative tone about the basketball program. The voices of the fans can be heard in a feedback loop on the very same media that disseminate the corporate, elite basketball product for their consumption. Fans are not passive consumers who accept whatever the media dispense. They develop opinions, express them in public, and so affect to some degree the product they consume.

Moreover, Internet and talk radio conversations point to the existence of a much more vast, though less audible, conversation that occurs in private, informal situations, after church, in the hallways of schools, or on the subway. It is ongoing, untraceable, unmeasurable, perhaps in the broad scope of things even negligible, but it creates the fabric of a vast and loose community. Through this conversation the ethic of the community is collaboratively constructed, meaning is produced, and emotions are communicated. Many of these values and meanings and emotions are the ones prescribed by powerful mainstream media, echoing the discourse of television commentators. But this conversation takes place in so many locations, in so many cultural contexts, that it cannot be controlled from the top down. Corporate media sports culture does not account for how basketball gets talked about in a gay bar, or in a fundamentalist youth group, or in the back alleys of Beirut, or even for that matter at the dinner table of a stereotypical middle-class American home. The conversation is too vast, too idiosyncratic and local, too personal to be fully determined. In contemplating this almost amorphous conversation, we arrive at the outer boundaries of the basketball community. If the run is the localized heart of the community of practice, then the casual conversation is the global sprawl—in a billion local contexts—of the community of interest.

Membership in the basketball community ranges from casual to obsessive. Some might watch the NCAA championship game and nothing else, or pick up a basketball at a family picnic. These peripheral members of the community do not derive significant elements of their identity from the practice. But on the other end of the scale, there are those for whom sheer repetition in the practice drives it to the center of their identity. Thad Williamson (2001) found in his study of UNC fans that 82 percent of them rearranged their schedules in order to see games on television. Other fans have the energy to fill out tournament brackets when they are announced, or they visit basketball Web sites, pore over box scores in the daily newspaper, or develop great impressions of Dick Vitale. They take time from family to watch games, or they pass the passion on to their families (72 percent of Williamson's subjects introduced their children to the UNC fan experience). For serious, "elite" fans, basketball is one of the important markers by which others recognize them and by which they describe themselves. Sheer repetition and commitment of time and emotion will guarantee that the practice will become a vital part of their identity.

For players, the force of repetition is even stronger. To be a regular player is to engage in a practice such as yoga or tai chi—deliberately chosen elements of everyday life, pursued in search of fuller knowledge, deeper appreciation, and richer experience. Playing the game requires re-arranging time around it—the time to play, to work out in preparation, to shoot around, to pack up clothes and equipment, to take care of injuries, to think about the game and replay it in one's head. Many players find a run that meets regularly, even daily, so that basketball is a routine element in their everyday lives. It can become, in the simplest temporal terms, a dominant theme in their identities. Of course in this sense basketball is not unique. I have had to call my wife in from working in the garden in the dark in the rain. Card players can become addicted to gambling, and teachers can be consumed by their jobs. These and all of the other myriad cultural practices can be pursued to a point at which the person becomes centered around the passion.

For basketball players this repetition works deeply because it oper-ates complexly on the body and the mind. People who play basketball become players right down to the synapses and muscles, the coordination of hand and eye. Mariah Burton Nelson, who played college basketball and is the author of *Embracing Victory: Life Lessons in Competition and Compas-sion*, evokes this embodiment eloquently:

> As I devoted myself to this basketball, learning to shoot it, catch it, pass it, and care for it, the basketball in return seemed to caress, care for, and even shape me, stretching my fingers, strengthening my willowy arms and legs, widening and length-ening my feet so they'd offer a good place from which I could jump and to which I could land. (1998, 210)

Players shoot around so that the process of shooting becomes unconscious, wired into the body. If you play all the time, the decision making, the subtle movements of the body in response to complex assessments of ongoing developments, and the uncanny communication with other play-ers become more deeply internalized and embodied, uniting body and mind around the intricacies of the practice. Again, similar processes occur in other practices—note the everyday, unconscious athleticism of baggage handlers, the deftness of nurses taking blood, the instantaneous negotiat-ing skills of great schoolteachers. Deep engagement in any practice begins to shape the mind and body of the practitioner. In fact, this shaping by repetition is a good overall definition of culture as such, which is acquired more deeply in unself-conscious routine than in formal learning.

In basketball, as in all cultural practices, the deeply embodied cultural lessons it teaches create a personal and community identity that rivals and cuts across the more intense, heavy affiliations of contemporary identity politics. These politics cannot be ignored, since they engage with real suffering and oppression, but they can be pursued with the realization that not all of our community affiliations fall into the familiar categories of race, gender, class, and sexual orientation. As Audre Lorde says: "Without community there is no liberation, only the most vulnerable and temporary armistice between an individual and her oppression. But community must not mean a shedding of our differences, not the pathetic pretense that these differences do not exist" (1984, 112). "Essentialism" is the temptation of those who are embattled, even if it often mirrors the prejudices of those who define the community from the outside. But all members of these heavy communities are also members of many communities of practice, each community bringing with it a distinctive cultural formation of its own. A black person who plays chess is not culturally identical to a black person who plays video games. A woman who lifts weights is not identical to a woman who does yoga. "Heavy" identities therefore do not tell the entire story of an individual's cultural identity or interpersonal connections.

Wegner understands identity formation to be the process of negotiating our complex community engagements, calling it "the nexus of multimembership." Individuals create their own identities over time, in a complex cultural terrain:

> We all belong to many communities of practice: some past, some current, some as full members, some in more peripheral ways. Some may be central to our identities while others are more incidental. Whatever their nature, all these various forms of participation contribute in some way to the production of our identities. As a consequence, the very notion of identity entails (1) an experience of multimembership, and (2) the work of reconciliation necessary to maintain one identity across boundaries. (1998, 158)

Or, as Michael Walzer puts it, we all belong to "a great and discordant variety of social unions" (1995, 64). We do not derive our identity from any *one* of those communities but from the specific combination that we have constructed in our everyday lives.

The category "cultural practices" is vast and varied, including work and professional life, games and hobbies, and chosen avocations as well as the necessary activities of everyday life. Lawyers share a practice, basketball players share a practice, and shoppers share a practice, as do parents and teachers and nurses and sales clerks and plumbers and electricians and skiers and hunters and priests and poets. The randomness of this list suggests the complexity of the phenomenon. And if all of these practices create the loose but potent community life that basketball creates, then the social and cultural structure of our world is infinitely complex. Putnam's (2000) argument in *Bowling Alone*, that community ties have diminished in contemporary American society, may be correct if we focus on official membership in established groups, but the communities created by cultural practices are more difficult to trace. They are taken for granted, nearly invisible compared to the politically motivated communities that dominate contemporary culture. At a time when community membership often seems divisive, when the definition of community seems indistinguishable from "interest group," the existence of communities of practice, characterized by loose ties and multiple membership, suggests that our national and even our global culture are more interconnected than we sometimes think. But because of the diversity of these practices, those interconnections do not add up to a unified and coherent cultural formation; rather, communities of practice interrelate in a complex overlay, creating rich and irreducibly complicated identities within a rich and complicated culture.

From this perspective, the communitarian worry that we have lost communal ties is unjustified, but the worry about the coherence of our identities stands. We belong to many communities, none of them internally coherent, and we do not derive from this diversity a coherent identity. The question is whether coherence is necessary for individuals and societies. Can the absence of coherence be thought of as an opportunity rather than a threat? In place of coherence there is the openness, the pleasure of difference, the negotiation of identity that communities of practice promote. Nikolas Rose says: "Community is not fixed and given but locally and situationally constructed. From this perspective, communities can be imagined and enacted as mobile collectivities, as space of indeterminacy, of becoming" (1999, 195). In such a cultural situation, selfhood requires "an ethic of creativity"—"the active, material, technical creative assembling of one's existence, one's relation to oneself, even one's corporeality" (1999, 196).

Basketball communities, organized around a practice with strong emotional resonance for players and fans, provide many of the benefits of community without some of the dangers. They provide a sense of belonging and identity, but they do not set themselves against other communities or create armed camps. In their loosest form, all they require is an interest in the game and a willingness to enter into the ongoing conversation. Basketball is a community of *practice*, and as such it brings people together around something they *do* rather than something they *are*. It provides much of what we want from a community—an ethic, a sense of connection, a way of looking at the world—but it does so at low cost, without evoking the passionate politics of identity communities.

We derive our values, beliefs, and ways of thinking, feeling, and relating from many sources, as many as there are practices in our culture. As Honi Fern Haber says, "Each of us is a member of many different communities, and these different communities do not form a coherent or unified, in the sense of essential or unchanging, whole" (1994, 1). As a result, we must "recognize both that the 'I' is plural and that 'I's' in the community are equally plural" (1994, 127). Understanding contemporary identity must begin with an acceptance of the fact that culture and identity are irreducibly complex and must be negotiated in the moment, on the run, in the open court.

Chapter 6

Basketball and Racial Identity

At its elite and most visible levels, basketball in America is a black sport. Black players dominate the game and the selling of the game. As a source of popular cultural icons, basketball provides some of the key images for blackness in our society. But the images of this black sport are then consumed in this country by a white-majority audience, through media that consciously shape the images for white needs. Within the community of basketball fans, white and black, basketball gets talked about routinely in a racialized discourse learned from the media and from conversations among the fans themselves. In this discourse there are "black" players and "white" players, and the color difference points to differences in style, attitude, and culture. As many critics of the game have noted, the "black" player is routinely depicted as a natural, a physical marvel, while the "white" player is a thinker, a hard worker, a coach on the floor. My goal is to bring this easy opposition into question and, more importantly, to show how the game itself questions the racism of its own discourse. More generally, I want to question the role that this racialized discourse of basketball plays in the cultural experience of the white, male fans to whom its images are directed.

As a member of the basketball community, I come to the topic of basketball and racial identity with a specific set of experiences and beliefs, like any American brought up in this divided but hybrid culture. So here is a quick race-identity sketch—Irish American, working-class Philadelphia family moving to the suburbs from a neighborhood changed overnight from all white to all black, fervent supporter and participant in the civil rights movement, educated in literary and cultural theories that

emphasize the social construction of personal identity, teacher in an overwhelmingly white Southern university, writer interested in the critical agency
of all subjects in postmodern culture. And here is a quick basketball re-
sume—lifetime mediocre but eager player, pickup games, intramurals, still
playing half-court games after twenty years in full-court oldguy games,
avid fan of basketball at every level, lover of the musty smell of gyms, the
hard asphalt of the schoolyard, the sweat of summer ball, the no-look pass,
the bump and grind of the low post, the grace and power of Michael
Jordan, the arrogance and wit of Charles Barkley, the awkward strain of a
nine-year-old child's first layup, the black-white game that is our country's
proud creation.

     In my analysis of the racial dynamics within the culture of basket-
ball, I am guided by a set of core beliefs about race, deriving from the
extensive literature produced by critical race theorists and black cultural
critics, and from my own experience in the game itself. First, I believe that
race is a function of culture rather than biology. As Henry Louis Gates puts
it, " 'Race' as a meaningful criterion within the biological sciences has long
been recognized to be a fiction" (1992, 48). Racial identity is constructed,
not given, though its constructed nature is hidden under the implicit claim
of biological foundations. "Race" is in a sense a verb, the act of defining
social and cultural groups in terms of their genetic heritage. These definitions
are acts of power, producing not just categories but hierarchies. The mo-
tive for invoking race is always political, always a way of imposing or
resisting or deconstructing power. Second, if race is a fiction, then it is no
less a lived reality for those who impose the definitions and especially for
those who have the definitions and the hierarchy imposed on them. People
kill and people die in the name of race. Racial definitions have effects on
movement through space, sexual choice, educational opportunity, health
prospects, residential patterns, self-concepts, psychological development,
economic opportunity, and a thousand daily feelings and choices. "Race"
may not have an ontological ground, but it has a deep hold on our cultural
common sense and thus on our daily lives. Third, racial definitions are
constructed by all groups and individuals in a society, not just by those at
the top of the alleged hierarchy. White-dominated mainstream media have
tremendous power to create racial definitions, but black culture and black
identity have been produced by the cultural work of black people struggling in an oppressive history. As a result of this discursive dynamic, our
culture has produced and still produces *competing* definitions of race, and
race politics can in part be understood as the conflicts among those
definitions. Fourth, this multiplicity of definitions means that there is no
such thing as a racial "essence," as purists of all races often claim. Neither
"white culture" nor "black culture" is homogeneous. Both groups are in-

ternally divided along lines of class, gender, ethnicity, sexual orientation, religion, region, and so on. And members of both groups also belong to many communities of practice and have internalized from these experiences cultural formations that *matter* in personal identity, complicating racial and other group identities. Also, all of these definitions have changed throughout history, and individuals change their self-definitions and their characterizations of the racial other throughout their lives. Essentialist definitions of race ignore all of these complexities in favor of simple dichotomies. Fifth, racial definitions in postmodern culture are produced in a media-soaked environment that creates complex representations and semiotic styles that come to be associated with different racial groups. Our thinking about other races in a still significantly segregated society often originates in those media images. Many white Americans "know" Michael Jordan more than they know their black fellow citizens, just as many black Americans "know" Larry Bird better than they know white people outside of the media experience. Televised basketball thus contributes to the construction of racial identities in America. Sixth, the question of race in America is not as simple as "black" and "white." In a multiethnic, multiracial society, racial definitions are constructed and contested along many axes. But to a significant degree basketball as a cultural practice organizes itself around a "black"/"white" dynamic, and its wider cultural impact consists of its construction of that opposition. The internationalization of the NBA may change that dynamic, but this simple racial binary still dominates the game, especially the televised game.

Basketball appears in many and diverse formats within the popular media. There is of course extensive television coverage of professional, college, and even high school basketball, and as Todd Boyd has pointed out, the game works perfectly for the sports highlight shows on ESPN and on the local news. Its percussive rhythm of dunks and blocked shots, desperation full-court heaves, impossible passes, and muscular rebounds can be edited into video sequences with great visual appeal (Boyd 1997, 117). And then there are the pregame shows, programs of discussion and analysis, features on basketball stars, appearances on talk shows, stories on news programs about scandals, arrests, and labor disputes, and endless call-in radio shows and Internet chat rooms. High-profile players also are featured in print and TV ads aimed at the youth market, and there is a long list of basketball-themed movies and television shows, all popular with white as well as black audiences.

And prominent in all of these formats are the bodies and faces of young black men, idolized at least in this context as marketable images for mass consumption. Lyndon Barrett's (1997) essay, "Black Men in the Mix: Badboys, Heroes, Sequins, and Dennis Rodman," to which I will return in more detail, is an extended reflection on the paradoxical centrality of images of black bodies in a popular culture aimed at a society that routinely despises and destroys black bodies and fears the physicality of young black men. Barrett's observations press the question: Why is basketball, routinely defined as a black game, so popular in the white cultural imagination? What roles do these images of blackness play in a culture that still feels comfortable with simple racial oppositions? Of course basketball is not the only black cultural practice that dominates American popular culture. A list that includes the blues, jazz, rhythm and blues as it transforms into rock and roll, rap and hip-hop, popular dance forms, and black speech styles and body language would suggest that even the most racist white American lives in a culture that owes much of its style to African American vernacular culture. I will pursue in this chapter some tentative answers to the question of basketball's popularity, some of them cynical, reflecting the irony of black cultural popularity and political marginality, and some of them utopian, reflecting white and black America's ability to imagine a social and cultural world that escapes simple and dangerous dichotomies.

But in addition, I would like to get past media images into the game of basketball as it is played on the streets and in the gyms, not by an elite, gifted few but by a huge, diverse population of church groups and families and friends and coworkers in rec leagues and pickup games and backyards and schoolyards. Only a few hundred players work in the NBA; some 35 *million* people in the United States alone play basketball in these less structured, local circumstances. In the vast world of pickup ball, black dominance, at least numerically, does not exist. Pickup players are black, white, Hispanic, Native American, Asian, and so on, in percentages no one can calculate. What role does race play in these games? How much influence do media images have on the racial definitions and identities of people who play for fun? Do these local games confirm or undo the images created by the media? I will argue that the race definitions that come out of this broader cultural practice are more subtle and less dichotomous than the media stereotypes. I have a strong faith that vernacular practices, though they are not untouched by the media, are healthier and more critical than the practices and discourses of mass culture.

Nevertheless, it is true that the discourse of basketball on all levels is thoroughly and routinely racialized. As Todd Boyd says:

> It seems as though sports, especially basketball, remains one of the few places in American society where there is a consistent racial discourse. This is not to say that there are not other areas of society where race is a significant part of the conversation,

but in basketball, race, directly or indirectly, *is* the conversation, at all times. (2000, 60)

On one level this discourse is discouragingly simple. The terms "white ball" and "black ball" are easy to decode for even the most casual fans of the game. "White ball" is routinely defined as hard working, "blue collar," "heady," self-sacrificing, team oriented, disciplined, and fundamentally sound—based on set plays, gritty defense, and submission to the coach's orders. "Black ball," in contrast, is seen as athletically gifted, creative, self-centered, stylized, improvisational, flamboyant, and expressive—based on individual freedom and the desire to please the crowd. Think of John Stockton versus Vince Carter. Think of Princeton playing University of Nevada at Las Vegas. These categories come easily to hand for sportscasters, journalists, players, and fans. Few people take them as absolutes, but they do serve as ready-made descriptive categories that seem to be confirmed enough by observation to be accepted as valid. They also draw their "validity" from their congruence with larger racial definitions that cast white people as systematized and productive and black people as intuitive and spontaneous.

Inevitably, these figurative oppositions also are hierarchies. In the commonsensical white racist view, "white ball" names the way the game should be played, and "black ball" names the corruption of the game. "Black ball" means excess, self-congratulation, thuggish violence, and ostentatious display. On the other hand, to many black observers, "white ball" is, in a word, dull. It is mechanical, unimaginative, earthbound, and overcoached. "White ball" is the name for how the game *used to* be played, before the truly gifted athletes took over. Black critics such as Nelson George and Todd Boyd have tied "black ball" into the Black Aesthetic movement and more generally into the African American improvisatory tradition that produced free-form jazz and the spontaneous oral creativity of rap. In *Elevating the Game,* George expresses his love for the Rucker League, the great Harlem summer league that attracted the best of New York's players, and he contrasts the theatricality of the black Rucker players with the "tightly choreographed patterns" of white ethnic New York ball. These players, he says, "ran through these patterns endlessly," in "standardized" formats that contrasted with the creativity of Rucker (1992, 75). Boyd, though he rejects essentialist definitions of African American culture, does see improvisation as a powerful component of the black artistic tradition, and this belief shapes his construction of "white ball" and "black ball":

Textbook basketball is akin to classical music, wherein performance is centered on the replication of a supposedly superior style. Musical sophistication is determined by one's proximity to the original; deviations are considered errors. This privileging of the original seems to permeate much of Western culture. Mastery of the form is achieved through one's ability to replicate at the highest level. With this in mind, those who operate in the tradition of textbook basketball can be clearly linked to this recurrent Western ethos of replication.

Playground basketball, on the other hand, is much like jazz in the sense that mastery of form depends upon one's ability to improvise, to create on the spot, to engage in full-court transition games that foreground style. The celebration of style through improvisation, consistent with much of African American culture, has had a great impact on the selling of the NBA to the American public through the mass media in the 1980s and into the 1990s. (1997, 116)

My objection to this line of analysis is that it seems to accept the white racist definitions of the game and of racial identity, and simply reverse the valence. The familiar dichotomies of system versus impulse and training versus gift remain, but they are placed in a different evaluative frame. My impulse is to deconstruct the opposition, to point to examples of players who confound the stereotypes, and to question the basis of the dichotomy. George and Boyd seem to conflate "playground" ball with "black" ball, as though those white ethnic kids never played except on organized teams, running through their coaches' patterns. And as a result they oversimplify the racial dynamic of the game.

In *Elevating the Game*, George tells a story about the origin of the fast break that seems to disconfirm his own oppositions. Nothing epitomizes the "black aesthetic" of basketball more than the fast break, where there are no set plays, only the improvisatory skills of the players on the run. One of the pioneers of the fast break was a black coach, John McLendon, who worked at North Carolina College for Negroes and Tennessee A&I, powerhouse black college teams before integration. But where did McLendon learn the fast break game? George tells us that it was from the game's creator himself, James Naismith, McLendon's white coach at Kansas. Naismith, who is now associated in the lore of the game with stuffy white YMCA ball from an era long before the soaring dunks of the 1960s and 1970s, in fact believed that the game ought to be played for maximum pleasure, as a full-court game, with no lags in the action, no walking the ball up the court uncontested. Naismith believed that the game ought to be recreation—fun—not the rote repetition of coach-designed plays. Certainly basketball does reflect African American culture, but this little history suggests that our culture's simple "black"-"white" dichotomies are inadequate to the beauty and complexity of basketball.

Boyd offers Michael Jordan as an example of a player who exemplifies the "fusion of the formal and the vernacular." Boyd sees this ability to "flip the script" as an example of African American cultural achievement analogous to the jazz player's ability to master formal musical modes and then bend them to his or her own creative uses (1997, 111–12), which it surely is, but I would argue that Jordan's game could also be thought about as an achievement that undercuts the opposition itself. His game is too rich to be fixed within dichotomies. His game is unthinkable outside of a tradition that goes back from Dr. J to Earl Monroe, Connie Hawkins, and Elgin Baylor (and Thelonious Monk and Duke Ellington too), but it also encompasses the court sense of Dean Smith, the defensive tenacity of Jerry Sloan, and the classic form of Jerry West. It is too simple to call his game a hybrid though; it is a unique creation that undermines racial oppositions and escapes categorization.

A similar argument could be made around figures such as Larry Bird and John Stockton, whose games often are seen as perfect examples of "white ball" and therefore underappreciated. Sportswriters and television analysts often cite Bird as an example of a player whose game is an intellectual achievement produced by a stereotypically white work ethic. But despite this media image, has there even been a more improvisatory player than Bird? His game may not have been in the air, especially as he got older, but his passing and his court sense were "black" to the bone. He even talked about making moves for their "degree of difficulty," just to keep himself from getting bored, thus suggesting an interest in style for its own sake that many critics and ordinary fans see as part of the "black aesthetic" of the game. John Stockton, who is white, famously matched with Karl Malone, who is black but often characterized as playing "white ball," also is caught in stereotypical characterizations. Maybe it is because of his undemonstrative style, but Stockton often was presented by announcers and journalists as the "white player" personified—smart, tough, cerebral, team oriented. He and Malone were tenth-degree black belt masters of the pick-and-roll, one of those stodgy "white" plays that George makes sound so dull and repetitive. But the pick-and-roll was absolutely different every time Stockton and Malone ran it. The basic structure of the play (Malone sets a pick and then rolls to the basket) is like the musical theme that these jazz (and Jazz) players run variations or riffs on, reacting in the moment to the moves of the defenders, creating the play on the fly.

I am happy and proud to say that my last couple of paragraphs could have been overheard in a sports bar or in a living room as a group of fans talk over a game. That is, the endless conversation about race that Boyd describes does not always simply reproduce dominant racial definitions. The racial dichotomies of basketball discourse are routinely deconstructed by fans themselves. Everyone around the game knows that there are black "white players" and white "black players," and players whose games cannot be categorized at all, and they could cite you plenty of examples. Categorize the following players from the history of the game by racial style: Bill Russell, Willis Reed, Lenny Wilkens, Tom Chambers, Bob Cousy, K. C. Jones, Maurice Cheeks, Dennis Rodman, Paul Silas, Jason Kidd, Christian Laettner, Sam Perkins. Ordinary fans know that "black ball" and "white ball" are names of styles only loosely connected to the "race" of players, which is to say that they know on some level that "race" is a cultural construction rather than a biological given.

One recent development in elite basketball that helps fans deconstruct race is the increasing internationalization of the NBA. Players from Serbia and Brazil and Mexico and China and Argentina do not fit into any easy racial categories. Some are easy to identify visually as white or black, but their cultural uniqueness defies reduction to "white" or "black." Many recent European players, such as Peja Stojakovich and Dirk Nowitzki, have very "black" games. They give full play to their athleticism rather than accepting the supporting role for which the "white" player is suited. They seem never to have been told that they are "white." They flow with the game and trust their skills, like a "black" player, or like a pickup player. Their success suggests, in fact, that many American white players have accepted the role of the "white" player as a self-fulfilling prophecy, limiting their games to fit the stereotype. Similarly, African players raised in France, Afro-Brazilian players, and other players from the global African diaspora do not easily assimilate into "black" cultural categories. Hakeem Olajuwan and Tim Duncan escape from easy racial categories. There may come a time when the globalization of basketball will make the "white player"/ "black player" dichotomy useless, but for now it plays an important structural function in the culture of the practice.

The "black"/"white" opposition does negative cultural work not only because it misrepresents players but because it misrepresents the culture of the game on a technical level. *All* basketball is improvisational, even in the most official, organized contexts. Coaches may design plays, but plays are just strategies for setting up opportunities to improvise. As with the pick-and-roll, set plays provide only the minimal structure necessary for players to be able to anticipate and communicate so they can make the split-second decisions that the game requires. And when you get away from organized ball, into the great uncoached world of pickup ball, there is nothing but improvisation, no matter what the race and cultural background of the players. Part of the magic of playing the game is the psychic communication that occurs among experienced players as they create the game. Basketball, and not just "black" basketball, is an improvisatory group movement system, unpredictable moment by moment, even when the moment calls for a "play" like the pick-and-roll or a backdoor cut. Does this creativity make all pickup ball "black"? I have seen it practiced by very white-bread players. Creativity derives from the practice of the game itself, which attracts improvisatory personalities, no matter what cultural tradition players bring to it. Of course great black players made improvisation increasingly accepted in the game, and they drew on the resources of African American culture to do so, but my guess is that pickup games in Latvia play like jazz, and that the game cannot and should not be simplified into a "black" and "white" duality.

The most grievous white error around these racial dichotomies is the conflation of "white ball" and white players with what I have called "ethical basketball." White players such as Bird and Stockton often have been deified by the media as models of basketball behavior. And black players such as Allen Iverson and Latrell Sprewell often are demonized as signs of the coming moral apocalypse. There is of course no correlation between race and ethical behavior in the game, but in a white dominated culture, it is not surprising that "white values" come to be the dominant values in a particular practice. There is journalistic glee when Allen Iverson or Latrell Sprewell confirms the gangsta stereotype. White culture can then take great pleasure in these confirmations of its own moral superiority. Basketball does have an ethic, negotiated on the spot in every game, and the idea that white players have a corner on that ethic is belied by even a moment's serious observation. Nevertheless, there is a persistent narrative among white fans that connects the black takeover of the game to the decline of its standards.

This conviction that black players are ruining the game has occurred at the same time basketball has achieved unprecedented popularity and symbolic force in white American popular culture. Criticisms of "black ball" serve as a cover for white fascination with the athletic black bodies on display in the spectacle of televised basketball. Black bodies are subjected to white moral codes, reaffirming white cultural hegemony. But the figure of the black player serves a more complex function in white America, as a screen on which fans can project their feelings about race, sexuality, morality, politics, and social structures. The televised game provides an opportunity for white fans to construct racial categories, working across the cultural productions of the black and white players themselves. Part of the pleasure of watching basketball for white people, as I will argue more extensively in the next chapter, is that they are situated at the power position of the spectator who imposes meaning structures on the images

provided by the media, images already structured by the rhetorical strategies of—white-dominated—television and journalism to reinforce meanings that serve white interests. White people are positioned to enjoy the
pleasure and power of looking and defining.

In *Playing in the Dark: Whiteness and the Literary Imagination*, Toni
Morrison (1992) sums up her discoveries about how white American writers create black characters:

> As a writer reading, I came to realize the obvious: the subject
> of the dream is the dreamer. The fabrication of an Africanist
> persona is reflexive, an extraordinary meditation on the self; a
> powerful exploration of the fears and desires that reside in the
> writerly conscious. It is an astonishing revelation of longing, of
> terror, of perplexity, of shame, of magnanimity. It requires hard
> work *not* to see this. (1992, 17)

Morrison understands that white writing about black characters in fiction
tells us much about the writer's self-definitions. I would contend that white
"fabrications" of the figure of the black player in the same way reveal the
self-obsessions of white fans, who *make use of* the black player as a way of
dealing with their own fears and hopes. They can do this because as the
dominant racial group in the society they have the power to impose the
dominant definitions. They claim the power to decide what blackness shall
mean as a popular symbol. As John Wideman says, "Race is not a set of
qualities inhering in some 'other'; it's the license to ascribe such qualities
allied with the power to make them stick" (1994, xv). Many white fans are
quite comfortable with the racial dichotomies in the game. The "black"
player is *not us*; his qualities define ours; he is what we are not. Just as
Morrison argues that the enslaved black defined the essence of white freedom, I would argue that the figure of the physically gifted, spontaneous,
creative "black" player defines by opposition the power of "white"
systematicity, discipline, hard work, and dedication. But it is not just that
the definitions suit white needs, it is that the act of defining brings with
it the pleasure of power, especially when what is defined is the physical
power of the "black" player. Whites get to trump on the level of representation the power of the displayed black body.

Gerald Early (1998) evokes the opening chapter of Ralph Ellison's
Invisible Man, "Battle Royal," as a symbol for the role of black athletics in
white America. This episode of the novel, set in the segregated South,
depicts a free-for-all fight in which young black boys, blindfolded, fight
one another for the amusement of a white audience at a smoker (the
opening act was a white stripper). The men in the crowd, watching the

struggles of these physically powerful and politically powerless athletes, revel in the pleasure of their white invisibility. They can call out threats, taunt the weak fighters, and enjoy the power of the strong ones, all behind the safety of their superior class and race status. An NBA game provides a similar racialized pleasure. Black players strive and display their prowess for an overwhelmingly white crowd that plays out its fears and fantasies in vicarious passion. The players, of course, are not the economic inferiors of the fans, as the fighters in "Battle Royal" are, but part of the charm of the game for white audiences is that many players act out an underclass, street-black persona that confirms white economic superiority as a group and reinscribes the gangsta figure as the dominant stereotype of contemporary African American masculinity.

White fans watch black players, with stylized, perfected black bodies. Many white women take from this experience a straightforward heterosexual pleasure mixed with racial taboo. For white men, all along the homosocial continuum, the experience is more complex. Sexual as well as racial taboos come into play. In Wideman's wry description of the sexual politics of the NBA, he creates an image of barnstorming black players,

> riding into town itching for a fight, archetypal American road warriors with enormous guns but corked up in blackface, a few great white hopes as sidekicks, forbidden, seductive black bodies on display for a night of G-rated fun. Indians posing as cowboys and they get paid to scalp the locals. Black over white in a country historically, fiercely, dedicated to just the opposite proposition. Michael Jordan in an ad, winking at two white girls who sit on a park bench checking him out, wishing away the emperor's trousers, speculating aloud about the style of his underdrawers as the bald, black prince strolls, struts, trots by. If it sells underwear, if it sells tickets, there's no rule that can't be broken, no stereotype not turned upside down, pulled inside out. (1998, 70)

For white male fans the key is "G rated." Sexuality is not on the official agenda. Those black bodies are not explicitly on display. They are engaged in a contest, one that the spectacle predicates would go on even in the absence of observers. "Display" is a by-product of the situation, not its sanctioned purpose. But display still happens. In televised basketball, for example, instant replays stop time and allow bodies to take an iconic form that captures the fierce kinetic beauty of players. For heterosexual white men in live and TV audiences there is a homoerotic charge in the gaze, most often unconscious and unacknowledged.

Cultural critic Kobena Mercer (1991) explores this cross-racial homoerotic gaze in an analysis of Robert Mapplethorpe's photographs of black
male nudes. His analysis of the power relations in these photographs stresses
the invisibility of the white spectator:

> Insofar as what is represented in the pictorial space of the
> photograph is a "look" or a certain "way of looking," the pic-
> tures say more about the white male subject behind the camera
> than they do about the black men whose beautiful bodies we
> see depicted. This is because the invisible or absent subject is
> the actual agent of the look, at the centre and in control of the
> apparatus of representation, the I/eye at the imaginary origin of
> the perspective that marks out the empty space to which the
> viewer is invited as a spectator. (1991, 170)

The formal postures of the photographs also have an important effect,
Mercer argues: "As all references to a social or historical context are effaced
by the cool distance of the detached gaze, the text enables the projection
of a fantasy which saturates the black male body in sexual predicates." And
this fantasy, Mercer says, is a fantasy of power over the—physically powerful—racial other: "The dynamics of this tension are apparently stabilized
within the pictorial space of the photographs by the ironic appropriation
of commonplace stereotypes—the black man as athlete, as savage, as mugger.
These stereotypes in turn serve to regulate and fix the representational
presence of the black subject, who is thereby 'put in his place' by the
power of Mapplethorpe's gaze" (1991, 175). Beautiful black bodies, iconic
forms, stereotyped identities, the power of the gaze—these conditions are
present for the basketball spectator, especially in televised sports that abstract
the game from its social and physical context and isolate the iconic moments, formalized and repeated in instant replay and stop action. In addition, the discourse of basketball coverage subjects the black body to a
range of symbolic meanings centered around the stereotype of "the black
player," which connects with the other "commonplace stereotypes" that
Mercer describes. Black bodies can therefore be simultaneously idolized
and contained; they are beautiful and sexual to the eye but subordinated
by the white power of cultural definition.

A vivid example of the power dynamic that Mercer describes can be
seen in the coffee table book *Soul of the Game: Images and Voices of Street
Basketball* (1997). This book combines photographs of street ball players,
by John Huet, who has worked in advertising for Nike, Reebok, and
Gatorade, with poems and short prose pieces written by rappers, street
poets, and the players themselves. Huet's photographs display with great

beauty the chiseled bodies and kinetic grace of these black players, visually abstracting them from their physical and social environment in order to linger over their physical beauty and their emotive expressions. The players sweat and strain, and we see up close their scowls of anger and competitive passion. What is unsettling about the book is that it provides a very thin cover story—a desire to honor local street players—for an unacknowledged desire to fetishize black bodies. The photos often dismember these bodies in order to focus on huge hands, straining muscles, expressive faces, complex cornrows, and smoothly shaven heads. It is downright pornographic, which would be okay if it were acknowledged as such, but the eroticism is packaged inside a sentimental narrative about the sacredness and urban grit of pickup ball. The book is an "artistic" version of the endless television commercials in which beautiful black basketball bodies are displayed in an effort to attach street credibility to mass-market products. The audience for this book and for those ads is heterosexual white men, and the erotic energy conveyed must be sublimated and denied in order to operate successfully in mainstream media. The reduction of dangerous black bodies to beautiful accessories that surround desirable products is a reassuring reminder to that audience of its cultural power over the black masculinity that it fears and desires.

The complex role of the black male body in the white male imagination derives of course from a violent, oppressive history. Part of the cultural function of elite, televised basketball is to allow straight white men to deal with that history and those complex feelings in a safe, "G- rated" environment. As the "white player"/"black player" dichotomy reminds us, the structure underneath the black-white opposition in our culture is the mind-body duality. White people are associated in our cultural imaginary with the life of the mind, black people with the life of the body. The "white player" is a thinker; the "black player" is a body in unself-conscious motion. This violent and dehumanizing opposition produces a complex black figure—gifted with a more perfect body, more in touch with visceral drives, impelled by emotion and instinct, unburdened with culture and history, more sexual, more violent, more intense, more authentic. "Whiteness" then comes to be associated with a disembodied rationality, alienated from primitive desires and powerful emotions.

Norman Mailer (1957) articulated these feelings more than forty years ago in his influential essay "The White Negro." Mailer is easy to criticize from our historical perspective, but his essay makes a complex point that should not be dismissed as simple white boy envy. And his emotional attachments to the figure of "the Negro" are still pertinent for understanding our own very different racial order. Mailer's essay comes directly out of the horror of World War II and the Holocaust. Mailer sees himself living in a world saturated by horrible and meaningless violence, produced systematically by the civilization that was created to repress it:

> If the fate of twentieth-century man is to live with death from adolescence to premature senescence, why then the only life-giving answer is to accept the terms of death, to live with death as immediate danger, to divorce one-self from society, to exist without roots, to set out on that uncharted journey into the rebellious imperative of the self. In short, whether the life is criminal or not, the decision is to encourage the psychopath in oneself, to explore that domain of experience where security is boredom and therefore sickness, and one exists in the present. (Mailer 1957, 192)

Mailer found his model for this authentic life in the figure of the Negro, seen as living the life of the body in a life-denying culture:

> Any Negro who wishes to live must live with danger from his first day, and no experience can ever be casual to him, no Negro can saunter down a street with any real certainty that violence will not visit him on his walk. The cameos of security for the average white: mother and the home, job and the family, are not even a mockery to millions of Negroes; they are impossible. The Negro has the simplest of alternatives: live a life of constant humility or ever-threatening danger. In such a pass where paranoia is as vital to survival as blood, the Negro had stayed alive and begun to grow by following the need of his body where he could. Knowing in the cells of his existence that life was war, nothing but war, the Negro (all exceptions admitted) could rarely afford the sophisticated inhibitions of civilization, and so he kept for his survival the art of the primitive, he lived in the enormous present, he subsisted for his Saturday night kicks, relinquishing the pleasures of the mind for the more obligatory pleasures of the body, and in his music he gave voice to the character and quality of his existence, to his rage and the infinite variations of joy, lust, languor, growl, cramp, pinch, scream, and despair of his orgasm. (Mailer 1957, 194)

I quote this passage at length because it articulates the messy mix of fear, sympathy, and condescension that characterizes white feelings about the black body. Mailer provides a perfunctory apology—"all exceptions admitted"—but then goes on without hesitation to identify "the Negro" with

Staggerlee, the "bad Negro," the street hustler who lives by his improvisatory wits and enjoys the pleasures of the powerful male body. "The Negro" for Mailer is a man, not a woman; he is poor and unemployed; he has given up on the life of the mind because it can only get him in trouble. Mailer's reductive characterizations could be dismissed as racist and arrogant, except for the fact that he makes it clear that the Negro's existential life in the moment is not a function of his "race" as such but of his socially defined racial status. In a world in which white people deny one's right to life, living for the moment is a strategy for psychic survival. "The Negro," Mailer suggests, has been forced by American racism to see the facts of all human life, which Mailer learned from the war and the Holocaust—that no real security exists, despite middle-class white illusions, and that an existential leap into a self-directed quest for authentic existence is the only solution for modern life.

In his critical rejoinder to Mailer, James Baldwin nevertheless confirms Mailer's image of the Negro as inevitable existentialist:

> . . . to become a Negro man, let alone a Negro artist, one had to make oneself up as one went along. This had to be done in the not-at-all-metaphorical teeth of the world's determination to destroy you. The world had prepared no place for you, and if the world had its way, no place would ever exist. Now, this is true for everyone, but, in the case of a Negro, this truth is absolutely naked: if he deludes himself about it, he will die. (1961, 183)

In Baldwin's characterization, "the Negro" is the great improviser, living in the authentic moment, facing the truth that white people have the privilege of ignoring. Since no place has been made for him, he must create his own identity "on the run," as a basketball player might say. Both Mailer and Baldwin see "the Negro" as a disillusioned figure who cannot accept conventional pieties because he knows the awful facts of life. He is in touch with the truth, living authentically in the real.

I realize that I am putting the best face on Mailer's essay, which on a deep level does buy into conventional white prejudices, simply redefining as hip the behavior white racists had defined as depraved. But Mailer does articulate a number of themes that help explain our own popular culture's obsession with the black male body: white inauthenticity and alienation, black sexuality and violence, black ability to improvise in the moment. For many white fans the black body on display in basketball is a fantasy figure, living as the white fan cannot. The fans' premise is that those black bodies are what we have repressed in the name of civilization and responsibility. To

be a white basketball fan is to get in touch with the inner Negro—the visceral
pleasure of the dunk, the blocked shot, the impossible rebound, the crossover,
the quickness. That *not I* up there *is I*, we assert, or at least an *I* that would
be ours if we were not so constrained by jobs and families and duties. White
fans identify with black players by casting them in the role of the repressed
self, the id, the dark force that civilization is designed to deny, and they are
not deterred in this identification by the stupidity of its premises.

These fan fantasies could be thought of as "primitivist," in the sense
of the term that Marianna Torgovnick (1990) proposes in her book *Gone
Primitive*. Torgovnick is interested in the ways in which Western intellec-
tuals have constructed the figure of the primitive as the natural human
opposite of the overcivilized Western subject. One aspect of that figure is
its physicality—the primitive is bodily:

> Within Western culture the idiom "going primitive" is in fact
> congruent in many ways to the idiom "getting physical." . . . As
> we have seen, Freud believed that civilization arose to protect
> humans from the uncontrolled imperatives of sexuality and
> aggression. In return it exacted the repression of sexuality and
> the control of aggressive impulses. The flip side of this theory
> was a widely shared, unexamined belief that "uncivilized"
> people—that is, primitives and certain marginal members of
> the lower classes—are exempt from the repression of sexuality
> and control of aggression. (1990, 228)

Western constructions of "primitive" physicality allow white people to
believe that oppressed groups such as African Americans are compensated
for their marginalization by a more authentic way of life, more in touch
with the real world of the body and nature. Suffering from what bell hooks
calls "cultural anhedonia," the affluent, white-collar fans of the NBA can
explain their condition by reference to their race, their noble but burdened
whiteness, rather than to their own life choices, and they can use the black
bodies on the court as tokens of what they as white people have left
behind. This strategy relies on race at the expense of a class analysis that
might see "cultural anhedonia" not as a racialized trait but as a class-
related function of bureaucratized and money-fixated yuppie lifestyles in
which black bodies reaffirm the "naturalness" of white privilege.

This affirmation requires the display of black bodies, but they must be
disciplined bodies. All players, black and white, must submit at least to some
extent to the dictates of "white ball" in order to survive in elite sports
organizations. They must be "coachable," willing to submit to someone else's
call in a game situation, willing to play within a team concept. The white

public, then, has the pleasure of observing a disciplinary system that it defines as its own, imposing its rules and patterns on black bodies. As John Hoberman says in his controversial book *Darwin's Athletes,* "The dissemination of aggressive black male images by corporations and their advertising media threatens to alienate the white public if displays of black assertiveness are not rationed and counterbalanced by others that domesticate and gentrify virile black men" (1997, xxi). The figure of the coach is an important relay position in this display of symbolic power. The racial identity of the figure of the coach is "white," whether the actual coach is black or white. The position of the coach, with its emphasis on system, teamwork, discipline, fundamental skills, strategy and tactics, motivation, and group dynamics, is coded "white" over against the "blackness" of the players. Hoberman says:

> Reinforcing the image of colonial hierarchy are countless television images of well-groomed white coaches who look like business executives, dressed in jackets and ties and appearing to be clearly in charge of their sweating, half-dressed black players. Here the integrated sports world functions symbolically as a modernizing school of discipline in which the wilder impulses of the black male are domesticated by putting him in a uniform and making his athleticism the product of an organization with white corporate values and organizational strategies. (1997, 935)

Basketball enacts a public psychodrama that teaches that the impulsive, creative, physically powerful "black" self must be controlled by the moral structures and productive practices of the "white" self. The coach serves as the "superego" in this scenario; he is the socialized conscience that makes repression possible. The white fan can therefore enjoy basketball as a display of his repressed "black" self *and* as a dramatization of the necessity for that repressive control.

Basketball fans need to have it both ways—they want to see physically powerful black masculinity, but they want to maintain white dominance. Lyndon Barrett, in his essay "Black Men in the Mix: Badboys, Heroes, Sequins, and Dennis Rodman," suggests how that desire can be fulfilled. The black players of the NBA are dangerous figures. They often transgress against the rules of the game, refuse to abide by genteel corporate imaging, and, in the case of Rodman, they even call gender definitions into question. But their enfoldment into televisual discourse domesticates them into white fantasies of consumption culture. Barrett says:

> Throughout the contests staged by the NBA, the specular pleasure of professional play is translated, via regularly aired

commercials, into anticipatory identification with some further moment of pleasure objectified in the form of a "readily"
acquired product and image. As stated earlier, this circuit centered "around the theme of consumption" entails the extremely
unlikely combination of blackness, masculinity, the market,
and an acute moral imaginary. Moreover, the circuit formed
by this unlikely combination is most effective and most ratio-
nalized when particularly adulated players in the mix of NBA
competition also occupy the narratives of exchange punctuat-
ing that play. In the most economical versions of NBA events,
indispensable catalysts of this phantasmatic production of
desire are select physically adept African American "young
guys" spectacularized within the acrobatics of the NBA as
well as proliferating within the commercial narratives under-
writing the broadcast. To identify with these figures in their
technological displacement from basketball courts to vignettes
of available consumption and new pleasures is to be bound
up in an extremely economical set of manipulations. (Barrett
1977, 115)

These figures of "black macho," dangerous and disruptive on the court, are
transformed in commercials into ordinary consumers or comic-harmless
characters in scenes of safe, domestic consumption. Thus their transgres-
sions are limited to the athletic sphere. Their danger is manageable, finally
not incompatible with mainstream consumer culture.

In some advertising the strategies of domestication are more subtle.
Many ads for basketball shoes and other youth-oriented commodities play
on the figure of the dangerous black man in its current form—the young
ball player as the gangsta rapper, posse in tow, party in mind, full of
underclass rage, ready to explode at the conventions of the game and the
hierarchies of society. That image sells too, as Todd Boyd and others have
pointed out. Black gangsta basketball style becomes a middle-class, white-
boy style of rebellion—a haircut, a brand of shoes, a stylish jacket. These
white boys are not rebels against the racial order but rebels against middle-
class sexual restraint, searching for a style of masculinity that defines them
as hard, unwilling as yet to become the sensitive man that white, middle-
class culture and schooling require. Boyd rightly asserts that the economy
of the NBA allows young black players to assimilate less to middle-class
norms—they can afford to keep their underclass style, to live large, and
they can create a public persona that refuses to be domesticated, smoothed
out for white consumption. But any public persona constructed through
the strategies of marketing and advertising is thereby domesticated, be-

coming just one more semiotic alternative, one more rebel style that finally confirms mainstream fantasies.

In the late 1990s a series of Nike commercials featured "the fun police," a group of what were then younger NBA stars who play the game with a tough edge, a snarling, macho style—Kevin Garnett, Gary Payton. These ads played cleverly with the racial stereotypes of the game. In one ad, "the fun police" arrest a young, middle-class, white kid who just cannot pass the ball, a "crime" that is commonplace in the white put-down of "black ball." But behind the clever ironies, the strategy of the campaign is to put dangerous black styles to work, selling Nikes in the suburbs. In another commercial the players become ushers at a fantasy game in which tickets for row A, held by white rich guys and their trophy dates, get them put in the last row of the house, and tickets in row triple Z, held by young black kids (with one white token), get them courtside, Jack Nicholson seats. The white guys in the last row, corporate types with a bizarre cameo by Donald Trump, make lame jokes about needing binoculars, while the kids revel in the electricity of the up-close game. The "fun police," of course, are on the side of the kids, indulging a fantasy of a world in which money does not buy privilege. This cynical and mean-spirited ad co-opts young black basketball style for empty corporate self-congratulation, for it is, of course, Nike and the sleazy money that surrounds basketball that have made the NBA the yuppie league, with tickets so expensive that no kid could afford even row triple Z. Those kids have been frozen out of the game, along with families who cannot even think about buying four tickets and parking and food, and along with almost everyone black in America. Only the corporate types that this commercial claims to mock can afford to see a game. The rest get to watch basketball on TV, surrounded by Nike ads. Fans watch the ads and buy the products, but they do not see the live game, thanks to Nike, thanks to the skybox-mad owners, and thanks to the very players who appear in the ad. Even dangerous styles can become domesticated, can submit to commercial discipline.

The disciplining of the black male body in the spectacle of basketball requires a strategy that simultaneously hypermasculinizes and feminizes the players. The bodies that televison displays are hypermasculine. The camera loves the slam dunk, the chest bump, the clenched fist, the high five. But the very act of putting a body on display feminizes that body. The subject in the position of arranging and framing the display is coded masculine, while the body to be displayed for aesthetic and kinetic appeal is coded feminine. As Kobena Mercer says, "Analogies between race and gender in representation reveal similar ideological patterns of objectification, exclusion, and 'othering' " (1992, 6). Similarly, Torgovnick notes that "those familiar tropes for primitives become the tropes conventionally used for

women" (1990, 17). Representations of black men as impulsive, emotional, creative, and closer to the body associate them with the feminine,
allowing the white male viewer to conquer the black male player, even on
the field of masculinity.

This double strategy of hypermasculinity and femininity can be seen
in more than just basketball of course. The figure of the sexually endowed
black stud has been a staple of plantation mythology, Reconstruction era,
Klan propaganda, 1970s' blaxploitation films, and contemporary hip-hop
videos. The black man's penis and his appeal to white women are legendary
elements in the dreams and nightmares of white men in positions of power
that they secretly believe they do not deserve. But as Susan Gubar puts it,
"The black man who *is* his penis neither has nor ever will have the phallus"
(1997, 54). The phallus, the symbol of a self-governance that also dominates
others, is not a function of physical power but cultural power. And insofar
as black men are *the represented* rather than the agents of representation, they
are feminized, in just the way the subjugation of women is in part maintained by the power of the male gaze. Basketball, as an arena for the display
of the black male body, contributes to these strategies of cultural power.

Gubar goes on to say that "as any orthodox Lacanian would immediately interject, all men have penises, but none possess the phallus. Not
a real organ but instead an attribute of power or meaning, the phallus
remains a signifier beyond the reach of all human beings" (1997, 54). This
message, that no one has self-possession and natural, authentic power over
others, has an acute recent history with white men, the group brought up
most powerfully under the illusion that they *do* possess the phallus. Feminists have made that illusion impossible to maintain under honest self-
reflection. In addition, the life of the workplace for yuppie white fans is a
disciplined and repetitive routine, one that serves as a constant reminder
of the limits of personal power. The black male body, then, serves as an
unconscious symbol for what was never possessed but feels just now lost—
total physical power, self-possession, the ability to *rise up over* the daily
constraints. And as a bonus, the symbol does not in the end threaten the
arbitrary racial hierarchy. Basketball is just a game, and its players can be
dismissed as grown up children whose achievements do not threaten real-
world economic power. For all their spectacular masculinity, they are less
than men, powerful only in the play world. Being cast in the role of "the
penis" or "the id" emphasizes their irresponsibility; their actions have no
serious consequences. They can serve as symbols of the phallus regained,
even as we rest certain in our own knowledge that they do not in fact
possess the phallus either, in spite of their physical prowess.

One consequence of this symbolic order is media caricatures of black
masculinity. The figure of the basketball player connects with other easy

stereotypes of the bad Negro, the thug in the street, the pimp with the razor, the figures of black macho. As a result, the real variety of masculine experience among black men is obscured. bell hooks writes movingly about the wide variety of black men that these cartoon figures may exclude:

> Though I admired my father, I was more fascinated and charmed by black men who were not obsessed with being patriarchs: by Felix, a hobo who jumped trains, never worked a regular job, and had a missing thumb; by Kid, who lived out in the country and hunted the rabbits and coons that came to our table; by Daddy Gus, who spoke in hushed tones, sharing his sense of spiritual mysticism. These were the men who touched my heart. The list could go on. I remember them because they loved folks, especially women and children. They were caring and giving. They were black men who chose alternative lifestyles, who questioned the status quo, who shunned a ready-made patriarchal identity and invented themselves. By knowing them, I have never been tempted to ignore the complexity of black male experience and identity. The generosity of spirit that characterized who they were and how they lived in the world lingers in my memory. I write this piece to honor them, knowing as I do now that it was no simple matter for them to choose against patriarchy, to choose themselves, their lives. (1992, 88)

Adapting hooks's phrase, I would say that the figure of the black player in the white imagination "puts in place of this lived complexity a flat, one-dimensional representation" (1992, 89). And the fact that this erasure of really existing black masculinity in all of its complexity serves the interest of privileged white men reminds us that the spectacle of basketball is an act of racial and cultural power.

But basketball does not function only to reaffirm racial stereotypes. It also embodies for many of its fans a desire to make connections across racial lines. The game presents the spectacle of black and white players cooperating as teammates and sharing energy in the emotional flow of the game, and the fans participate vicariously in the emotions of the players, creating strong affective ties, even in the hearts of hardened racists. Put simply, basketball fans *love* the players on the teams they root for. They feel that players *represent* them. The players' excellence at the game stands for their own quiet aspirations. And race matters little in their affiliations. When the "blue-collar" Charles Oakley and the warrior Patrick Ewing and the brash, fearless John Starks—all African Americans—played for the Knicks, fans of all races felt that these players represented the city of New

York and its roughhouse culture. It is easy to dismiss these feelings as sentimental self-delusions, as John Hoberman does by calling basketball a source of "the propaganda of racial bonhomie" (1997, xxiii). But positive feelings across racial lines count heavily in a culture that so often encourages ignorance and suspicion. It is of course highly questionable how much of that affection crosses over into more deeply held racial attitudes or behaviors, and as a worst case it can be used as a cover for racial fear and hatred. But precisely because of its strong emotional pull, basketball provides white and black fans with the opportunity at least to rethink conventional racial hierarchies. Players such as Michael Jordan or Hakeem Olajuwan or Grant Hill are not just figures of physical prowess in our culture, they also are moral figures whose actions seem to embody a certain ethical character. Racial hierarchies in the popular imagination are in small but significant ways challenged when public figures of moral excellence are black, not white.

Basketball serves the positive cultural function of creating bonds of affection among men brought up not to share or even acknowledge their feelings for one another. In basketball this affection crosses racial lines, creating an opportunity for white and black men to express their desire to overcome racial separation and to connect as men and as human beings. Basketball can therefore be seen as a utopian project, open to all of the cynicism that the awareness of real-world injustice can bring, but holding out as a desire a society in which race counts only as respected difference and what matters is shared effort and fellow feeling. I would point to the fans' pleasure in those great moments of ecstatic joy that follow a comeback win, when a team gets on an unstoppable run, driving the home crowd into a frenzy, ending in a team embrace, white and black players together, lines of demarcation lost in Dionysian joy. How much do those moments count? Grown men are brought to sentimental tears by them. They feel themselves in the presence of a privileged moment, a vision of a better world, as though the tragedy of race in America were bypassed. Wounds feel healed, fears seem irrelevant. Of course the racial horrors of our history never disappear, and they continue to structure even these utopian desires, but maybe the illusion that history can be escaped is necessary to the politics of real racial healing, which must still of course occur in the midst of that history, not in some theater of spectacular brotherhood. But not even the most guarded, most pragmatic racial politics can occur without some utopian vision.

I have so far written this analysis of basketball and racial identity mostly from the position of the consumer or fan of the game, invoking the political problematic of the position of the spectator, which provides the white fan with a complex experience of power and affiliation, politics and

eros. Media presentations of elite basketball foster simple racial dichotomies but also provide an opportunity for fans to deconstruct the oppositions. But if we now turn to the pickup game, we see that for players the
ability to deconstruct racial oppositions is simply a survival skill. If you
cannot see and behave beyond the cliches of "black" and "white," then you
cannot play the game effectively. In the game as it is played outside the
elite, organized leagues, there is no privileged, spectatorial position for the
white player to inhabit, and for actual black players, the iconic figure of
the "black" player does you no good if you cannot play. Pickup players
experience rich local cultures as well as the national media culture that
many fans are limited to, and local cultures produce more diverse and
unstable meanings. Race in pickup ball is thus a more fluid category, shaped
by local circumstances and personal histories. The global racial oppositions do not disappear, but they are modified, complexified in the rough-
and-tumble of the local game.

    This is not to say that race does not matter in the cultural practice
of the pickup game. Players do not magically divest themselves of stereotyped racial identities. Any black player has to deal with the expectation
of an excellence conferred by blackness itself—in fact, I know black guys
who will not play the game even thought they love it, because they know
they cannot live up to those media-driven expectations. And any white guy
in a mixed-race game has to deal, at least at first, with the fear of being
thought a chump. But after some testing out, players are forced by the
game to deal with the real strengths and weaknesses of actual players
rather than with race-defined stereotypes. It makes no sense to throw an
alley-oop pass to a 5'9" earthbound black guy on the mistaken impression
that he is Tracy McGrady, and you can get burned fast if you mistake a
quick and high-flying white guy for the stiff that the stereotype defines him
as. The moment-to-moment exigencies of the game require players to
observe and respond to the actual individuals assembled on the court,
where simple dichotomies are not helpful.

    On the court, complex readings of the bodies and skills of other
players are required at every moment. Those readings proceed, as I argued
in my chapter on decision making, by means of a complex heuristic, a set
of rules of thumb, shortcuts necessary for quick assessment and decision.
For most players in this country at least, race is one of those heuristics.
Players do make assumptions about each other on the basis of race, but
those assumptions are instantly tested by the flow of the game. One black
guy I have played with and against has a simple, direct style. He is relentless
and aggressive and uses his strength to get to the basket. Players who come
to his game with the assumption that because he is black he will play
"black" keep waiting for him to do something fancy, and he keeps pounding

away in the lane, playing the game that plays to his strengths. Only a basketball idiot would persist in the stereotype rather than adjust to the reality. Once the stereotype is put aside, the thousand other assessment techniques of the game come into play. Can he go left? Protect the ball? Play defense? Shoot from the outside? The "race" heuristic no longer operates.

Bill Bradley (1998), in his book *Values of the Game*, claims that race virtually disappears for players. What matters in basketball, he says, is not race but character. Who can you rely on? Who will put in the practice time? Who will stay focused at the crisis moment? The answers to those questions are more immediate and pressing than who is black and who is white. They determine the moment-to-moment decisions in the game, which always rely on a knowledge of the other players' histories and tendencies. Who should you pass to when your team needs a basket? Who can you rely on to block a shot so you can risk a try for the steal? On defense, players do not think, "Where's the black guy?" They think, "Where's the shooter?" Bradley's analysis recalls Martin Luther King's famous hope that people could be judged by the content of their character rather than by the color of their skin, and he offers basketball as a privileged cultural practice in which that ideal is made real and serves as a model for our lives outside of the game.

I believe that Bradley's analysis is too optimistic; it underestimates the power of racial categories and oversimplifies the lessons of the game. Basketball simultaneously *establishes* racial dichotomies and provides opportunities to unthink them. It does not guarantee that race will disappear; in fact, for many fans it reinforces conventional definitions. But Bradley does remind us that players are in a better position than fans to think their way through dangerous stereotypes. While watching television, which does so much to turn the "white" player and the "black" player into icons, fans have to *work* to decode the powerful visual images and the racialized discourse of game analysts that operate as confirmation of these racial assumptions. For pickup players, the decoding is easier: You cannot pass the ball to a "black player" or a "white player," you can only pass to that particular player—black or white—over there. It would be a rare American who could forget or would not notice the race of that player, but any player who lets racial definitions determine his or her game is living in an interpretive delusion and cannot play effectively. The game reinforces subtler and more personal methods of analysis and decision.

Probably the best player with whom I ever played was a black guy who played briefly in the NBA. In our oldguygame, he could have used his size and skills to dominate the game. He could have set up inside and dunked the ball whenever he wanted. But this guy was too smart to let the game get so dull. He instead indulged the desire of all big men to play point guard, to handle the ball and make creative passes. He became Magic Johnson, running the court and finding the open shooters, having a kind of fun that he could not have in games on the elite level, where his size would put him back under the basket. His negotiation of the politics of "black" and "white" was subtle and complex. He decided not to be the big "black" player who throws down athletic dunks, but rather to do as Magic did, to bring some "black" flair to the "white" job of distributing the ball and running the offense. His performance of this role was highly theatrical. That is, he knew what the stereotype of the "black" player was, and he played with it ironically, bringing some fun to his sometimes all-too-"white" teammates. He would woof at and tease people, as they might have expected from a "black" player, but he never let them put him in an easy category. He had the highly developed interpretive ability of an experienced player—he could see people's specific strengths and weaknesses and use their distinctive skills in the game he was creating. His performance of race left all stereotypes behind, because it was too complex to allow the other players in the game, black or white, to fold it into their racial cliches. He enacted for himself and made possible for the other players a street deconstruction of racial categories.

Bradley also wrote a book in 1976 called *A Life on the Run* about his experiences as a player with the championship New York Knicks of the early 1970s. He played on that team with such iconic black players as the courageous Willis Reed, the smooth and stylish Walt Frazier, and the ultimate schoolyard player, Earl "The Pearl" Monroe. Bradley was a Princeton All-American, a Rhodes scholar, a white boy from middle-American Missouri. Many of the players he came to know had vivid and bitter memories of segregated America, and they shared the militant attitudes of black activists in the 1960s and 1970s. Bradley says that his experience as a white player in the black-dominated NBA taught him that he knew *nothing* of the lives and struggles of black people in America. He learned that the black players who were his teammates had been brought up in a different world, and he had the good sense not to presume that he could offer any simple insight into their experience, just because he had played with them.

While I admire the honesty and cultural realism of Bradley's statement, I would like to put a different spin on the experience of race for players. Surely Bradley was right to say that playing a game does not lead to privileged sociological knowledge. But in our still very segregated society, the basketball court *is* one place where black and white people meet and experience some form of interpersonal knowledge. That knowledge is game-specific but not merely technical. Players do not just know whether a specific player will pass or shoot, they also develop more personal, subtle understandings in and through the culture of the practice. Does the player enjoy the game? Is he mean when he is ahead? Does he respect the game? In the context of the game these are intimate knowledges, insights into the structural determinants of identity. The game requires players to quickly learn the *games* of other players, and in knowing a player's game we learn something of a player's soul. This deep and specific personal knowledge is routine in the game, and it routinely crosses racial lines. How much does such knowledge count in undoing simple racial stereotypes? The answer to that question is local and individual. Some games are racially polarized; in other games, race is never an issue. Some players question the stereotypes, while others put them into play unself-consciously. But for most players the game is an opportunity for complex interpersonal knowledge, and in a racially polarized culture, such knowledge is good anti-racist politics.

In *Hoop Roots* John Wideman (2001) contrasts media images of basketball, which function to "embody racist fantasies, to prove and perpetuate 'essential' differences between blacks and whites, to justify the idea of white supremacy and rationalize an unfair balance of power, maintained by violence, lies, and terror, between blacks and whites," and the experience of pickup ball, which "transcends race and gender because it's about creating pleasure, working the body to please the body, about free spaces, breaks in the continuum of socially prescribed rules and roles, freedom that can be attained by play" (2001, 167). In the act of playing, the exigencies of the practice count more than the prejudices and preconceptions that players bring to the game. I am not as confident as Wideman that basketball can *transcend* race—cultures do their work in games as well as in the "serious" institutions of social life—but I do believe that basketball is one of the cultural sites where Americans have the opportunity to do productive work on race. Their perceptions of the game are thoroughly racialized, sometimes overtly, but more frequently as a persistent, unconscious category of understanding. The game can therefore reinforce racist hierarchies and embody our worst cultural politics, but it also provides a modest, everyday opportunity to bring those unconscious structures out into the open, to reveal them as intellectual shams, unworthy of the game.

Chapter 7

Televising Basketball

Spectacle and Representation, Display and Control

So far in this book I have been writing as a basketball player, as a participant in a cultural practice. I have tried to provide an insider's perspective, reporting on the felt experience of the game. In so doing, I often have found myself at odds with the critical perspective on sport provided by cultural studies scholars. While I understand and accept the critique of sports as practices that can be used to establish and reinforce dominant ideologies of race, gender, and sexuality, I also have felt that the texture of the play experience and the pleasure of the game are lost in these sweeping condemnations, just as they are lost in the conservative representation of sport as builder of character. So I have wanted to report the complex experience that occurs inside the practice of the game, in its movement style, its decision making, its ethical processes, its community formation, its racial dynamic. Certainly basketball, along with other institutionalized sports, does contribute to racism and sexism and homophobia, but it simultaneously provides—as do all complex cultural practices—an opportunity for players to question and challenge its own ideology. But when I turn now to an examination of television representations of the game, I will adopt the critical perspective without much reservation. There is no denying that basketball on television delivers a strong dose of conservative ideology. It does so by editing out most of the cultural subtlety of the game, framing it within familiar visual and discursive structures, and telling simple stories about courage and team spirit, hard work and family values.

On a recent Atlantic Coast Conference (ACC) tournament broadcast, I heard the following moral values cited with the confidence of common sense in the routine coverage of a random five minutes of game: teamwork, sportsmanship, discipline, respect, toughness, hard work, patience, aggression, poise, rising to the challenge, talent, intelligence, confidence, and pride in achievement—predictable civic virtues in the conservative corporate and community culture that the telecast addresses. Right after this five-minute game sequence, in fact, there was an ACC promo for its "corporate sponsorship program," in which the league enters into partnership with "companies who share our commitment to excellence." The work of ideology is sometimes not subtle.

In pickup basketball, which is conspicuously absent from television, the culture of the game is so local and various that it is hard to generalize about its ideological implications. Some games are viciously competitive, some are easygoing and friendly, some are hyper-macho, some are played by men secure enough in their sexual identity not to need to proclaim it, and some are played by men, by women, by mixed groups, by gay men, by lesbians, by white players, by black players, by church groups, by soldiers, by lawyers, by convicts, and so endlessly on. They may live in South Philly or in South Dakota or in South Africa. They bring their own unique motives to the game and mix with the other players present in order to negotiate the culture of their game. The values and practices of that game are impossible to predict until the negotiations begin, and so generalizations about the ideology of pickup ball must be tentative, open to the vagaries of local negotiations.

Organized basketball is much more predictable in its political implications. The litany of conventional virtues proclaimed in that ACC game was not invented by the telecast. Elite, organized basketball almost always explicitly promotes those conventional values, along with an implicit sexism, racism, and homophobia, without the help of media representations. Coaches and youth group leaders have always pitched it as a disciplinary strategy, a place where young people can learn to be good, productive citizens, a practice that requires ruthless competition, that encourages the manly virtues, where women are marginalized and homosexuality is closeted at best. Television emphasizes and codifies those values, and by a feedback loop it affects the culture of the game, right down to the schoolyard. Almost no one who plays basketball comes to the game *without* those media representations. They are part of the set of expectations that players bring to their experience in the game, and they shape players' behavior on the court, even in the most casual pickup games, far from the eyes of the media. Pickup players will naturally try the moves they see on TV, and they bring the values of the TV game along with the moves. The representation

is always part of the practice. There is no version of the game untouched
by media representations and the ideologies they enforce. As a result, any
study of basketball has to take into account the media version of the
practice. Basketball is omnipresent on television, in films, in popular music,
and in advertising—throughout popular culture. Basketball gets played in
driveways and schoolyards and local gyms, but for millions of people it
occurs primarily within the frame of the television screen in the living
room. There the game does the same job as all television content—it
reinforces the values required of good citizens and eager consumers—and
it exerts cultural power over players and spectators alike.

As a player I participate in the game for the pleasure of play, but as
a fan I witness a practice constructed for visual consumption, a spectacle.
Elite, competitive basketball may give its players the pleasure of participation, but the game exists as entertainment for paying fans and for a television audience. As many scholars have noted, sports in the age of media
have been carefully reshaped *for* the media. Even the court itself is bor-
dered by placard advertisements that the television viewer cannot escape.
Sut Jhally has argued persuasively that professional sports served business
interests long before the coming of television, but he also has enumerated
the many ways in which elite sports leagues were more than ready to adapt
to the needs of TV: "sports leagues changing the rules of the game to
provide a better television package; clubs moving from one city to another
based not upon stadium support but upon the television audience; the
flow and momentum of the game being interrupted for time-outs that are
called so that television can show commercials; the creation and destruc-
tion of entire sports leagues based upon whether or not television support
could be found; and the ability (or inability) of teams to sign players,
depending on the size of the television market a team controls" (Jhally
1989, 80–81).

This domination of media over sport has led Garry Whannel to
comment that "In a very real sense sport has become a branch of the
advertising and public relations industries" (1992, 2). And Richard Gruneau
(1989), in "Making Spectacle: A Case Study in Television Sports Production," has demonstrated the easy collaboration of television production
personnel with event coordinators and their corporate sponsors, eager to
make the live event suit the needs of the media production. Elite basketball
is a more than willing subject of media representation. It presents itself
precisely as a spectacle to be represented, in a shape designed for television
coverage. Television does not capture and represent basketball as recalci-
trant material to be forced into media structures. Elite basketball repack-
ages the game for that capture. Nevertheless, television does impose its
own forms and discourses on the game. Put simply, seeing the game on TV

is not the same as seeing it live, and certainly not the same as playing it. Televised basketball must be understood as *television*, demanding many of the same perceptual habits and interpretive responses from viewers as do other kinds of television programming. Television wants viewers to believe that it does not impose a form on reality, that it provides immediate and live coverage of the real. But as many television scholars have noted, television creates a highly mediated experience, with its own rhetoric and aesthetics. John Corner, in *Television Form and Public Address*, calls TV "a veiled social practice which passes itself off as either technologically necessary or as simply professional 'common sense' " (1995, 17). Television places basketball within an unacknowledged complex of visual and discursive frames that will serve at once to display and control the game.

Insofar as basketball is a mass spectacle staged for corporate media, it should not surprise us that the values espoused by the spectacle appeal to the large consumer market it seeks. The carnivalesque elements that surround the game—trickster ticket scalpers, bettors and bookies, drunken fans, vulgar taunts, petty fan violence—are edited out of the television spectacle, or are reduced to stereotyped and sanitized cameo appearances. Television presents basketball cut off from its local social context, from the lives of its players and fans, from the social nexus that gives it its full cultural meaning. What is left as a television spectacle is best understood in terms of Guy Debord's (1983) famous claim in *The Society of the Spectacle*, that "the spectacle's form and content are identically the total justification of the existing system's conditions and goals. The spectacle is also the *permanent presence* of this justification, since it occupies the main part of the time lived outside of modern production" (1983, 6). Televised basketball is a gigantic business operation, involving colleges and universities, professional leagues, television production companies and broadcasters, advertisers and corporate sponsors, and agents and lawyers. It reaches millions of viewers in America and countless millions around the world. Billions of advertising dollars depend on the huge reach of the televised game. So much money is at stake and so many social subjects are available for media delivery that it makes almost inevitable economic sense that only the most mainstream messages are allowed in basketball coverage. Jimmy L. Reeves says the following in "TV's World of Sports: Presenting and Playing the Game":

> Television processes and re-presents social reality by translating the conflict and contradictions of the modern world into terms that are accessible and forms that are comprehensible to a vast, heterogeneous audience. In framing, focusing, and narrating the commonsense world, then, television is also engaged in an on-

going rewrite—or re-*vision*—of the American way. In this rewriting ritual, television contributes to the reproduction, maintenance, repair, and transformation of social reality. (1989, 205)

The technical and discursive frames that shape the spectacle must be reliable for commercial sponsors and familiar and comforting to viewers, for *comfort* is one of the chief pleasures of television. Roger Silverstone, in *Television and Everyday Life,* argues that television provides stability and continuity in the lives of postmodern subjects whose social relationships have become attenuated and unsatisfying. Television provides a sense of ontological security without personal contact. The TV screen is a "transitional object," says Silverstone, a replacement for the security and permanence created for the infant by the mother. Television is always available, reliable in its daily and seasonal rhythms, predictable in its modes of presentation, its genres and formats. It may present us with disturbing scenes or tragic news, but it contains them within its powerful visual and discursive frames. As Silverstone says, television is "a secure framework for the representation and control of the unfamiliar or threatening" (1994, 21). David Rowe (2004) explains the function of sports on television as a perfect combination of novelty and predictability. Games are always new, with the promise of an open future, but they also are predictable, arriving during the same season each year, packaged in a familiar format, recurring with the formal precision of ritual. Their function is to reinforce cognitive and moral habits, even when they present content that might challenge those predispositions.

So what is it in basketball that must be contained, that is so unfamiliar and threatening? Why do we need to frame and thus control it? The most direct, political answer is that basketball at the elite level is perceived as a *black* game, more and more associated in the public mind with young, flashy, gangsta-style players connected to the scary streets of black America. One of the challenges facing televised basketball is to package that dangerous black masculinity for white Americans. Todd Boyd, John Wideman, and many other black cultural critics have commented on the ways that televised basketball allows white America a vicarious, safe taste of street life. Television must therefore *frame* the blackness of the game within "white" systems of visual presentation and discursive practice. I will later examine how those systems work, but what they work *on* is blackness, with all of the unsettling connotations that that word still holds for white America.

Basketball also must be framed and controlled because it is a practice of the body, an aggressive and even violent practice that reminds us of the physical impulses that we deny ourselves in the bureaucratized daily world. These imposing bodies, moving with speed and intensity, come to represent the body itself, a symbolism reinforced by the fact that they are mostly black bodies, which have long represented for white people in America the physical power and danger of the body itself. Television loves the speed and physical power of basketball, the slam dunk, the decisively blocked shot, players throwing themselves onto the floor or over the first row of spectators, so great is their energy. And because basketball players are often superb physical specimens who wear no pads or protective masks, they are visible and available as sexual images. They combine sexuality, aggression, grace, and beauty in ways that attract the male and female gaze. The erotic element in watching basketball cannot be denied, but it is part of what must be contained, even while it is made available for enjoyment.

Television also displays and contains the masculinity of the game. Coverage of men's basketball overtly proclaims traditional masculinity, but it also acts to contain it. Virtually every game includes a reference to a player who is *the man*, or who steps up to *be the man* or who plays like *a man among boys*. And there is the endless procession of thinly coded masculine values cited in every broadcast—great players are competitors, aggressors, leaders, perfect manifestations of a patriarchal dream. John Fiske says, "The sporting male body is . . . an active hegemonic agent for patriarchal capitalism, and as such fits neatly with sport's embodiment of our dominant ideology" (1987, 248). But even while televised basketball showcases masculinity, it contains that masculinity in a nonthreatening structure. Basketball is *playing at* traditional masculinity. The players are only engaged in a game, without real-world consequences. As Fiske also says, television images "exist in their own flickering domain and never come to rest in a firm anchorage in the real" (1987, 116). The masculine physical power of the players is therefore safe, confined within the rules of the game, the limits of the court, the frame of the screen. In a postindustrial social environment in which aggression and physical power, the ideals of traditional sporting masculinity, are so infrequently necessary or desirable, televised basketball displays masculinity but simultaneously segregates it from real social life.

Televised basketball also segregates the game from its local context. Pickup ball is radically local—its culture is created by the players who show up for the game, and they bring with them their histories and their connections to the locale where the game is played. Performances of elite basketball reduce this local quality by submitting the game to official rules rather than local negotiations and by staging the game as a predictable spectacle. Almost all professional and major college games are now highly "produced" in what Jon Wertheim (2005) calls a "Vegas style," with music, dancers, promotional gimmicks, laser shows, fireworks, and sideshows, framing the sport itself within what Robert E. Rinehart (1998) calls "the sporting experience," an evening's live entertainment, within which a basketball game occurs. These shows are numbingly similar, from one huge corporate arena to another, with the result that any local flavor is drained out of the game. And then when that spectacle is repackaged within the visual and verbal discourse of television, almost all local culture is lost. Pickup ball is exactly not a television event. It is too local, too unpredictable, too complex as a cultural practice to fulfill the need for predictability in television programming. The closest television gets to pickup ball is "streetball," which turns the pickup game into an MTV-style highlight reel, with NBA wannabes showing off their flashiest moves in a crowd-pleasing spectacle. Even this "street" version of the game is transformed into a familiar media text.

Lastly, television frames and contains the *beauty* of the game. Basketball is a game of grace and coordinated, symmetrical movement, a source of visual, aesthetic pleasure. Think of the slow motion replay, in which the grace and beauty of the players are lovingly displayed. In our artistic tradition as well as in mass media, visual beauty—for all of its appeal—is almost always *framed* and therefore controlled. The physical frame around the work of art is intended to detach the art from its surround, to draw attention to its singular beauty. The frame of the TV set serves the same function, to emphasize the beauty of the visual, even when the content of its images is disturbing. But along with the display function comes the control function. Beauty must be kept within boundaries. It is disruptive, even disheartening. It ill suits us for the scruffiness, the randomness of daily life. We need *doses* of it, but we cannot live with it too much. It reminds us of our own limitations, our frailty, our mortality. It has to be kept in a frame. And since basketball displays the beauty of powerful (often) black (usually) men, it can be broadcast only when all of these elements are disciplined within severe constraints.

Televised basketball does play positive roles within the culture of the game. It gives players and fans the opportunity to see the game played at the highest possible level. They can see the skill and the beauty of players, in images delivered with all of the technical skills of the best television production personnel in the world. Hans Ulrich Gumbrecht (2006) argues in his book *In Praise of Athletic Beauty* that the experience of seeing that beauty is a powerful good in itself, even for those who never play the game. We get to invest our passions in the fortunes of teams we love and to connect with other fans who share our passion, and we get to take pleasure in excellence embodied as beautiful movement. Gumbrecht also points out that television allows those who are inside the practice to *analyze* those performances and expand their knowledge of the game by seeing it played at an expert level. Great moves in the elite game routinely filter down into pickup ball. But the cost of these benefits is that basketball must be subjected to the visual and ideological disciplines of television, abstracted from its local context, transformed into a safe morality tale for a mainstream audience, framed and displayed in a predictable, endlessly repeated style.

VISUAL FRAMES

One powerful element of television's framing power is its small size. It miniaturizes the human form rather than creating the larger-than-life images of the film screen. Television brings the world into the domestic space, but except in homes with giant screens, it does not dominate the visual field. It reduces the sweeping events of the world into compact and unthreatening images, confined within the small frame of the screen. It can turn seven-foot tall, 330-pound Shaquille O'Neal into a tiny, cartoon figure, radically *smaller* than life. A viewer immersed in the game and knowledge-able about the physical strength it takes can certainly feel Shaquille's power in these images, but to the viewer who engages in what John Ellis (1982) calls "the glance" rather than "the gaze," these powerful athletes are reduced to manageable visual data like any other experienced on television. All of the dangerous elements of the game—the aggression, the macho—are contained in a small rectangle placed within the reassuring predictability of the domestic space.

The camera work and editing of broadcast basketball also construct predictable frames around the game. Watch any game in any league, tele-cast by any production company or network, and you will see the same visual design. In fact, a similar visual design is used in almost all team sports. One camera is placed at midcourt, shooting from a high angle, creating a long cover shot or establishing shot for the game, panning to follow the action as it moves from one end of the court to the other, and zooming in and out to create the effective frame for the scale of the depicted action. At either end of the court are handheld cameras, mobile units that provide the medium shots, the close-ups, and the reaction shots that personalize the game. Editing practices are equally predictable, following a long-established practice of long shots for continuous action, punctuated by cuts to reaction shots during pauses in play. Whannel (1992) has traced these sport broadcast practices back to the early days of the BBC and of American broadcast systems, and they have become so standardized in contemporary basketball coverage that they have become invisible, as if the game inevitably required exactly the coverage it gets, as though no aesthetic and rhetorical decisions have been made. It is this invisibility that requires us to look at these standard practices closely in order to uncover their ideological implications and their effects on how we see the game.

The long shot from above midcourt is the dominant shot in basketball coverage. It is even charted out in Herbert Zettl's (1997) *Television Production Handbook,* the standard textbook in TV production classes. This camera placement in effect puts the TV audience in the best seat in the house, in the tradition of early Hollywood films that thought of themselves as filmed theater. This position reads for viewers as a default setting, the commonsensical place from which to watch a game. We are distant enough to see the whole court but close enough to feel a part of the game. The camera placement flatters us, informs us that the game is staged in honor of our presence. But our presence is unobtrusive—it does not affect the game, it simply witnesses. At this site we do not feel the influence of mediating structures, just privileged placement. Of course even this commonsensical perspective is a mediating structure. It is more focused than the view that a human eye present at the spectacle would deliver. It frames the game more tightly—it leaves out much of the crowd and the surrounding arena—and more steadily—it is never distracted. But this long shot is more than "the best seat in the house," it is mobile. It not only pans as the human head would turn, it dollies—the entire camera moves to follow the action. The camera also moves virtually, by zooming subtly in and out, as the action demands. Zooms and dollies create an endlessly changing but always perfect frame for our viewing. This changing perspective creates for the audience a dreamlike mobility of observation. It allows us to go effortlessly to the perfect spot for seeing every moment of the game. It creates a detached omniscience, a fantasy of total visibility. Foucault would call it the "panopticon shot."

The flattery implicit in the shot does the ideological work. The long shot puts us at the center of the apparatus. The game is staged for us; the television production contrives to place us as the perfect observer. The entire corporate and organizational effort behind the televised game works in our interest, serves our needs. The audience is thus characterized not as "eyeballs" being delivered strategically to sponsors but as the privileged benefactors of a complex administrative, technological, and corporate project. In the same spirit, commercials then offer us their wares, provide us with information and images that facilitate our choices as imperial consumers, served by the corporate world: "We do it all for you." This ideological work, this placement of social subjects in an imaginary version of real economic life, happens routinely without the awareness of either viewers or production personnel. The viewer is watching *through* the frame and thus not attending to it, and the producers are presenting the best view of the game that their professional expertise can create. None would acknowledge that the goal of the shot is ideological flattery, but the attraction of the televised game is built on that foundation.

One recent alternative to this high-angle establishing shot is the floating camera suspended above the court. The NBA play-offs in 2006 were often shot in this style, with the camera looming above the action, free to move to any position necessary for optimal coverage. This strategy places the camera where no live spectator could be, creating a televisual image freed from the theatrical style of the midcourt shot, which delivers the perspective of a perfect seat in the arena. The result is a strangely beautiful, slightly disorienting view of the action. "No one could possibly be here," you think, even as you take pleasure precisely in the visual experience of being there. This shot puts the viewer in a godlike or an angelic position, with what seems like infinite mobility, hovering over the players, seeing their interactions in ways not previously possible. It remains to be seen whether this perspective will become a permanent part of the visual repertoire, but it does flatter the viewer even more than the midcourt shot, allowing for a feeling of omniscient power over the players below.

In the conventional style, the establishing shot is supplemented and enlivened by medium and close-up shots provided by handheld cameras usually stationed at either end of the court but able to move down the side of the court and into an infinite number of perspectives. Whannel (1992), Margaret Morse (1983), and other television scholars have commented on the complex roles that the close-up shot plays in sports broadcasting. Morse (1983) especially, in "Sport on Television: Replay and Display," has examined the gender dynamic of this visual strategy. Since the telecast assumes a male audience, it follows "self-evident" gender rules. That is, the long shot is the default setting because it appeals to the detached, distant, male consciousness constructed by traditional gender roles. The close-up, on the other hand, creates an intimacy, a personal relationship, that appeals to traditional femininity. Morse notes the ways that sports close-ups, especially when replayed in slow motion, emphasize the beauty, individuality, and sexuality of the athletes. And she argues that "in a culture where the female image is proliferated and exchanged among and between both sexes, national spectator sports are *the* place where the male body image is central, if disavowed" (1983, 45). This image must be disavowed, of course, because it might provoke homophobic panic. The male audience must not be allowed to think of itself as taking pleasure in the masculine body. Morse argues that it needs a "license" to look, a justification for what would otherwise be disallowed. For Morse the license is provided by the fact that the close-up and the slow motion replay are presented by the announcers as aids to understanding, extensions of our ability to *know* the game, know it even better than the players and the referees, who lack this perfect seeing. Morse says: "The technique of slow motion allows the analysis and appreciation of body movements which are normally inaccessible to view; this capacity has justifiably lent slow motion an aura of scientificity. Slow motion replays are treated as part of a hermeneutic process of scientific discovery, which, among other things, allows viewers to outguess the referee and see what 'really' happened" (1983, 49). Thus the close-up, often replayed in slow motion, is legitimated as an element in a masculine visual discourse.

Close-ups and medium shots from handheld cameras serve several functions in the production and for its ideology. Close-ups from many angles add to the omniscience effect, enhancing the fantasy of infinite optical mobility. Because the camera operators are knowledgeable professionals, they are almost always in the perfect place for the revelatory shot. How did that ball go out of bounds? Here—instantly—is the close-up replay that answers the question. We get to see what we missed from our detached point of view. We are moved *into* the action. Because cameras can get so close, and because they use lenses that project our vision forward, we see events as though we were on the court. For example, handheld cameras sometimes deliver a shot following behind the ball as it moves up court. We get the perspective of a player trailing the play, as though the audience were a necessary participant in the developing action. Thus in addition to an imagined omniscience, the audience is granted an imagined participation. The couch potato becomes the virtual elite athlete, invited into a flattering identification with a fantasy figure.

Close-ups can invite identification because they enlarge the human image, relative to the small size of the TV screen. In action close-ups the human body often fills the frame, creating a sense of explosive—though contained—kinetic energy. And because they enlarge the face, which in basketball is not hidden behind a helmet, close-ups also create personality, turning the players into characters in the ongoing narrative of the game. We see the players' reactions to events, their elation at a close win, their anger at a bad call, their cool under pressure. As fans we are feeling the same emotions at the same time, and our imagined proximity adds to the sense of identification. Ideologically, the strategy is clear. If the players are constantly described as models of mainstream masculine virtue, then audience identification helps to transmit those values, to remake the audience in the desired pattern.

Morse sees in the slow-motion close-up a media version of the dream state, in which the human body is freed from the constraints of time and space: "The frequent repetition of the same play in slow motion marks the game on television as no longer occurring in a world subject to the laws of ordinary linear and uni-directional time. Within the compressed space the body covers ground effortlessly, while the slowness of the motion seems to free it from the pull of gravity" (1983, 49). This "oneiric world" transforms speed and violence into beauty and grace, creating a physical and perceptual utopia in which grace exists and is available to our perfect seeing. These "scientific," perceptual, and ideological pleasures provide cover for and make possible the pleasure for a heterosexual male audience in seeing a beautiful male body. Basketball's camera coverage is often close and tightly framed. It renders players and their beautiful bodies intimately visible, available for sensory pleasure. And for homosexual male and heterosexual female audiences, these excuse discourses at least do not get in the way.

The long shot and the close-up put the viewer firmly in visual control. It is *the audience's perspective* that is privileged. The technology allows us to gaze with an enhanced vision, from what seems like all angles, all of them perfect. The frames the cameras impose on the action focus our vision and hold the game within the televisual apparatus. They create a dream environment, that for all of its apparent documentary realism sets up the game as a place apart, a ritual space in which the force of the dominant culture can be applied with great power. While creating the illusion of a powerful and perfect knowing, televised basketball in fact creates a powerful and perfect space for imposing dominant values and controlling disruptive pleasures.

Another effective framing device in the visual presentation of basketball is created by the editing process. If camera work puts a literal frame around the action, then editing creates temporal and cognitive frames for our perception. The temporal experience of live basketball for players and live spectators is radically linear. The past cannot be revisited, and the game moves relentlessly to the end of its time. Televised basketball disrupts linear time. The regular use of replays throws us back in time, often repeatedly, seeing the same action from different perspectives, as real time moves forward. Editing in basketball coverage happens live, not after the game in an editing suite. It presents the audience with multiple sources of information, from multiple sites, creating a pastiche of images in a complex, temporal array. And yet for viewers, the coverage seems simple, smooth, predictable, invisible. The game must *feel like* a linear narrative that unfolds over time, while providing many sources of information in a nonlinear presentation.

This pastiche of images obviously includes the establishing shot and handheld shots, but the broadcast also includes instant replays, clips from other games, network studio feeds, and archival footage. While the action of the game is in progress, the establishing shot dominates, though on occasion the ongoing action will be covered by a handheld camera. After a score, as the players run to the other end, reaction shots from players, fans, or coaches are inserted. And when the action stops, replays are woven into the coverage, while the discourse of the announcers turns from narrative to analysis. On occasion images from a player's past performances can be inserted in this spot in order to personalize the game, giving the player a history, a character developed over time. Or a stoppage in play might allow the coverage to switch to another game, as at tournament time, or to a network studio for a promo for an upcoming game. Editing moves us back and forth in time, provides us with constantly changing visual perspectives, and moves us around in space, presenting information from many sites in one broadcast.

The resulting complex pattern is an instance of television as postmodern textual practice. Its viewers have become accustomed to nonlinear, multiple sources of information, instantaneously juxtaposed. The complexity of information delivery is incessant, creating for the audience a montage of *different* frames, packaging the action in different ways, replaced by another package in the next second. Of course this complexity is omnipresent in television. We have all learned to follow from shot to shot within the show, from show to commercial, from commercial to commercial, from news bulletin to weather forecast to promo for future shows, back to the show, and back into *its* pattern of cuts and cognitive relocations. Add to that mess the fact that almost all viewers surf through many shows and networks with similarly complex sequences and you have a fundamentally discontinuous cognitive experience. As David Rowe (2004) says in *Sport, Culture, and the Media*, basketball is perfectly suited to the MTV-era "culture of fragmentation," with its fast-paced editing and its aesthetic of discontinuity (2004, 189). And yet ordinary views are the easy masters of this complex domain. They know at every moment where they are in that matrix. They can surf and return with perfect precision. They are rarely confused by this decentered mix that seems so complex to describe.

If the editing practices of broadcast basketball rely on their viewers' skills as adept postmodern thinkers, then they also construct simplifying visual strategies that master the apparent confusion. For example, all cuts within games are clearly motivated, making visual connections that follow emotional or cognitive logics. Usually the close-ups are reaction shots, showing a player's or coach's emotions in the dramatic situation that has just been depicted in the long shot. Archival footage is verbally keyed to the present moment as explanatory background. Cuts to studio feeds or other games are cued verbally and make situational sense, for example, during play-off seasons when important and related games are going on around the country simultaneously. Images also are connected by sheer technical skill. The audience very rarely sees a cut to a camera that is unready or out of position. Cutaways are always done in time to get back to the action focus. Mistakes are so rare that they are highly noticeable. In fact, I would maintain that much of the pleasure of televised basketball, and of television itself, is the technical brilliance of coverage, knitting together the disparate elements of the broadcast.

The result is a juxtaposition so seamless that the audience forgets the fact that disparate elements have been juxtaposed. As Reaves (1989) puts it in his essay "TV's World of Sports": "The behind the scenes labor of producers, directors, sound technicians, video editors, and camera operators is masked, or made invisible, by conventional production techniques. Unless the conventions are violated, either by error or by design, the visual processing of the sporting event generally remains inconspicuous, submerged in the conscious mesh of the taken-for-granted" (1989, 209). The resulting visual style is comparable, as Whannel argues, to "the well established conventions of realist cinema" (1992, 33). "Natural" camera placement, motivated edits, smooth transitions, adherence to the "180-degree rule" (all cameras on the same side of an imaginary line drawn horizontally across the court)—all of these techniques are aimed precisely at making technique invisible, so that the audience can have the experience of imaginary immediacy. The audience wants to be made to feel that the television production is only "channeling" the events of the game, bringing them to the audience with minimal interference rather than "mediating" the event, packaging it in visual and discursive frames of reference. John Corner, making use of this distinction originally proposed by Stuart Hall, tends to see television as "mediation" *posing* as "channeling" by means of a "veiled social practice which passes itself off as either technologically necessary or as simply professional 'common sense' " (1995, 17). Gruneau, in his close study of the production process behind the telecast of a ski competition, observes the huge number of decisions made by production personnel, but he also notes how the technicians routinize those decisions, as though they had no ideological import. The result is that "these production 'values' tend to express dominant ideological tendencies" (1989, 135). The visual presentation is so smooth and natural that the conventional ideological content of the images seems similarly inevitable.

DISCURSIVE FRAMES

The frame around the game is a hybrid structure, combining visual and discursive elements. Narrators and analysts talk over the visuals, shaping the audience's experience of the game as it unfolds. For the viewer, a complex relationship between visual image and spoken discourse is set up. The visual frames would do their work even without the verbal structures—the omniscience effect of camera work and the ideological effects of invisible editing occur even with the sound off. But the verbal discourse also constructs cognitive and emotional frames around the action, subjecting it to preexisting, predictable patterns of understanding. The play-by-play announcer and the color commentator are powerful presences in the fans' experience of televised basketball. They shape the emotional tone of the game and place it in historical and cultural contexts. They define its significance, explaining why it matters in the context of the season, in the tradition of the opposing teams, and in the emotional lives of players and fans.

The spoken discourse that is part of this visual-aural hybrid is itself a hybrid discourse. It combines in complex ways narrative, analytical, and moral discourses. The conventional division of these discourses is between the play-by-play announcer, who is the narrator, and the color commentator, who analyzes each play and provides moral and ideological exegesis. But in practice the roles often are shared, the two voices producing an improvised discourse that shapes the reactions of viewers as events unfold, while connecting the present to the preceding action and creating anticipation of the emerging future. The discourse they produce exerts control over the viewers' reactions to the game, placing them inside a complex structure of narrative, analysis, and moral commentary.

The narratives are conventional, with predictable ideological effects. The narrators are constant voices in the audience's ear, never allowing events to go untold, always providing commentary to lead audience reactions. It is the job of the announcers to turn the game into a narrative, with a strong plot line, recognizable characters, and a coherent theme. Literary critic J. Hillis Miller defines the rudimentary requirements of narrative as a protagonist, an antagonist, and an observer who learn from the story. The announcers in basketball broadcasts are the observers who learn and who pass on the lesson to the audience. The protagonists and antagonists are the players and coaches who are precisely *turned into* characters by the ongoing narrative. The plot, the conflict, is in part shaped by the developing outcome of the contest but also by the predetermined expectations of the narrators who create a narrative out of the raw materials of events. Rowe says that this narrative function "extends [the] range of meaning and cultural resonance" of games, allowing them to become "imbued with significance." Without this narrative, he says, "all sport looks like a series of bizarre manoeuvres observing arcane rules for no apparent reason" (2004, 178). Rowe, I think, overstates the role of television narration—after all, a spectator in the stands at a game makes sense of the action without a narrator's guidance—but for the televisual spectator, the game occurs only within the narrative framework created by the broadcast.

One of the most important tasks of the narrator is to transform players into characters. Much of this work is accomplished visually, by close-ups that humanize the figures in motion and by replays that allow viewers to gaze at length on the bodies and faces of players. These personalized images can then be assembled into highlight shows and player profiles that provide for the audience a visual archive of the player, a virtual memory that gives depth and temporal continuity to the characters. This corporate-produced, star-making apparatus allows the narrators to craft the specific story of any given game, relying on backstories that they can assume viewers already know. Nevertheless, much of the work of characterization is created by the announcers in the moment of the game, as they improvise a narrative over the unfolding events.

Many of the characters are one-dimensional, predictable, with little personal nuance, created by a process of abstraction. Narrators fix on one apparent aspect of a player's style or demeanor and detach it from the complexity of lived experience and performance. I say "apparent" because there is no way for the viewer to know whether the media-created character is an accurate representation of the real-life player. Thus Karl Malone is a warrior, Walt Frazier an icon of cool, Tim Duncan stands for moral purity, and Magic Johnson plays for the joy of the game. These simple characterizations obviously do not do justice to the players as persons or even to their games. But once established, they shape our perceptions of the players' future actions, so that what we tend to see on the court is what the stereotype allows. These powerful athletes are thereby reduced to manageable clichés that we can comfortably fit into our habitual cultural categories.

Sometimes the characterizations are more subtle, with the internal contradictions and psychological nuances of complex literary characters. Magic Johnson, for all his joy in the game, becomes the tragic victim of a stigmatizing disease. Michael Jordan, for all his regal bearing, has a trash-talking, arrogant streak. Dennis Rodman, for all his carnivalesque excess, plays the game like a blue-collar worker. These more complex characters create the sustained human interest that an ongoing narrative requires. Most teams have a "marquee player" or two, and the rest are "role players," terms that suggest the ways that the discourse of the game derives from the discourse of narrative. The "marquee players" are ideally both great players and compelling characters, and game narratives usually are built around them. Either the star steps up in the clutch moment (Larry Bird, Michael Jordan) or he becomes invisible at the moment of greatest need (Wilt Chamberlain, Dirk Nowitzki). He becomes the hero of the day or the tragic failure who did not live up to his potential. The role players are then the reliable forces against which the more mercurial lead characters are contrasted. The role players are presented either as physically limited—when a star is taking advantage of their weakness—or as canny professionals who do the dirty work of the game—when they set a good pick or make a good pass to a star. The mix of those characters over time, their shifts of teams and allegiances, their growth and maturity, and their changes in new circumstances can all provide the emotional continuity that the narrative needs.

The stars in these narratives are "known" by fans in rich detail. The ordinary events of their lives cause media frenzies. We know about their scrapes with the law, their marriages and divorces, their car wrecks and bar brawls. We know their salaries and endorsement deals, their troubles with coaches and agents. We know about their brave single moms or their proud fathers. We meet their posses, tour their homes, get glimpses of their Benzes and Escalades. We know how they were recruited for the college game, or even for elite high school teams. We know the history of their successes and failures, their conflicts with coaches and other players, their reputations as solid citizens or head cases. And so when an announcer is weaving the narrative of the game, he can rely on this shared personal knowledge to give depth and complexity and magnitude to the story. Games are elements in the ongoing narratives of larger-than-life figures, and in turn the status of the figures gives weight to the game. If you have ever seen the opening introductions of players at NBA games, with laser lighting, smoke and fireworks, and an arena announcer who enunciates each name as though it were the name of a Greek god, then you know that the game creates narratives that claim an epic status, that seem to occur on a level above the everyday.

Critical commentators on sport broadcasting have tended to see these narratives in gender-inflected terms. Gina Daddario's (1998) study of Olympic TV coverage in the 1980s and 1990s contrasts the detachment and relative impersonality of event coverage, which appeals to traditional masculine ways of knowing and feeling, with the emerging "up-close and personal" coverage of athletes' personal lives, triumphs and sorrows, which appeals to traditional feminine sensibilities. Daddario argues that Olympic broadcasters consciously shifted their style to the feminine side in order to attract a larger viewing audience than would be available among men who are enthusiasts for the games themselves. Since the moment Daddario describes, sensibilities have changed, and the "feminine" emphasis on personal history and relationships is now an accepted part of almost all sports coverage, including that which is aimed almost exclusively at men. In fact, the game narratives themselves would not be possible without being implicated in the personal gossip that surrounds the game, because it is the gossip that creates audience identification and loyalty. If TV sports broadcasting has now taken on the emotional register of the soap opera, then it is a soap opera for men as well as women.

One way that basketball coverage particularly resembles the soap opera is its emphasis on interpersonal relationships. When Shaquille O'Neal and Kobe Bryant do not get along, we all know. Viewers are constantly informed about the delicacy of team chemistry, how one head case can disrupt the flow of a team full of solid, professional role players, or how a star without the required humility can try to "force it," to take over a game without trusting his teammates to support him. Players are defined as characters not simply by their style of play or their individual personalities but by their involvement in complex emotional relationships. These group stories can of course be spun out infinitely, as in a soap opera, creating long-term viewer loyalty beyond the detached appreciation of athletic achievement.

Since most players who figure into these narratives are African American, these narrative techniques become forms of racial profiling. A white-dominated medium tells stories to a white-majority audience about the lives of black people. The predictable result is a stereotyped array of black character types, from the dangerous man (Gary Payton) to the paragon of virtue (Michael Jordan, whom Mary McDonald has called "the anti-OJ"), from the gangsta (Isaiah Rider) to the crazy man (Dennis Rodman). It would take a separate study to describe the array of black characters displayed in the game by white networks for white consumers. But that array is a form of control, an acceptable range of character types, which even if they are at times dangerous are reassuringly familiar. White players are stereotyped as well, either as sharp minds and fierce competitors, or as hapless dorks, or rarely as athletes so gifted they are almost black. Televised basketball contributes powerfully to our culture's discourse on race, and although some viewers may see through the stereotypes, the force of these narratives moves toward characterizations that reinforce dominant racial formations.

Basketball narratives also reinforce traditional gender roles, despite the efforts of many women players and TV commentators. The range of characters in the men's game is extremely narrow, and traditionally masculine. "Fierce" is a term of high praise, and "soft" is one of the worst terms of contempt. It may be that the gender language of the game is a case of overcompensation, since basketball is viewed by many football players and fans as a "soft" game—real men play football. But for whatever reason, basketball characters are almost always described in terms that reaffirm traditional masculine roles. Players are warriors, winners are aggressors, games exist only for the competition. In fact, in recent televised basketball, exaggerated masculine displays have become the norm. Huge yells of dominance after a dunk, chest thumping, throat slashing, taunting, and self-display are part of the entertainment package that the game offers.

They make the highlight reel, and they send a surge of adrenaline and testosterone to the viewer. Players express themselves in the style of a masculinity free from social constraints. Televised basketball uses its mostly black characters to reassure its mostly white male audience that it too is at least vicariously connected to the primal male. The actual practice of playing pickup basketball encourages a more complex performance of masculinity, but televised basketball is unambiguous in its reinforcement of traditional manhood.

In narrative coverage of the women's game, the gender politics are more complicated. Many commentators have noted the attempts in the Women's National Basketball Association (WNBA) and Olympic coverage to emphasize the traditional femininity of the players. Lisa Leslie, who is a model in her off-court career, is often presented as the image of the league. But there are many characters in the televised women's game who do not fit that stereotype, and no attempt is made to make them fit. Teresa Witherspoon is an icon of toughness. University of Tennessee coach, Pat Summitt, is as macho as Bobby Knight. And the WNBA has developed a very physical style as players have become stronger and more athletic. The danger of the players' physical strength, and the danger of their challenge to traditional feminine images, is contained not so much by images of frilly femininity as by narratives of wholesome, pure team basketball, played by women who are connected to family and community. Players often are presented as the heroines of excited young girls in ponytails and gym shorts who look up to the players as models of female strength and independence. Athleticism for girls is presented as a wholesome outlet for their natural skills, supported by families and local communities. What might otherwise be troubling signs of excessive masculinity are recuperated as actions that bring people together, as elements in a web of interpersonal relationships, as expressions of a traditionally feminine interest in social connection and cohesion.

Televised men's basketball thus reinforces traditional masculinity, while women's basketball communicates a more complex message. Women's athleticism is still problematic for our culture's gender definitions, so that even as television displays the beauty of women's bodies in motion and the intensity of their will to win and excel, it must compensate by framing their power within a rhetoric of relationship and community. Nevertheless, their physical power and their joy in play are visible on the screen, thus complicating our sense of appropriate feminine behavior. Many of the play-by-play and color commentators on the women's game are women who have played the game, often during a time when their efforts were completely ignored. As a result, the narratives of women's games carry an emotional charge associated with a pleasure finally allowed to be spoken in public. It is now okay for a girl to want to be an athlete, and it is okay for women to enjoy watching the game. Women's basketball has a very large following in the lesbian community, which testifies to the forthright way that televised women's basketball has handled gender complexity. The women's game loosens up our culture's rules, while the men's game tightens them.

The formation of characters in basketball has a moral function as well as a role in cultural politics. Basketball characters are used as figures in a moral allegory, as teaching devices intended to shape the values of young people, as models of the moral life for all. The cultural work of the game to a large extent happens here, in the construction of character types that foster hegemonic values. Michael Jordan has become a character of this type. David L. Andrews has edited a collection of essays, *Michael Jordan, Inc.*, which explores the political significance of Jordan as a media icon. Michael Danzin, in his essay "Representing Michael," describes the figure of Michael Jordan as "translating blackness into a non-threatening Reaganesque masculinity for male youth" (2001, 7), and C. L. Cole (2001), in "Nike's America/America's Michael Jordan," casts Jordan as an icon of individual effort and moral uprightness, in contrast to which black crime can be portrayed precisely as a *failure* of individual effort rather than as a symptom of urban decay. Jordan's image can be put to this use not because he personally holds these beliefs but because he has been transformed into a moral icon within the narrative of the game.

Because of their success in creating recognizable characters with rich interpersonal histories, it is easy for basketball narrators to create the plot devices necessary for a successful narrative. These plots almost always take a reassuring, familiar, and even primal form. Opposing forces engage in conflict until one of the forces prevails. The conflict is resolved, one way or the other. This binary competition is the plot of *The Iliad, High Noon, Hoosiers,* and every televised game. In addition to following this simple opposition, it is the job of the narrators to create the specific conflict that any given game takes on. They can draw from the history of the characters to create this conflict. Maybe the coach of one team used to coach the other. Maybe the stars of both teams are feuding. Maybe these teams have played for the championship three times before, maybe one team is a small-town high school and the other is a big-city team, maybe the two teams play distinctly different styles, maybe one team is young and the other old—the simple fact that the teams are opposed in their pursuit of a win is always *inflected* by some more character-driven opposition. These inflections give a distinctive human shape to each game, which might otherwise seem like a virtual repetition of every other game. What makes basketball narratives intelligible is the clarity of their conflicts—I mean, the opposing sides are wearing different *clothes*—and the certainty of their resolutions, and what gives them cultural resonance is the value conflicts evoked by the human dimensions of the created narrative. Think of Bill Russell and Wilt Chamberlain. The consensus narrative of their conflicts was that Chamberlain represented the body, the pure gift of athletic excellence, while Russell represented the mind, the will, anticipation, and strategy. Every game between Chamberlain and Russell, between Philadelphia and Boston, no matter the outcome of the competition, contributed to an ongoing public reflection on the nature and moral value of competing forms of excellence. Every basketball narrative evokes some similar cultural conflict, and while those conflicts might be undecidable in everyday life, they are brought to a decision in these narratives, at least at the moment of competitive resolution. Tonight, at least, athleticism wins, and we must take that settled fact into account.

Narratives require forces in conflict, but they also put the audience on one side of the conflict, hoping for a satisfying resolution. That is, these stories have a *protagonist*, a force the audience is intended to feel sympathy for and identify with, and an *antagonist*, a force that opposes the desire of the protagonist and thus of the audience. But in a basketball game, who is the protagonist and who the antagonist? The answer is that it is up to the narrator. This is obvious in games that are being broadcast simultaneously by announcers who represent both of the teams—say the Lakers and the Kings. For the Los Angeles announcers the Lakers are the heroes, the ones whose fates concern us, and the Kings are the force that wants to deny our desires. For the Sacramento announcers, the conflict and the sympathies are reversed, and they create an *essentially* different story. One event, two stories, and two explorations of "cultural resonance." The extreme example of this practice is "the homer," the announcer who outright roots for the home team and demonizes the opposition. But neutral announcers also produce a story line in which one team or the other is featured. For example, one team might be undefeated, or another might be dealing with injuries or even personal tragedies. The narrators will make the game a story about one of the teams and reduce the other to bit players. Of course, basketball narratives must be flexible and open to the actions that develop. A story about an undefeated team fighting to save their perfect season might turn into a narrative about an amazing upset, David overthrowing Goliath. Either our team wins, and we experience the satisfaction of desire, or it loses, and we undergo the minor tragedy of frustrated hope. Either way, the conflict comes to a conclusion that evokes an appropriate emotional response. Even the pain of loss is rendered intelligible, as the logical outcome of a clear contest.

Despite this experience of resolution, basketball narratives can still create an unsettling experience, or they would if their postmodern style were not so common in popular culture. One of the complications is that sports narration, unlike most fictional or historical narratives, occurs simultaneously with the events it narrates. That is, the narrator does not know at the onset of the narrative how the conflict will be resolved. The events play out before his eyes, beyond his control, though he retains the power to shape their significance. As Whannel says, the outcome of the game is "genuinely uncertain" (1992, 113). Fictional narrators, except in the occasional experimental novel, do not begin to tell the story until it has been resolved. They know the outcome before they begin, and they construct a narrative that leads believably to the inevitable conclusion. Basketball narratives, and live sports narratives in general, are much more open. The narrator shapes the story of the conflict even though the future is radically open and unknowable. But this temporal complexity is further complicated by a final simplicity. That is, game narratives are open and indeterminable at every moment except the last, at which point the openness is transformed into radical closure. The conflict is resolved, the outcome is public, quantifiable, unchangeable. Such narratives require great strategic skill, so that the openness of the outcome is maintained, even when a rout is under way and the winner is predictable. The convention of the sports broadcast is that the game is not over until the fat lady sings, so the story must be told in a prospective, open mode. But in the midst of this temporal openness, the narrator also must keep the cultural conflicts clear, so that when they are resolved by the outcome, they can be put into perspective, reflected on, "wrapped up." The radically open narrative must have a reassuring and an unequivocal resolution.

ANALYSIS

One of the distinctive features of sports broadcasting is that narrative and analysis are brought together in a hybrid discourse. The team of announcers works together to create a unique discursive form, a narrative interwoven with its own instantaneous analysis, as though a novel included its own critical interpretation or a film included its own reviews. And all of this verbal discourse, narrative and analytical, works in complex relationship with the visual discourse, forming a complex hybrid text. The analytical function of the text puts the game inside frames of information, interpretation, evaluation, and moral commentary, and more than any other of these framing devices, analysis domesticates and controls the game, subjecting it to modes of knowledge familiar and comfortable for its largely white male audience.

Basketball analysis occurs in the midst of the action and its narration. It also occurs during pregame, halftime and postgame segments, and during *SportsCenter* every night, and in shows such as *Inside Stuff* and other broadcasts dedicated entirely to sports analysis. And surrounding the televised game are radio call-in shows that allow fans to analyze the game, in addition to the huge array of print journalistic coverage. In fact, for fans, part of the pleasure of watching basketball is engaging with this vast world of commentary and analysis. Talking about the game frames the experience of watching the game, and fans engage in analysis just as much as the expert commentators. Viewers want to *know* the game, mastering the physical within a mental framework. I will focus on the analysis that occurs at the moment of the event and its narration, but this instant analysis can only be understood within the whole multimedia matrix of sports commentary. Game analysis creates a sense of transparency, as though the game were open to a knowledge that needs no extensive reflection, no systematic thought. The event occurs, it is narrated at the same moment, and it is *known* at that very moment, made sense of, while the bounce of the ball still echoes.

The authority of game analysis derives from the fact that the analyst is usually an insider, a former player or coach. He or she can speak with the authority of experience and knowledge built up over time. The analyst usually has been a part of the game's repertoire of characters for a long time, and viewers therefore read the analysis as authentic and trustworthy. Of course, viewers often disagree violently with the analyst, a point I will return to later, but they do so *in spite of* the structural authority of the analyst's position. The analyst expresses that insider status in a number of ways. Part of the job is to provide an insider's understanding of game situations. What is the coach likely to be saying during the time-out? How does a certain player react to pressure? How does a certain coach deal with an uncooperative player? The analyst is the person who is supposed to know, to draw directly from experience as an insider, which is by definition unavailable to the average viewer. The analyst also uses an insider *language*, which is uniquely suited to the event being described, and which connects the analyst to the knowledgeable viewer. As Rowe says, "This specialist form of sports discourse binds producer, reader and text by the force of its own conventions and rules" (2004, 98). Over years of viewing, the audience comes to feel comfortable with the insider talk, even if it has never been an insider itself. It can therefore indulge in a fantasy of belonging, of membership in the sports community, as though it too was part of the team.

Analysts also bind the audience to the broadcast by using *direct address*. He or she not only talks *about* the game but *directly to* the audience, as though a conversation among equals were occurring. We are looking at the game together, the analyst seems to say, and so what I see is what you see. As Jane Feuer (1983) has pointed out about TV talk shows, the mode of direct address creates and reflects an ideology of family and community, as though we are all members of the same insider group, all sharing a knowledge and an attitude toward the events we are watching. Direct address is inherently flattering. The audience is addressed as a peer by a famous person, one for whom it has long-term feelings of affection and respect. The audience is therefore set up to see the events as the analyst sees them, and to accept his or her instantaneous interpretations and framing devices. Despite the formal, apparent equality between analyst and audience conferred by direct address, the analyst is still in discursive control. He or she is the source of information and insight, and the audience is the silent beneficiary of the analyst's multiple ways of knowing.

The analyst's most obvious task is to comment on the unfolding narrative. This commentary takes the form of explanation, interpretation, and evaluation. Many color announcers are ex-coaches, and some broadcasts take on the feel of a coaching clinic. Game analysts spend a lot of time on the "x's and o's" of the game. That is, they explain how a certain play works, or why it did not work. These explanations tend to occur during stoppages of play, in combination with slow-motion replays, often with literal x's and o's superimposed on the screen. Marv Albert, one of the great play-by-play announcers in the game, loves as a joke to call his color man, Mike Fratello, an NBA coach, the "czar of the telestrator," because Fratello so often uses this superimposition technology for a teaching moment. In these situations, the authority of the analyst is very high, since he is working out of a career dedicated to understanding and explaining the game to players. The viewers are addressed as those who do not know—they receive the information the analyst dispenses.

The effort of explanation also includes an extensive use of statistics. Game analysts have rich stores of information at their disposal, and they legitimate their explanations of the game by citing the appropriate statistics. They know who is a good foul shooter and who is a strong offensive rebounder, or who leads the league in steals, or which team has a higher shooting average, so they can explain the choices of coaches in strategic situations, or they can account for the dominance of one team in a certain aspect of the game. These statistics convey an air of objectivity and authority, and they send the message that the game—and maybe, by extension, experience in general—can be *known* in a detached and numerical way by those who make it the subject of their expertise. Basketball analysis, that is, is the discourse of the expert, encouraging the belief that professional expertise is the legitimate source of knowledge, rather than what seems like the amateur observations of the nonexpert fan. Many fans resist this subservience, but the discourse of the expert still legitimizes the frames of understanding that the program places around the events of the game.

The statistics cited by the analyst often produce a literal, visual frame around the game. That is, statistics are displayed graphically in computer-generated data presentations, often under the action or super-imposed over a replay or close-up. The production of the game becomes a problem in information delivery and data display. Replay of the action often is accompanied by verbal commentary and visual data, creating a convincing rhetoric based on multiple sources of information. The visual image of the game is not left unmediated for the viewer's independent analysis. It is packaged as a visual display inside the information that provides its authoritative explanation. These production techniques presume that a viewer is a veteran television watcher and is therefore capable of processing these multiple and simultaneous sources of data. This visual as well as verbal framing of the game only works properly with fans who are expert viewers and who have been educated in understanding both the game and its modes of presentation.

In addition to these explanatory frames, analysts also impose interpretive frames. That is, they claim the ability to get into the minds and hearts of the players and coaches. They try to read the mind of the coach who is setting the strategy. They speculate about the motivation and emotions and psychological makeup of players. These forms of knowledge do not have the authority of statistics or objective ways of knowing. They rely directly on the analyst's history within the game. The analyst can claim to know how others are thinking and feeling because he or she has gone through the same kind of experience, or because of personal relationships with the participants in the event. Like all interpreters, they rely on experience and personal history rather than on more detached ways of knowing. Their interpretations must stand the test of events. Does the coach decide to call a time-out, as the analyst predicted? Does the player choke with the game on the line, as the analyst tells us this player has done before? The authority of the analyst in these matters must be built up over time, depending on a felt reliability rather than a demonstrable truth.

In these interpretive acts, the analyst not only *explains* the developing narrative but also *contributes* to it. In the effort to explain on-court events, the analyst often cites the psychological or emotional state of the characters in the narrative. For example, play-by-play announcers often noted that recent Los Angeles Lakers teams lacked offensive coordination. In order to explain this observation, analysts routinely referred to the widely reported personal conflicts between Kobe Bryant and Shaquille O'Neal. As I said earlier, we viewers have no way to know if those reports are true, since we have only media access to the events, but each time a game analyst refers to this interpersonal conflict, he reinforces our sense of these iconic characters, and their character traits are then used to tell the story of a particular game.

The basketball analyst, armed with this interpretive knowledge of players and coaches, can shape the plot of the unfolding narrative. The analyst becomes an expert on group psychology, sensing changes in momentum and team morale, reading the outward signs of players' facial expressions and physical postures in order to understand how the game changes, or to put it another way, how the plot develops. They half perceive and half create turning points in the game, crucial moments when the momentum changes and the energy shifts from one team to the other. After all, games take over two hours of real time to play, so the narrator/analyst must keep audience interest by segmenting that time, dividing it into emotionally meaningful units. And basketball is in fact a game of runs, when one team will seize the advantage, feed off the energy of its own success, and change the direction of the game. The game itself has the makings of a plot, and the narrator/analyst senses the shifts and enhances their drama.

The analyst also is a critic, an evaluator of players' and coaches' performance. Some analysts—I am thinking of Billy Packer, for example—seem to think of their job primarily in terms of pointing out where players and coaches go wrong. The outcome of almost every play seems in Packer's eyes to result from some error or weakness. On the other hand, some analysts—I am thinking of Dick Vitale, for example—lavish praise on every play, turning a routine layup into a superhuman effort. For some commentators the outcome of the game is a result of the coach's genius or his strategic errors; for others, it derives from the interaction of the players' skills. Analysts are extremely hard on what they see as the coach's strategic errors, especially in managing the clock or in endgame situations, and on what they perceive as players' laziness or lack of concentration and will to win. Analysts, then, critique the events of the game, or more to the point, they critique the plot developments in the stories they themselves are creating.

Game analysts also construct a moral reading of the game. That is, they see the game as a moral allegory, an opportunity to see character in action. A player plays through the pain of an injury, and the analyst drives home to us the moral courage of his decision. A star player reins in his game so that it integrates better with the skills of his teammates, and the analyst turns him into a hero of selflessness and teamwork. A coach turns down an offer from a bigger school, and the analyst sets him up as a paragon of loyalty, or the coach accepts the big job, and the analyst sees him as a good father and husband who wants the best for his family. A player commits a flagrant foul, and the analyst gets the opportunity to lament the death of sportsmanship. A player forces a shot, and he is turned into a symbol of selfishness. A player confronts a coach, and the player comes to represent the moral failures of the younger generation. These judgments are routine in game broadcasts, and they are as predictable as they are frequent. Playing pickup basketball may teach a subtle, local, and situational ethical style, but *watching* basketball places the audience in the land of the uplifting sports cliche. The moral judgments are very rarely surprising. They almost always read predictable values out of conventional interpretations of game events. The values routinely evoked in the analysis of game narratives are the values that viewers have heard since they were children from teachers and coaches and preachers and bosses. They are the virtues of the good, subservient worker—selflessness, acceptance of rightful authority, commitment to the team, willingness to work within one's own limitations, acceptance of proper roles. These are the elements of the moral frame that the analyst places around the game, transforming it into a simple lesson in character development.

The moral frameworks are elements in a complex, interlocking system of frames that television places around the game. The frames are visual and verbal, narrative and analytical, political and moral, and though they are complex, their function is to simplify, to reduce the game to manageable proportions. This reduction aims to satisfy the needs of the audience that the broadcast addresses. It is certainly not the job of basketball broadcasts to challenge the beliefs or upset the expectations of their viewers. Basketball broadcasts are strictly formatted so that the audience gets what it expects, and their cultural messages are intended to flatter the audience's values and beliefs about the game and the issues it raises. This audience is overwhelmingly white and male, and the frames that the broadcast places around the game are designed to make sense and appeal to that dominant group.

The whiteness and maleness of these frames persist despite the great efforts of black and female announcers who attempt to give the game a countercultural or multicultural twist. Despite the fact that there are great black and female sports announcers, the default setting for the role of sports announcer is white and male. At the beginning of almost every game we see two white men in jackets and ties setting the scene while black players warm up in the background. Because the role of the announcer is coded white, black announcers have to make sure that they keep their black styles within comfortable white norms, and because it is coded male, female announcers have to be able to present themselves successfully in the mode of the conventional male sports announcer before they can even think about inflecting their presentation in a style that might appeal to female viewers. Stuart Scott and David Aldridge and Kenny Smith and Charles Barkley may one day transform broadcast basketball into a black cultural practice, and Robin Roberts and Cheryl Miller may give women's basketball its own language and culture, but all of them now work in a broadcast system set up for the easy consumption of white men. To get a sense of how white and how male broadcast basketball really is, try to imagine a game produced for television with a predominantly black or predominantly female audience in mind. Such a change would affect every frame we have discussed, visual and discursive. The game would be shot differently, edited differently, narrated differently, and analyzed differently.

Whiteness puts its mark on all of these framing devices. For example, the invisible style of camera work and editing, borrowed from mainstream Hollywood films, was developed with mainstream white audiences in mind. It reads for these audiences as a transparent means of access to the truth about the world, hiding and denying the way it frames the world into the shapes of their needs and desires. The statistical frames placed around the game are particularly designed for white male sports fans—they express an outright geek desire to quantify, to categorize, to master by a detached, objective knowing. The whiteness of basketball broadcasting is particularly significant, of course, because its subject matter is so much a part of black culture. These black players are placed within a white visual frame and within white cultural frames, by means of which they are transformed into commodities for the white marketplace. Part of that transformation requires players to keep their blackness to themselves, or to display it within structures set by white tolerances. More fundamentally, they must buy into white cultural beliefs in order to gain celebrity. They have to learn the cliches, follow the conventions of white discourse. These players and their game have to be folded into dominant media discourse, in which they are tamed and tempered along with all of the other potentially dangerous images that television mediates.

The maleness of the frames around the game is less visible, because the game itself is coded as masculine in our culture. It becomes most visible in broadcasts of women's basketball, which has yet to develop its own distinctive visual or discursive style. The broadcast conventions remain male—only the participants are female. In broadcasts of the men's game, the masculinity of the frame seems natural and thus naturalizes conventional masculinity. The focus is on competition, on conflict, on physical courage, playing with pain, putting in hard work, accepting rightful discipline and authority. Physical strength, aggressive attitude, and cold-minded strategy are constantly featured in the broadcast's visual displays and its cultural messages. These traditional masculine values are offered as ideals of human behavior, reinforced and embodied by the almost super-human beauty and power of the performers. This combination of domi-nant ideology, kinetic beauty, and comforting presentation is almost irresistible. Basketball on television works to reinforce traditional gender definitions, as well as traditional beliefs about race, sexuality, and morality.

I say "*almost* irresistible" and "*works to* reinforce," though, because no cultural message can guarantee the terms of its reception. That is, receivers of the message, as Stuart Hall in cultural studies and the whole reader response movement in literary studies remind us, are not passive recipients of the media texts they consume. Broadcast media do have the power to determine the messages available to viewers, but they do not have the power to determine the interpretive work that their viewers per-form as they make their own sense of the messages. This is not to deny the power of media texts. They are clearly designed around powerful rhe-torical strategies intended to shape the responses of their viewers. And over a lifetime of media consumption, viewers learn predictable ways of interpreting texts that are suitable for and responsive to these strategies. Otherwise, media texts would never succeed on their own terms, which they clearly do. But viewers also learn from their own life experiences and from the media themselves ways of questioning those strategies, ways of resisting those messages, "reading against the grain."

In fact, viewers of broadcast basketball often violently reject the in-terpretations and the narrative frames offered by game announcers. One source of this resistance is partisanship. Fans of a particular team often are disappointed and angry about how that team is covered on television. For example, when a college team makes the NCAA tournament, it becomes the subject of national media attention, over and above the often extensive regional coverage received for each one of its games and each nuance of its program. If you are a rabid St. John's fan, for example, you probably know more about the players and coaches and traditions of the school than the national network announcer assigned to the show. Your knowledge comes out of local media coverage, Internet chat rooms, sports talk radio, campus rumors, and other forms of local knowledge. As a result, the announcer's status as an expert comes into question, and his or her inter-pretations of the action may seem either inaccurate or obvious. Worse, the announcer may cast your team as the antagonists in the plot, focusing attention on the fate of the other team, which may have a more prominent national brand identity. In such a situation, partisan fans may end up screaming at the TV, focusing their attention as much on the stupidity and unfairness of the announcers as on the game itself. I know North Carolina fans who watch the visuals on nationally covered Carolina games but listen to Woody Durham on UNC's sports radio network so that they do not have to contend with pro-Duke announcers such as Dick Vitale and Billy Packer (though, of course, many Duke fans feel the same announcers are biased toward UNC). Such fans do not respect the authority of the broadcast and may mock and jeer at the cliched moral lessons intoned by the announcers. Basketball often is watched by groups of friends and family, either at home or in sports bars, and mockery of the broadcast can be part of the social fun.

Certain elements of the broadcast itself encourage an active, critical audience response. For example, the fact that the narrative and its interpretation are offered by many voices, which may well disagree, weakens the authority of the broadcast messages. A game analyst may correct an error by the play-by-play announcer, or one analyst may disagree with another. Bill Walton is often upbraided by his frequent broadcast partner, Steve Jones, for his, to put it mildly, counterintuitive observations. Part of the pleasure of their broadcasts for the viewer is hearing them undercut each other's authority. John Fiske also points out in *Television Culture* that in sports broadcasts the visuals often undercut the commentary (1987, 237). Play-by-play announcers are especially vulnerable to this conflict, because they are working in real time, and errors are inevitable. The camera clearly shows a fact different from the one being reported. Such small errors are mostly inconsequential and are almost immediately forgotten, but taken together they turn the announcer into a slightly unreliable narrator. And even the analyst, who has at least a small amount of time to reflect, may produce an interpretation that can easily be challenged by viewers who have the same access to visuals and who may make entirely different sense of what they see.

But although viewers may be routinely critical of game narratives and commentary, they are much less likely to be critical of the visual frames that television places around the game. My own sensitivity to those visual strategies is a function of my background as an occasional teacher of film studies. But most viewers do not think consciously of how an establishing shot flatters them or how invisible editing hides its own ideological strategies. So even when they are reacting critically to many aspects of the broadcast, fans are still subject to its implicit ideology. Fans are not the easily manipulated dupes that some versions of cultural studies make them out to be, but they do not and cannot make themselves immune to the shaping forces of their culture, no matter how critical they become.

The cultural impact of televised basketball is therefore considerable. Its overall effect is to simplify the game. I feel a sharp contrast as a player between the game I practice and the representations of it on television. The practice of the game, as I have argued throughout this book, promotes very specific and subtle ways of thinking and feeling. The ethic of the game is local and contingent, its engagement with issues of race and gender is complex, and the relationships it fosters are deep and compelling. But on television the game is flattened out, reduced to a set of reassuring conventions. On television the game is all about competition; in the gym sometimes the game is all about pleasure. On television the lessons of the game are easy to put into capsules; in the practice of the game, the lessons take a lifetime to learn. On television players are hypermasculine warriors; in the gym, they can be tender and compassionate. On television the story of the game is simple; in the game itself, the experience is so complex that it would be hard for players to make a story out of it that would be adequate to their experience. Unfortunately, basketball plays its role in American culture more as a media event than as a daily practice. And as a media event it is part of the apparatus that keeps people in line. It naturalizes our culture's hierarchies and ideologies, presenting them in a beautifully framed composition.

So what then should we make of the pleasure that watching basketball provides for the fan? Should it be dismissed as the sugar that makes the ideological medicine go down, the new opium of the people? The connections that fans feel with basketball are deep, and its visual and emotional pleasures should not be underestimated. Televised basketball provides kinetic visual beauty, an opportunity to express local loyalties and connect with other fans, and an occasion for reflecting on the issues that the game raises. The fans' pleasure at the beauty and complexity of the game, however, should not blind us to the cultural work that basketball is made to do as a media presentation. The game is bigger and richer than its representation, but its representation plays a bigger role in our culture.

Chapter 8

Representing the Culture

Movies about Basketball

I n Gina Prince-Blythewood's film *Love and Basketball* there is a series of
scenes in which Lena Wright and Quincy McCall, a girl and boy who
grow up together and fall in love around their shared passion for basketball, play one-on-one games that reflect the changes in their relationship
and in their basketball lives. As preteens they battle on the court over the
fact that he cannot accept being beaten by a girl; as young lovers they play
strip basketball, connecting their physical love of the game with their
physical love; as troubled young adults, they play through injury and
psychological pain, which we can see in their striving, emotive bodies.
They play their games in domestic spaces—driveways, backyards, bed-
rooms. There are no spectators (except us), no coaches, no institutional
sponsors. When they play they bring their whole lives as characters with
them. We know that her mother disapproves of her athleticism and competitive drive; we know that he has been disillusioned by the father he
idolized. They are both star players in elite basketball, and we see them
playing in those contexts as well. Both make it to the professional leagues
(Lena to the brand new WNBA), and we see them competing at the highest
levels in the biggest spectacles. But in this film we see not just their official
basketball lives but their personal lives, and we see the ways that the game
shapes and is shaped by their personalities, their relationships, and the
fabric of their everyday experience. We see, in other words, what we cannot see in basketball games on TV, which abstract the game from its culture
and its connection to the lived experience of its players. Television basketball

195

can provide its audience with knowledge about game tactics and playing styles, but it cannot otherwise capture the culture of the game, which exists in relationships and histories and local contexts that cannot be broadcast live. In order to see basketball culture represented in mass media, we have to go to the movies.

Television images tend to flatten and narrow experience, simplifying the game so that it fits broadcast conventions and audience expectations. The strict visual and discursive conventions of game coverage tend to simplify and prepackage basketball into an embodiment of sports clichés and corporate values. Television coverage abstracts the game from its lived culture and presents it as pure spectacle, on display so that it can be framed and domesticated. Every game *looks* the same on TV, because of the exigencies of production conventions, and every game *means* the same on TV, because of the ideological requirements of sports broadcasting. The game loses the lived complexity present in communities of players in real social circumstances, surrounded by dense local cultures. In TV coverage, the cultural gap between the practice and its representation is at the maximum.

In recent American films about basketball, on the other hand, the representations of the game are fuller, more complex, more realistic. Films capture the culture and the subjective feel of the game, not just its spectacular performance. They take their audiences into practice gyms and pickup games, into schoolyards and backyards, and into the local cultures that surround the game and shape the lives that the players bring to the court. Films have this power because the genre of realistic narrative, with its emphasis on character, setting, and point of view, can convey the personal, social, and cultural complexity of the game. The cultural style of the practice lends itself to a media genre that is designed to focus audience attention on personal lives and interactions in a believable visual space. Recent American basketball films, even the ones that are less than satisfying as films, do collectively construct a rich and various portrait of the game. I take it as axiomatic that no representation does full justice to experience, since the rules of its medium always reshape the patterns of the practice, but movies are better adapted to basketball culture than television, with its much more limited narrative resources.

In this analysis of media representations of basketball as a cultural practice, I am evoking two—to some extent—contradictory traditions of thinking about the role of narrative in human understanding. The first sees narrative as a falsifying, ideological, deceptive imposition of simplifying structures on complex experience, functioning as a legitimation of prevailing political realities. The second sees narrative as a privileged mode of knowledge that recognizes its own subjectivities and cultural positions but engages with the felt complexity of experience—less detached, less systematic, more engaged, more opportunistic, more improvised than empirical approaches, and therefore more appropriate for cultural studies.

Television's basketball narratives elicit the first critical tradition for me, because they are so highly stereotyped in plot and character and so thin in their physical and social setting. There is a very limited repertoire of plots operating in televised basketball—David versus Goliath stories, vengeance scenarios, transformation narratives—and these plots are imposed on the unfolding events of virtually every game. They demand stock characters, easy to recognize and evaluate, easy to fit into comfortable categories of race and gender and comfortable moral discourses of selflessness and heroism. This radical simplification of events in turn *requires* a thin sense of context and locale. Simple stories are imposed for the very purpose of repressing the complexity of contexts—television stories must be "universalized," abstracted, portable, open to many cultural uses. Context and complexity attach stories to the local, the interplay of human histories and styles, the improvised world of daily practices. The purpose of highly stereotyped narratives is to reduce practices to formulas that serve as conceptual and affective comforts, reassuring reminders of the status quo.

Basketball movies are open to the same critique. They too rely on stereotyped characters and predictable plots, sometimes in the worst Hollywood style. But unlike the simple narratives imposed at the moment of play in live televison coverage, basketball movies have the time and techniques necessary to create more complex characters enmeshed in thicker environments, even if they do often sell out to easy plot devices. As a result, they provide more complex and sophisticated narrative understandings of basketball's everyday culture. Mainstream Hollywood narratives are of course highly conventional, playing to the largest audience possible, but the conventions of realistic fiction, in which a complex and believable character is placed within a recognizable social context and engages in psychologically believable action and interaction, make it an appropriate genre in which to explore the personal, interpersonal, and local nature of basketball practices.

One of the most arresting sequences in a film about basketball is Spike Lee's lyrical opening montage in *He Got Game*. This sequence articulates a personal and political perspective on the culture of basketball in a highly charged visual style, the kind of style that television does not allow. The sequence feels like a personal exploration of what the game means to Lee himself, at least in his most utopian moments. In this sequence basketball is presented as the essential *American* game, in the most inclusive sense. Set to the stirring music of Aaron Copeland, Lee's montage claims for basketball, so central to the modern black experience, a role at the heart of the American character itself, not transcending or forgetting race but simply recognizing that basketball is part of the everyday lives of all kinds of Americans. The montage generates intense visual energy with its swooping camera work, lyrical editing, and scenic variety. It takes us from barns with nailed-up backboards to courts in trailer parks and at gas stations, to pickup games on college campuses, to courts overlooking the Pacific and courts in the shadows of the projects, to sacred basketball sites such as Chicago Stadium with its statue of Michael Jordan, and the West 4th Street courts in Greenwich Village, home of the best pickup ball in the world. On all of these courts players of all kinds are engaged in every aspect of the game, shooting by themselves, running drills, playing half-court and full-court. The players are white and black, male and female, privileged and poor, and old and young, all caught up in the joy of play, moving to the energy of the emotive music.

What saves Lee's montage from sentimentality, from an easy, happy multiculturalism, is the way the sequence unfolds. It moves from the rural to the urban, from the all-American players bathed in sunlight to the gritty courts of the city, from white to black. Lee wants simultaneously to claim basketball as the *American* game and to claim it as a *black* game, played by men and women in desperate and racist circumstances, in a corrupt and dangerous world. The sequence expresses a utopian desire and a harsh realism—in fact, it ends with a black man shooting a ball in a maximum-security prison. In a brilliant edit, Lee cuts from a player shooting a ball in a pickup game at the projects, while the ball is in flight, to what seems to be the same ball spinning through the air past a prison guard with a rifle, peering down at the lone shooter. The shooter at the projects is the son, while the shooter in prison is the father. They have the same beautiful jump shot form, with a perfect release that creates the perfect spin, which provides Lee with the visual cue that connects the two characters. Lee suggests that basketball may be an American game, but it also is a black game, one that is connected to the harsh political realities of daily black life.

But despite the critical political stance, the sequence still surges with utopian desire. The players in the sequence are caught in the beauty of their movement, in lyrical slow motion. There is a short sequence in the montage in which two girls playing pickup execute a perfect give-and-go, with the ball coming back to the passer in the rhythm of her full stride as she lays the ball in. You can feel Lee's pleasure at the coordination of the play and the coordination of the camera with the players' movements. All of the players in the montage are full of joy and kinetic pleasure, even in the harshest of social and personal circumstances. The montage sets up a central contrast in the film between the purity of the game and the corruption of the basketball business and the society that surrounds it, with its slick and sleazy agents, its coldly calculating coaches, its white college girls looking for black studs, and its corrupt politicians and racist system of justice. Within this sequence, that is to say, Lee articulates a complex, distinctive point of view on basketball as a cultural practice, and he does it through his manipulation of the resources available to him as a filmmaker. As a result, he succeeds in representing the game in its cultural context, not from a disembodied perspective but from his own position as a black man living in the same society that his film depicts. This sequence makes its own distinctive political point, and there are many other basketball films that express a particular point of view and represent the game in all of its local diversity.

For this chapter I have focused on fourteen recent films that I believe taken together give a rich portrait of the practice of basketball. Two are documentaries with strong narrative styles and serious ethnographic goals: *Hoop Dreams* (1994, d. Steve James) and *Soul in the Hole* (1997, d. Danielle Gardner). Four are dramas on other topics in which basketball plays an important narrative or symbolic function: *Grand Canyon* (1991, d. Lawrence Kasdan), *Basketball Diaries* (1995, d. Scott Kalvert, based on the writings of Jim Carroll), *Smoke Signals* (1998, d. Chris Eyre, based on the writings of Sherman Alexie), and *O* (2001, d. Tim Blake Nelson, based on Shakespeare's *Othello*). Eight are films concerned centrally with basketball, in which the game provides the plot structure: *Hoosiers* (1986, d. David Anspaugh), *White Men Can't Jump* (1992, d. Ron Shelton), *Above the Rim* (1994, d. Jeff Pollack), *He Got Game* (1998, d. Spike Lee), *Finding Forrester* (2000, d. Gus Van Sant), *Love and Basketball* (2000, d. Gina Prince-Blythewood), *Coach Carter* (2005, d. Thomas Carter), and *Glory Road* (2006, d. James Gartner).

These films vary in quality as films and also as depictions of basketball and its culture, and they approach the game from many points of view. But taken together they represent effectively the diversity and complexity of the game. No basketball film is going to find the perfect perspective on the game, one that captures the practice in its totality. No such perspective exists, and no such totality exists. Basketball, like any cultural practice, needs to be represented from many perspectives, in many voices, since the game itself occupies so many different social and cultural positions. Robert Stam (1991), in his article "Bakhtin, Polyphony, and Ethnic/Racial Representation," argues that the measure of success for a representation of a racial or an ethnic group is not its "accuracy," since there is no essential truth about such groups, but rather its ability to include a number of voices and perspectives, in order to represent the complexity of experience and the fact that there is no privileged perspective for objective observation. Similarly, I would argue that no one of these films represents the cultural practice of basketball adequately, but taken together the films provide the polyphonic, multiperspectival approach that Stam desires. These are films by insiders and films by outsiders, films about organized ball and films about the pickup game, films about men and about women, films about small town teams and about ghetto high schools, films about Native Americans and African Americans and white boys, films about the purity of the game and films about its corruption, films that in very different ways represent the texture of basketball experience—playing games, practicing, shooting by yourself, bonding as a team, loving and hating your team-mates, and learning and failing to learn the lessons of the game. All of the aspects of basketball culture that I have identified in this book are present in these films, seen from different perspectives with different emphases, not so much cohering as accumulating into a rich and detailed represen-tation of basketball as a cultural practice.

VALUES AND ETHICS

Throughout basketball culture, from the local backyard to the giant arena, there is an endless, ongoing negotiation of ethical standards and practices. The game itself requires virtues that arise from the goals and procedures of the practice. In order to engage in the game fully and take maximum satisfaction from it, players learn and accept such values as selflessness, teamwork, attention to fundamental skills, and a willingness to expend maximum effort. These virtues are preached by coaches and TV pundits, but they also are recognized and rewarded in the most informal pickup games. Of course players do not always live up to these values, but they know when they are not, even when they express that knowledge by covering it up with an arrogant sneer. Many basketball movies preach these values overtly, packaging them either as a philosophy of life or as a recipe for success in mainstream American culture. Others examine the virtues of the game more critically, pointing to the hypocrisy of businesses and in-stitutions that preach the virtues and practice the opposite—cynical coaches, greedy owners, predatory agents, all with their own selfish reasons for preaching selflessness. David Rowe has argued that sports films "tend to be allegorical, framed as grand moral tales in which sports is represented as a metaphor for life" (2004, 192), and basketball films are no exception.

But basketball culture does more than teach a set of values—it also teaches a distinctive ethical *process*, a way of negotiating ethical practices at the local level. Every pickup game, without referees or coaches, requires its players to negotiate on the spot how the rules of the game will be applied and how the personal values and beliefs of all the players will be accommodated. This negotiation is difficult for an outsider to observe, since much of it is nonverbal and the rest is accomplished in the insider language of the game. When a player growls "Give up the damn ball" to a teammate, he or she is attempting to create a certain ethical tone, moving the ongoing negotiation toward the virtues of communication and mutual responsibility. Players need not and most often do not think of themselves as producers of an ethical culture, but they do so in their words and deeds on the court. Many films about basketball document this process, simply by depicting the game itself, not in the abstract formats of TV coverage but in a style that allows us to hear the players and see their interactions on the court and in their personal relationships.

Some basketball films, such as *Hoosiers, Coach Carter,* and *Above the Rim*, are explicitly didactic. They identify in basketball the all-American values that they wish to convey to their very different audiences. These films are based on the premise that there is moral confusion in our society, and that the values of basketball, properly understood, can return us to moral clarity. Others, such as *He Got Game* and *Hoop Dreams*, depict very powerfully the moral corruption of the business of the game, and by extension of society at large, but they see basketball as a vulnerable refuge from that corruption rather than a solution to it. Still others, such as *White Men Can't Jump, Above the Rim,* and *Finding Forrester*, manage to capture the ethical process of the game, the ongoing negotiation of ethical behavior that is a hallmark of basketball culture.

Hoosiers is the most overtly didactic of basketball films. It now seems more than ever a product of Reagan-era America, with its nostalgia for a time before what it sees as the corrosive moral—and racial—confusion of the 1960s. *Hoosiers* is explicitly about basketball as character education, embodied in the person of Coach Norman Dale, played with great energy by Gene Hackman. Dale coaches with a military-style conviction that authority must be respected, and that his orders must be followed without hesitation. He wears his basketball values on his sleeve. At a pep rally where his team is disrespected by the student body, he gives a stirring speech about the values of the game—hard work, sacrifice, commitment, respect. In practices his values are equally clear, embodied in every drill and coaching lesson. He teaches the importance of fundamentals, working as a team, passing the ball, playing tough man-to-man defense. Following the genre conventions of the uplifting sports film, his values of course drive the team to the state championship, and of course they also transform the lives of the players and the community. The plot of the film is almost completely predictable, but it produces strong emotional reactions. Moral behavior in this film gets its just rewards, and the story therefore satisfies a utopian and nostalgic desire for justice in a world with a clear moral structure.

Hoosiers has social and cultural objectives that go far beyond basket-ball—it is a 1980s conservative condemnation of the culture of the 1960s, a reclaiming of traditional moral codes. It takes us back to 1951, a time when Dale's authoritarian style would be accepted almost without argu-ment, a time before moral relativism and youth rebellion, when young men rightly submitted themselves to righteous authority. In this moral allegory the character of Shooter, performed memorably by Dennis Hopper, plays the central role. He is the father of one of Dale's players, an irresponsible man, drowning in alcohol, marginalized and despised by the community, desperately in need of the kind of discipline that Dale teaches. Dale has the insight to see that the best cure for Shooter is to *impose* responsibility on him, to give him the opportunity to use his basketball knowledge for the good of the team, especially his estranged and embarrassed son. *Hoosiers* is too good a film to make Shooter's transformation unproblematic. In fact, he fails at the crucial moment to live up to that responsibility, still vulner-able to his addiction, but by the end of the film he has clearly turned a corner toward sobriety and responsibility, toward reconciliation with his son and his community.

It is the presence of Dennis Hopper in the film that suggests the larger cultural implications of the moral allegory. Because of *Easy Rider,* Hopper is a 1960s icon, associated through that film with drug use, hedo-nistic individualism, and rebellion against authority. Shooter as a character takes on the resonance of Hopper's persona, and his salvation can be read as *Hoosiers'* hope for its own cultural moment, a desire to save America from all that Hopper as 1960s icon represents. Basketball is presented in the film as an anti-drug, a place where respect for authority can be learned, and where the highest goal is to serve the team and the larger community. I will argue later in this chapter that *Hoosiers'* cultural message has a strong racial charge—the 1950s in this film can also be seen as the time before there were Negroes to worry about—but for me the most fundamental ethical problem with the film is that all of the values that basketball teaches must be accepted by the players simply because Coach Dale demands it of them. If not, then they must leave the community of the team, no discus-sion or negotiation possible, and thus tempt the fate of Shooter, the self-destructive, undisciplined outcast.

There is, of course, a Coach Dale in every sport, men with strong convictions who believe that their tough love is required for the produc-tion of true masculinity and maturity in the young. They love their kids, with a love that allows for emotional and sometimes even minor physical abuse. I am not talking here of outright violent psychopathic coaches, most of whom are weeded out of the profession. Coach Dale sincerely believes that moral life requires submission to authority, that part of adolescent development is an acceptance that other people know more than you do and so must be obeyed without question, and that the process requires harsh challenges, rites of passage, and emotional and physical ordeals. Thus they can yell at and manhandle their players, then declare their love at the end of the process (the last line of the film is "I love you guys"). But even granting their sincerity and the authenticity of their feelings, such coaches are fundamentally out of step with the culture of basketball. Once the players get on the court, even on the most organized of teams, *they* are the ones who set the ethical tone of the game, who decide how to negotiate the values that will guide their practice. Coach Dale wants to take that negotiation out of the game, to keep all ethical power in his own hands. The political allegory is clear. *Hoosiers* teaches that righteous authority exists, and that the ethical life requires submission to its power. It teaches that citizens require discipline, that they must give up their own ethical instincts and follow values imposed from above. This belief in ethical discipline is a powerful strain throughout the culture of organized sports, connecting sports with family, religion, schools, military life, and workplaces as institutions of political authority. The joyful play of pickup ball, with its negotiations, its improvisations, and its moment-by-moment creation at the hands of interactive subjectivities, runs counter to this conservative rage for order and submission.

For me what saves the film from this benign fascism and makes it interesting on the ethics of basketball is its insider's awareness of how the values of the game are inherent in the everyday details of play. Coach Dale is a fanatic about fundamentals. He knows that if he forces his players to play as he wants them to, his moral lessons cannot be escaped. For example, he demands that team members develop the physical and mental skills to play man-to-man defense, in spite of their athletic limitations and their local traditions. He sees the zone defenses they have been playing as abdications of individual responsibility and man-to-man defense as a righteous affirmation of self-determination and moral maturity. On offense, he demands that team members play a game of constant movement and pinpoint passing, which requires players to master the discipline of the crisp, two-handed chest pass. Practices are devoted to fundamental skills, not to scrimmaging and shooting at will. It is in the daily practice of the disciplines of the game that the coach's values can be imposed. In its best moments, *Hoosiers* is a movie about basketball *practice*, its dailiness. The big wins that the team achieves are seen as the inevitable result of the values imposed in practice. And though I reject the assumption that values should and must be *imposed*, I do honor in the film its sense that what happens on the court *matters*, that styles of play have moral implications.

The 2005 film *Coach Carter* owes much to *Hoosiers*, transplanting its message about the necessity for discipline to the rough Richmond district of Oakland. The Coach Dale in this story is Ken Carter, played by Samuel L. Jackson, a former star at Richmond High who returns to the school as coach in order to replace an older coach who has lost his enthusiasm for the game. Coach Carter has become a successful entrepreneur, and he sees his job as teaching more than basketball—he wants to teach his players how to succeed in life and to move up the economic ladder. The players are tough kids who bring the street ethic of self-preservation and self-aggrandizement onto the court. Coach Carter's message centers on discipline, fundamentals, and conditioning. Any resistance to his authority is punished by push-ups and suicide drills, and anyone who cannot accept the program must leave the team. His conviction is that many of his players lack discipline in the home and therefore need to learn the lessons of respect and obedience from the team. In *Coach Carter*, sports definitely build character, and in the ghetto world the film inhabits, it seems nothing else does.

The central conflict in the story develops out of the contract that the coach requires of his players—they have to agree to attend all classes and maintain a C+ average. And even though they accept his discipline on the court and start the season with a long undefeated streak, they do not come through as students. They cut class and fail to put in the necessary work. Since they have broken the contract, the coach takes the controversial step of cancelling practices and then games, maintaining that they must be students first and athletes second, and that they have to apply the ethic he has taught them on the court to their lives as students and members of the community. What is interesting is that almost no one supports his ethical stand. The players mutiny, their parents complain, and the community rejects him. The argument against him is that basketball is the only positive activity in these kids' lives and in the life of the community, so why take it away? When the coach refuses to compromise, the players themselves come around. They organize their own study sessions and commit themselves to his principles. They return to their success on the court, and even though they do not win the big game at the end (a *very* unusual outcome in a basketball film), they have learned the ethical lessons the coach professed.

As this outline of the conflict suggests, *Coach Carter* is a conventional moral tale. The coach is right, the kids are wrong, the community that supports them is misguided, and the righteousness of his convictions transforms them. They see the truth, accept the discipline, and live better lives because of the influence of their coach. The moral simplicity of the story is of interest mainly because of the social complexity of its context. Coach Carter teaches his traditional values not in rural Indiana but in a multicultural, economically depressed, decaying urban neighborhood. The coach dresses like a businessman, teaches "white ball," refuses to allow his students to call each other "niggaz," and preaches the virtues of upward mobility and middle-class deportment. But the film resolutely refuses to engage with a racial dynamic. The coach is simply right, and his lessons are presented as universal. He preaches the ethic that anyone needs to succeed, and any social analysis of racial and economic discrimination is simply an excuse, a refusal to accept the code of individual responsibility by which the coach lives. Basketball in this film is a means to an end, a way of teaching lessons that the players cannot learn anywhere else in their culture.

Above the Rim places basketball in a more complex moral universe, but it has an equally strong and simple moral message. And like Hoosiers it has a powerful but unacknowledged racial agenda. In Above the Rim the value in question is selflessness, playing for the team rather than playing for oneself, and the film clearly intends to use the values of basketball to make a larger sociocultural point. The conflict between selflessness and egotism is played out in the high school career of Kyle, a great inner-city New York guard who is being scouted by Georgetown. He is so confident in his abilities that he tends to take the game into his own hands, disappointing his coach and the Georgetown scout who value him only if he keeps his individual game inside of the team concept. The broader moral and social issue is raised by the film's personification of the conflict between team and ego in the form of two brothers, Shep and Birdie, who come into Kyle's basketball life. Shep is a security guard at the high school, a guy who used to be a star in the neighborhood, until he lost a friend in a tragic (and to my mind ridiculous) accident. He is loyal to the coach and to old-school values, and he is a stand-up man in his community. He is played by an actor named Leon who turns him into a wooden hero, even though the character is supposed to be tormented by guilt over his friend's death. Birdie, played memorably by Tupac Shakur, is a local drug lord and stylish thug, who stands for the menace of street life, the life of ego and selfishness. Despite the problems caused by the fact that Birdie is a much more compelling character than Shep, the film makes perfectly clear that basketball virtue reflects real-life virtue. If Kyle plays for the team, he will turn out like Shep. He will get an education, play in the league, and become a responsible member of society. If he plays for himself, he will end up on the street, running with Birdie, swept into a life of license and violence.

The ethical contrast is racially marked. Kyle has a white coach, a Coach Dale in fact, who preaches the virtues of the game and who wants to pass Kyle on to John Thompson, a black coach who at that time taught those same virtues at the college level. We find at the end of the film that Shep will take over as coach at the high school, ensuring that the white coach's legacy will continue. The film also racializes the ethical conflict in

Shep's story. His tragic past involved an accident during a rooftop game in which Shep and his friend got into a how-high-can-you-jump contest. After Shep taunted him, the friend tried so hard to outjump him that he jumped off of the roof! To me the silliness of that premise undercuts the rest of the film, with Shep brooding about his guilt and Kyle learning to avoid the same selfish fate. But the silliness of the plot should not blind us to its simple racial profiling. Shep and his friend are trying to outleap each other, as of course all black players do, and they are woofing at each other, as of course all black players do, and it is the blackness of their game that kills. Kyle has to reject the "blackness" of his game, to accept the "white" game, with its ethic of selflessness. Of course he does accept the "white" game, does go on to college, does make the play that wins the championship. Shep does take his rightful place in society, and Birdie does get killed by his selfish ways. The social message of *Above the Rim* is that if black folks would just start acting like white folks then the evils of the world would be defeated by the virtues of the game when it is played by the rules of white culture. Basketball is character education, and its values can save even the most underprivileged players, even our corrupt society itself.

In movies such as *Hoosiers*, *Coach Carter*, and *Above the Rim*, basketball is depicted as a powerful element in the moral education of young people, and the films see themselves as reinforcing that moral work. They focus on organized basketball, with its coaches and rule books and ethos of institutional responsibility, rather than on the pickup game, with its negotiated, improvised ethical style. The virtues of the game are seen as the products of institutionalized discipline, a set of drills and fundamentals, along with a willingness to accept top-down authority. Basketball, that is, is part of *schooling*, training body and mind in the ways of living that make profit in the world. The films teach a complex mix of individual responsibility, selflessness and teamwork, and submission to authority, and the potential conflicts produced by that mix of incongruent values are simply plot points on the way to a success that the form of the story itself guarantees from the beginning. Challenges arise, but virtue wins out, and the narrative becomes a conventional inspirational tract.

More complex moral issues are at play in Spike Lee's *He Got Game*, though Lee's film is based on a similar contrast between the ethical purity of the game and the corruption of the society that surrounds it. However, in *He Got Game* it is the organized game at its elite levels, dominated by commercial interests (sometimes thinly veiled), that is the source of the corruption, and it is the street game, in all of its improvisatory beauty, that stands for the utopian possibilities of play. Lee loves the game, but he is alert to the cynicism and hypocrisy surrounding it. In this film, the very coaches and sports bureaucrats who invoke for public relations purposes the conventional values of the game—like Coach Dale—are complicit in a corrupt system of covert payoffs and institutional power. Schools provide illicit money and willing women, and the pros offer a life of unthinkable personal wealth, while the game is promoted by these very institutions as a lesson in selflessness and discipline. In contrast, *He Got Game* idolizes the beauty and righteousness of the game itself. Following its lyrical opening montage, all of the depictions of the game are loving tributes to its athleticism, grace, and joy. They are beautifully lit, dramatically edited, and full of slow-motion sequences that aestheticize the bodies and skills of the players. The beauty of the game stands for its purity and simplicity in a corrupt, evil world.

In *He Got Game* there are no easy moral nostrums that save our characters and master that cruel world. Politics do not go away, and injustices are not overcome by a simple moral code, as they are in *Hoosiers, Coach Carter*, and *Above the Rim*. Jesus Shuttlesworth, Lee's high school phenom, has a Coach Dale for a father. Jake, played by Denzel Washington, has tutored his son in the toughness that he thinks a great ballplayer needs. They play endless one-on-one games in which the father gives no quarter, trying to tear his son down so he can develop a man's toughness. But this Coach Dale allows his own toughness to go too far, abusing his son and causing his wife's death. Neither Jake nor any other authority figure in the film can pass a moral code on to Jesus because all are morally compromised or outright corrupt. All Jake can offer is his own growing moral awareness of the limitations of his macho toughness and his continuing belief in the beauty and purity of the game itself, symbolized by the matching beauty of the father's and the son's jump shots. In the film's somewhat strained magical-realism conclusion, the father throws a ball out of the prison and into the arena where his son is playing, passing on a legacy of devotion to the game, not as a moral force that can cure the world's problems but as a refuge, a pure experience, good in itself, in the midst of an ugly, inevitably corrupt world.

The moral world of *He Got Game* also is racialized. The game in its purity is black, and the corruption of the game is white. There may be black street agents and coaches, but they serve white institutions that buy and trade and discard black flesh. As an antidote Jake evokes Earl Monroe, "The Truth," who stands for the pure pleasure of the game, a freestyle game that throws off the shackles of institutionalized ball. That kind of purity may lead to mainstream success, or it may never transcend the local court, or it may land one in prison, but for everyone who plays the game it represents the possibility of a life better than the corrupt and pampered subservience offered by the self-serving white world. The complexity of *He Got Game* derives from the contrast between this racialized moral opposition and the

pan-racial inclusiveness of the opening montage. Lee blames white institutions for the corruption of the game, but he offers the pure practice of
the game as a holy pleasure available to anyone of any race who understands the beauty of a perfect jump shot in an imperfect world.

The contrast between the corruption of elite, mass-media sports and
the integrity of amateur, local play provides a visual foundation for the
moral perspective of Lawrence Kasdan's *Grand Canyon*, a multiple-narrative
melodrama that intertwines the stories of an affluent white family and a
working-class black family in Los Angeles. Basketball plays almost no role
in the plot of the film, but it serves an important symbolic role. The film
opens with a montage of Simon (Danny Glover) playing in a serious pickup
game. The sequence is shot in black and white, with beautiful close-ups
and slow-motion effects. The players are intense, totally caught up in the
moment of the game. The camera zooms out to reveal the busy, dangerous
city in which this great local game thrives. Then a jump cut takes us inside
a huge arena for a Lakers game, seen from the perspective of Mack (Kevin
Kline), a wealthy lawyer with an even wealthier friend (Steve Martin), who
has floor-level seats for the game. The camera, now in garish color, focuses
on the glitz of the game, the Laker girls, the trophy wives, the fat cats, the
celebrities. This game is clearly just a corporate spectacle, an opportunity
to enjoy the power of money and to indulge in male fantasies of physical
and sexual power. Simon, established in the opening sequence as a man of
integrity, becomes the moral center of the film. He adheres to a convincing
moral code, based on mutual respect tempered with an awareness of the
harshness of life. Simon, who drives a tow truck, saves Mack, whose Lexus
has broken down in a bad neighborhood, from a car full of gang bangers
looking for an easy mark. Simon talks his way out of the situation by
evoking a simple moral vision. He acknowledges that the kids live in a
tough world in which the violent and powerful hold sway, but he stands
for the possibility of a world of mutual respect where people have the right
to feel secure in their persons and to do their jobs, fulfill their responsibilities. Simon's on-court integrity is the foundation for his real-world
integrity, and it leads Mack away from his self-centered, privileged, inau-
thentic life, symbolized by NBA glitz, and into a more engaged, connected,
responsible life. Basketball—and especially pickup basketball—in this film
stands for the life lived with integrity, even in a harsh world.

This moral contrast also has a racial dynamic. Simon is an example
of a recurring character type, the working-class black character who provides commonsense, earthy wisdom to the alienated, abstracted white
character. Simon plays, Mack watches. Simon teaches, Mack learns. And in
exchange, Mack tries to intervene in the dangerous world in which Simon
lives, tries to provide opportunities that his position of privilege makes

possible. The black character provides authenticity and naturalness, and the white character provides compassionate liberal schemes for social amelioration. But it is to the credit of the film that Mack recognizes the awkwardness of his gestures and the compromised morality of his position as a white guy with a good heart. Basketball in this film stands as evidence of the fact that integrity and authentic connection can exist, even in a world beset by racism and economic injustice.

On the contrary, *Hoop Dreams*, the acclaimed documentary by Steve James, sees basketball as a dangerous illusion, a false hope for ghetto black kids, and as a corrupt institution, one that takes advantage of those young hoop dreamers. The film is full of real-life examples of the same hypocritical coaches, unscrupulous agents, and hustling recruiters that Lee fictionalizes in *He Got Game*. Not one of these representatives of elite basketball pays more than lip service to the values of the game. In fact, the game itself seems unimportant even to the players, except as a way out of the ghetto and up into the dreamworld of professional ball, with its instant wealth and ultra cool pop-culture visibility. Basketball for them is no longer about play, about the pure joy of the game, as in *He Got Game*. It is just a strategy, and a failed strategy at that. William Gates and Arthur Agee, the two young players the film follows as they grow from freshmen in high school to freshmen in college, are survivors who learn the harsh lessons of elite sports, but the game itself is not their source of strength. They get their moral stability from their street-smart understanding of life's difficulties and from the other survivors in their family and community. And they need those strengths to survive institutionalized ball, which has misled them and discarded them when they were no longer useful. The moral vision of *Hoop Dreams* is the darkest of the films I have discussed so far—it places its characters in the corrupt world of *He Got Game* without the utopian hopes that Lee sees in the game. Agee and Gates are okay at the end, but the moral lessons they have learned have not at all derived from the values of the game but from the experience of contriving survival strategies within the corrupt institutions that sponsor the game.

The films I have discussed thus far focus on the values that the game teaches and the corrupt institutions that surround it. But the ethics of basketball are not just a matter of static, standard values to be consumed by passive, blank-slate players waiting to be instructed. Basketball ethics are at their root a product of negotiations in the moment of play by players who create the ethical tone of the game out of their own subjectivities and their interactions with the other players present. Coaches and commentators often reduce the game to a moral lesson, but players recognize that every single game, even the most casual one, produces its own specific and nonrepeatable ethical tone. And basketball films capture that process much more effectively than televised games.

In *Finding Forrester*, for example, a high school phenom named Jamal Wallace (played by Rob Brown) gets a tryout at an elite prep school that is trying to recruit him away from a public school that cannot provide an education appropriate to his academic gifts. He is recruited as a student but also as a player, and on his visit to the school he is asked to play with the prep school's players in a pre-season pickup game. He goes into the game thinking it is a friendly run, but he finds out quickly that the stakes are high. He is matched up against the team's only black player, the current star of the team, who sees Jamal as a threat to his dominance. Jamal finds out quickly that his rival has stepped up the level of intensity in the game. He crowds and bumps Jamal, asserting his dominance. At this point Jamal could choose to step back, to play the friendly game he expected, but he decides to respond to the challenge, to take his own game up a level in intensity. The two players without a word have negotiated an ethical climate that allows more intense competition, more physical play.

Finding Forrester is particularly acute in placing this instantaneous ethical negotiation in a rich physical and social context. The pickup game is played on a beautiful rooftop court overlooking Central Park, in marked contrast to the Bronx tenements and playgrounds that Jamal is used to. His opponent, who at first seems to be another street player brought in to strengthen the team, is in fact a rich kid who is used to the position of power both on and off the court. Jamal has to negotiate the ethics of this pickup game, but he also has to negotiate his position as a working-class scholarship boy in an elite, upper-class school. The film offers his ability to negotiate the game as a sign of his more general social and cultural abilities. *Finding Forrester* takes us into a basketball world that really exists, the world of the elite school that can afford to recruit the best players, even those who will find themselves in social and cultural situations completely foreign to their personal and athletic histories. *Hoop Dreams* depicts the cutthroat atmosphere in such institutions, which will use up and discard such players if they cannot negotiate the difference. *Finding Forrester*, at least in this pivotal scene, is interested less in the corruption of the institution than in the ethical strategies that players devise in order to survive on the court.

White Men Can't Jump is all about ethical process and negotiation, not just on the court but as a lifestyle, a way of being in the world. The players in this film are hustlers who use their basketball skills and their street smarts to make money off of the game. Their hustle involves taking advantage of people's racial assumptions. Billy Hoyle (Woody Harrelson) is a white boy who can play but skillfully pretends he cannot. Black guys jump at the chance to bet against him, and then he outplays them and takes their money. He pulls this con on Sidney Deane (Wesley Snipes), the king of the Venice Beach courts in Los Angeles, and Sidney realizes that they can play the con together. Sidney bets local court heroes that he can beat them, even if he is forced to play with the white geek. Then he and Billy take them apart, often using race to provoke the other team into hotheaded, undisciplined play. Sidney then pulls the con on Billy, intentionally losing to friends and dividing up Billy's money. Billy feels betrayed, but Sidney argues that all is fair in the world of the con. Through the intervention of the women in their lives, the partnership is saved, and by the end of the film Sidney and Billy seem to be moving out of the world of the hustle and into more responsible adult roles.

As a reflection of the ethics of basketball, *White Men Can't Jump* is skewed by the fact that these players are hustlers who are fundamentally dishonest, who misrepresent themselves. They are playing under false pretenses. Billy presents himself as a weak player, and Billy and Sidney hide the fact that they know each other. On one level the con has its narrative charms, since it takes advantage of prejudices that deserve to be laughed at and rebuked. But in terms of the ethic of the game, the fact that the con requires them to hide their friendship is more problematic. Putting the racial dynamic aside, their con takes advantage of a basic element in pickup basketball psychology. Pickup players know that playing against players who already know each other, who arrive at the court together, is different from playing with a true pickup group. Friends have specific moves on which they have worked in a million games. They know each other's games and thus can anticipate the action, and they feed off of their preexisting emotional bonds. It is fair enough to take advantage of people's racial stereotypes, but it is not fair to take advantage of an unwritten rule of the game, one of the assumptions in which players must have confidence if there is to be fair play and satisfaction in the practice. As Billy and Sidney mature in this film, they learn that playing cons on and off of the court can have real consequences in people's lives, and they seem ready at the end to use their street smarts in more responsible activities.

But if this film ultimately is about the need to grow out of the world of the con, it also revels along the way in the fun of the hustle. Billy and Sidney have to grow up, but they do not have to lose the suppleness and creativity of the thinking that the con requires. After all, the con is based on a very basic basketball move—the fake. Often in the game the strategy is to pretend to be doing one thing and then to do another—show the ball as if you are going to pass and then drive in for the layup—pretend you are overplaying to one side but be ready to counter the offensive player's overreaction. The fake takes advantage of the other player's assumptions.

It gets him or her to place a certain interpretation on events and then acts in ways that take advantage of that interpretation. The fake is the con in a nutshell, and Billy and Sidney use it as a template for survival tactics off of as well as on the court. The con is their way of negotiating the complex reality of street life. Neither of them has a regular job. Both survive by one hustle after another, as part of the "scuffle economy," the working life outside of regular jobs and benefits, the economy inhabited by millions of Americans. In that economy there are no corporate guidelines for behavior, no preset rules. All must be negotiated, created on the fly. And one common method of negotiation in that context is to survive by one's wits, one's ability to put down a good fake, to take advantage of others' weaknesses, prejudices, habits of thought and behavior. All basketball players are, in a way, hustlers, making the game up on the run, in the absence of moral absolutes, within the loose framework of the practice. And despite the fundamental dishonesty of their hustle, Billy and Sidney do honor the game. Once play begins, they operate within broadly accepted ethical frameworks. They do not call every tiny foul, they do not engage in violence, they do not taunt and distract their opponents. They run their con, but they play the game straight up.

This complex moral state is the film's comment on life in marginalized America. It is the battle of each against all, with no institution to regularize experience, fit it into preset patterns. In such a "pickup" world the skills of the basketball player work as survival skills. And if survival requires a fake, a con, then so be it. Basketball teaches the ability to negotiate, to take advantage of the moment. But it also teaches that players can together produce rough justice and a fair playing environment, based on their commitment to the game and to each other. Billy and Sidney are con artists, but they also are righteous players. And as they play together they develop a personal connection that keeps them from taking advantage of each other. The ethic of their game derives from their personal relationship, as all basketball ethics do. At the end of the film one gets the sense that these men will grow out of the con but hold onto the ethic of the game as they face a life in the open court.

THE BODY, MOVEMENT, SPACE

For depicting the pure kinetic beauty of basketball, television and film have roughly the same visual and technical resources. In both mediums, cameras can be placed at the perfect angle to capture the physical beauty of the game. Both can use slow-motion techniques to linger over the beauty of the athletic body, caught with a precise but dreamlike intensity. Think of the slow-motion replay of a fast break in which a great guard makes a spin move and no-look pass; we can see the precise footwork, the grace, the exquisite, improvised collaboration of bodies in movement. We can see such sights in the carefully choreographed opening montage of *He's Got Game*, but we also can see them in the most ordinary television production of any college or pro game. Indeed, one of the reasons basketball has gained its global cultural appeal is that television does beautifully represent the visual, physical culture of the game.

Where basketball movies have their advantage is in placing the beauty of the body in movement within the broader culture of the game and within the lives of the players. Films can show that kinetic bodies in basketball are not simply beautiful—they also have profound personal, social, and cultural meanings. Basketball is a cultural practice of the body, subjecting it to the disciplines of the game, engaging it in complex physical and emotional relationships with other bodies, expressing through it the players' subjectivities and histories. These cultural implications are much harder to depict in the decontextualized visual field of televised basketball. But in basketball films—as in basketball games—the body in play can express its own emotion, relate to other expressive bodies, and operate within a rich cultural environment. Or to put it in narrative terms, the beauty of the moving body can express character, generate drama, and live within an evocative setting. The body in basketball movies is *situated* and *expressive*, not simply beautiful. Basketball movies can therefore capture the physical culture of the game in ways that television cannot.

In *The Basketball Diaries*, Scott Kalvert's 1995 film version of the autobiography of punk musician and poet Jim Carroll, the bodies of basketball players have a powerful visual and emotional significance. Early in the film, set in the 1960s, basketball is presented as part of the tough white street kid life, a way of expressing aggression and youthful arrogance. The Carroll character, played by Leonardo DiCaprio, moves from court aggression to real-life aggression, fueled by heroin addiction and despair. Basketball remains in his life a reminder of lost joy, as we see in a scene in which he plays ball with Reggie, played by Ernie Hudson, an older black guy who has become his mentor and father figure. They play for the sheer pleasure of it, and their friendly game stands for the life Carroll has lost, a life in which basketball can be just a game, not an act of violent self-assertion. After a friend is killed by a life in the streets, there is a powerful scene in which basketball becomes a physical outlet, a way of expressing inarticulate emotion. Carroll and his gang are wandering the streets at night in despair and grief, and they return to their playground court, lit dramatically by the lightning of a driving rainstorm. The boys strip off their jackets and shirts and play desperately, in the pouring rain, their wild energy the only available expression of their emotions. The scene is set to the driving beat of Carroll's great song, "People Who Died," and the music intensifies the feelings visible on DiCaprio's face as he hangs on the rim and shouts out his pain.

This scene is a dramatic reminder of a fact of basketball culture—players do not leave their emotive lives on the sidelines. They bring their emotions onto the court, and their play is in part a function of those subjective states, visible in their demeanor and movements. Televised basketball cannot capture this emotional reality. We can see on TV when a player is angry or joyful, but we have no access to the sources of those emotions in the player's life. Players in pickup ball are keenly aware of emotions in the game. If a player comes to the court tensed in anger, then other players will leave him alone, not wanting to tangle with someone else's emotional business. If a player cannot focus full attention on the game—players will say "I'm just not here today"—then other players sense this emotional state and take it into account as they make the million strategy decisions that comprise the game. No TV coverage that I have seen can display this daily reality of basketball, but films can provide the life context that gives meaning to the actions of the bodies on the court.

Emotive bodies are everywhere in basketball movies. In Tim Blake Nelson's O, an adaptation of Shakespeare's Othello set in the world of prep school basketball, we see in Odin's body and his play the sexual and racial jealousy that is destroying him. In Hoosiers we see the growing confidence and love of the game that Norman Dale has produced in his players. In He Got Game we see the anger and frustration of a father schooling his son in the harsh reality of court life. In Soul in the Hole we see the anger and aggression of players who walk onto the court carrying the anger and aggression of the streets. In Hoop Dreams we see hope and despair play out on the bodies of the two young players the film documents. And as I mentioned at the outset of this chapter, in Love and Basketball we see bodies at play fueled by the sexuality of their relationship. In all of these films the kinetic bodies of players are represented beautifully, but they also are presented in the context of their off-court lives.

If basketball bodies in films are expressive, then they also are situated in a realistic cinematic space, open to the surrounding world, in contrast to the decontextualized spectacle of television coverage. Every television game occurs in the same space, a rough rectangle defined by theatrical lighting and a border of faceless fans. As a result, television cannot represent the spatial culture of basketball, which is always rooted in complex physical and social locations, fashioned and interpreted by the social action of the players, and conditioned by powerful social forces. To understand the culture of basketball one needs to begin with local spaces, integral to the social and cultural geography of communities. Every gym, every playground, every driveway, and every arena for that matter, may be the sacred space that Huizinga (1950) defines as the play space, but it is still radically open to local cultural practices. Basketball films have the resources and the motivation to place basketball visually in a local environment, which is where the game always happens. The motivation for this effort comes from the desire to create a rich setting for the characters in the drama, and the resources are mobile cameras with greater depth of field, able to cover the game but also to *see through* the game into the world around it.

Basketball films are almost always shot on location, and as a result they have the cultural authenticity of local geography. In *Smoke Signals*, the film adaptation of stories by Sherman Alexie, we see glimpses of basketball as it is played on Native American reservations. Basketball plays an important symbolic role in the film, but the symbolic effects would not resonate as they do unless they arose out of the local details of the game. Two scenes take place in a school gym, which reminds us of the pedagogic role of sports on native reservations, and another takes place on a hard dirt court with a metal backboard and no net, next to a trailer, which reminds us of the poverty and oppression that fuels the native appropriation of the white man's game. Official, organized basketball may be taught in reservation institutions such as school and church, but it has become an integral part of many tribal cultures, reverberating to ancient Mesoamerican origins, the beat of the ball on the court recalling the beat of ceremonial drums. The symbolic climax of *Smoke Signals* occurs in a father's mythic retelling of the story of the time he and his son defeated two missionaries in a two-on-two game. For the father, who is standing on that dirt court when he tells the story, that long-ago confrontation in the school gym has become a myth of poetic justice, symbolic revenge for the indignity and cultural violence imposed by white Americans. I say "myth" because in the story the son flies like Michael Jordan, like an avenging spirit, lifting the game into legend, into the father's personal mythology. What grounds this mythic story and connects it to the real world lives of its characters is its visual placement in culturally significant physical spaces, where the game is in fact played and where its political and cultural implications are visible.

Another school gym that operates symbolically is the beautiful home court in *Hoosiers*. This intimate, familiar environment is the place where the lessons of practice are learned and then displayed for the community. In the logic of the film, *practice* is the process by which the ethic of the game is learned, and *community* is the source of that ethic. We see the team learning the fundamentals, learning how to operate as a team in that gym, and then we see the gym filled with the people of the community, who see the team as a representative of their values. Of course basketball is played in thousands of such gyms in every town and city in America, which explains in part the emotional power of the film for audiences far from its Indiana locale. Despite its media representations, basketball is much more a game of such local courts than it is a game of the massive, interchangeable arenas that dominate big-time, televised basketball. And in *Hoosiers,* even when the plot takes us to such an arena, where the state championships are played, we see it not from the familiar perspective of the television camera but from the fresh perspective of these small-town kids who come to the big city. To them the arena looks like a cathedral, a sacred space for a game that transcends their small-town experience of it. No television coverage has ever conveyed that perspective, that way of turning a faceless civic structure into the projection of a naïve but powerful dream. Part of the power of *Hoosiers* is that basketball is played in spaces suffused with the feelings of the players and fans rather than in the antiseptic space of media ball.

One of the most distinctive local spaces in basketball movies is the Venice Beach court in *White Men Can't Jump.* In this film, director Ron Shelton and cinematographer Russell Boyd manage to frame the court action in understandable basketball terms and simultaneously to reveal around the court the social and cultural carnival that is Venice Beach. Boyd, whose long and varied career includes work on *Picnic at Hanging Rock, Gallipoli,* and *Tender Mercies,* moves the camera onto the court as the hustle goes down, but the camera also sees *through* the action to the sideline gawkers and folks just passing by, evoking the tough but vital cityscape of Los Angeles, the world that makes sense of the peculiarities of this local game. The crowd is fundamental to that game. Billy and Sidney take advantage of the fact that their opponents put their local status on the line. They do not want to be played as chumps in front of the people who respect them, so that when they realize they have been conned, they lose their temper and play ineffectively. And the streets play a fundamental role in the game as well. The same improvisational skills are necessary on and off of the court, the same ability to sell a fake, to take advantage of others' perceptions. Movies such as *White Men Can't Jump* restore basketball to its daily *visual* surroundings and therefore to its local social surroundings.

Soul in the Hole, a 1997 documentary directed by Danielle Gardner, did not receive the acclaim of *Hoop Dreams,* but for me *Soul in the Hole* is a stronger film, exactly because its cinematography, by Paul Gibson, has the same depth of focus that I described in *White Men Can't Jump,* but with a more serious ethnographic intent. *Soul in the Hole* makes it visually clear that basketball is part of, integral to, the street life of Brooklyn, not a space apart, a safe haven, cut off from the complexity of daily urban life. Gardner and Gibson's camera moves fluidly from the action on the court to the action around the court. There are beautiful street-level long shots in which pickup games on project courts are just one part of the scene, otherwise occupied by moms and kids, old folks sitting on benches, dealers and hustlers, boys on bikes, girls jumping rope, life proceeding. There are no theatrical lights to frame the game, no loving, slow-motion replays to fetishize its beauty. Basketball is just one practice among many, one of the ways of operating in a complex and dangerous environment. But not just dangerous. One of the great strengths of *Soul in the Hole* is that it displays the energy and vitality of street life along with its dangers. "Booger" Smith, the playground wizard who is at the center of the film, is torn between the upwardly mobile life that organized basketball can give him and the disreputable life of street ball and street hustling. *Soul in the Hole* makes the conflict real by portraying street ball and street life as plausible choices, with their own rewards and attractions. This is not a romantic film—the street is a violent and harsh place—but too many basketball films (I think of *Above the Rim*) oversimplify this choice by demonizing the streets—on the one hand, squalor, on the other hand, wealth and celebrity. No rational person could make the other-than-prescribed choice. *Soul in the Hole* poses that choice as a real set of alternatives. "Booger" has around him players and coaches who preach the mainstream road, not as a fairy-tale moral path but as a realistic way of improving his own life and the community's life. But by placing the game in a vital, intense, and appealing social world, this film truly dramatizes that choice by visualizing the context in which it occurs.

Because they keep us in touch with the body in the game, basketball films also are good at depicting the intense emotional relationships—positive and negative—that physical contact can generate. Basketball films show us the hypermasculine aggression and violence that the game can foster, as well as the toxic relationships that can develop among players. The camera loves players who beat their chests and pump their fists and swagger over the opponent they have knocked to the floor. On television, in game coverage, highlight shows, rap videos, and commercials for teen products, these expressions of rage and physical power are commodified, selling mostly black male bodies that express in exaggerated form the repressed emotions of their mostly white audience. Media coverage exaggerates this violence for narrative and theatrical effect, but basketball in itself does sometimes encourage aggression and regulated violence. Insofar as basketball, like other sports, is an element in the traditional pedagogy of gender, it teaches men that such violence is natural, part of the game, a force that can be made use of, sublimated into hustle and team spirit. But even within that traditional pedagogy there is an understanding that this force is not always successfully sublimated, that it can turn personal and vengeful, that it can defy the ethical constraints and turn to outright criminal violence.

These outbreaks of male violence of course make strong plot points for basketball films. In Tim Blake Nelson's *O*, an adaptation of *Othello*, the toxic potential of ultracompetitive basketball is explored. Odin is the black stud brought in to play at an otherwise lily-white prep school in Charleston, South Carolina. Hugo is the son of the coach, now relegated to a supporting role on the team, setting the picks and fighting for the rebounds that make Odin's high-flying game possible. Hugo's desire to play the leading role, to demand the full attention of his father, fuels his jealousy of Odin, against whom he plots and schemes. Nelson's understanding of the racial politics of the game grounds the plot. Odin plays the dominant and spectacular "black" game, while Hugo plays the supporting role with his fundamentally sound "white" game, reversing the racial hierarchy in America and for sure in Charleston. Hugo's anger seethes throughout the film as Odin displays his talent, mesmerizing the father and the prize girl at the school, the daughter of the dean. Where Shakespeare grounded Iago's anger at Othello in the griping of a blue-collar soldier who feels his contribution is taken for granted, Nelson grounds Hugo's anger in the resentment of a blue-collar white player against a great black star. Because of this foundation in believable basketball politics, *O* provides a powerful critique of the role that sports play in encouraging a bitter, angry masculinity that seeks outlets in violence.

There are moments of violence in virtually all basketball films, from the verbal violence of woofing to the routine spats that can erupt in any game, all the way to intentional acts of violence with intent to injure. In *Hoosiers* there are conflicts with rival towns, in *Above the Rim* there are thugs working for the dealers who try to take out opposing players, in *Soul in the Hole* there are battles over street rep, in *Basketball Diaries* there are mean-spirited games that lead out into street violence, and in *White Men Can't Jump* there is constant woofing and the danger of revenge from those who have been conned. This motif of violence suggests that films can commodify male violence just as much as television. But in all of these films, violence and excessive aggression are condemned as betrayals of the game, unethical and downright mean. Of course these films retain the visual spectacle of male violence even as they condemn it, but they at least place that male violence in a complex human context.

Basketball films also manage to capture the physical pleasure of the game and the friendly connections it fosters. The easy physicality of the game and its comfortable intimacy of touch tend not to be plot points but routine moments along the way. There is such a moment in *Smoke Signals*, when some players who have just left the court sit and talk. I recognized the sheen of sweat, the comfort of well-used bodies, the easy connection among them. In *Finding Forrester*, there are scenes of intense competition verging on violence, but there also are pleasant scenes of Jamal and his friends shooting around at their local court, scenes that ground Jamal in a web of relationships that sustains his talents. In *Love and Basketball* there are friendly locker room scenes in which women who play the game together tease and joke with the ease that comes from shared effort. But the film that best depicts this aspect of the culture of basketball is *White Men Can't Jump*, which depicts it on the court. The games in the film are all shot intimately, with characters in close physical proximity, and with the camera right on the court so the audience shares the intimacy. *White Men Can't Jump* is a strong visual reminder that the basketball court is a small space occupied by bodies in complex motion. As a result of that kinetic and somatic energy, players develop a casual ease with one another, whether they like each other or not. For me this is the positive contribution that basketball makes to the formation of masculinity—the physical intimacy of the game can create positive and nonviolent connections among men, over against the ultracompetitive violence that also is part of its culture, and basketball films capture both aspects of the game's complex physical culture.

COGNITIVE STYLES

One would think that the cognitive practices of basketball culture would be invisible, unavailable to the camera or to the naked eye. And in a way that is true. One of the great pleasures of watching basketball is the display of pure creativity that leaves one wondering, "How did he see that?" "What was she thinking?" There is a mystery to the game, an uncanny quality, because so much of the game is mental and therefore in a sense invisible. Nevertheless, basketball films do capture the mental game, do let us see the cognitive style that the culture of the game promotes. In fact, both films and television have visual access to this cognitive dynamic because basketball requires *embodied* cognition, *kinetic* cognition. That is, the mental processes of basketball are so complex, operating at such high speeds, processing so much information through such a finely articulated grid, that these processes *must* be deeply embodied, practiced into the synapses and nerve endings and eyes and muscles of players. To watch these bodies in motion is therefore to watch cognition in action, the instantaneous, improvisational cognitive style of basketball culture.

The mental game of basketball requires a group of players to make frequent and instantaneous decisions together, to improvise plays in the moment, to create the game on the fly. In basketball movies this cognitive improvisation is evident in the most routine game footage, simply because it is always part of the game, even in the most ordinary pass or shot. Whenever two or more of us gather together, we will improvise the game. It is easy, natural. You can see it in the friendly schoolyard games of *Finding Forrester*, in the intense pickup games captured in *Soul in the Hole*, in the WNBA games of *Love and Basketball*, in the driveway game of *Grand Canyon*, and even on Norman Dale's very coached team in *Hoosiers*. The embodied and therefore visible cognitive style of basketball culture is captured naturally by these films, along the way to telling their stories. This cognitive style is so embedded in the culture that you could not make a film about basketball without displaying it. Even TV coverage gets it right, at least visually. Slow motion and replay can *show* us what the great player saw, how the great, unexpected decision was made. What basketball films do is connect that cognitive style to the life of characters and to the culture of the game and of the society in which it is embedded.

In *He Got Game*, for example, the pure freedom of Earl Monroe's improvisation stands as a symbol for the game that Jake Shuttlesworth wants to pass on to his son Jesus. For Jake, Earl Monroe is "The Truth," a player who cared only about the beauty and creative openness of the game, not about the money or the prestige. Jesus Shuttlesworth has to face the corruption of the pro and college game, and Jake wants him to have an image of the game's improvisatory beauty in his head as he tries to hold onto authentic play in a world that does not respect it. In *Soul in the Hole* and *White Men Can't Jump*, the mental game becomes a metaphor for the characters' ways of negotiating daily life. "Booger" Smith, the central figure in *Soul in the Hole*, is a creative master on the court. He can handle and pass the ball in ways that defy reason. And his life off of the court is similarly creative. "Booger" cannot follow the prescribed, respectable path toward college ball and the pros; he is addicted to the improvised daily life of the street, where his court skills he hopes will translate into hustling skills, survival skills. The film makes it clear that those skills probably will not be enough, without the support of a team, a family, some social structure that cares for him, but it also understands the appeal of leading a life without a script, a life in the open court.

In *White Men Can't Jump*, which I believe has the best cinematic depiction of pickup ball in a mainstream film, Billy and Sidney have to learn a similar lesson about social ties. The film beautifully visualizes the interplay on the court, the group improvisations that are pickup ball. There are Hollywood excesses—improbable trick shots, show-off camera angles— but the film does capture the fact that Billy and Sidney understand each other's moves and decisions, that they share a cognitive style. In fact, all of the guys they play against have the same "instincts," the same ability to make rapid decisions in a fluid information environment, in concert with other decision-making subjects—in other words, they are all ballplayers. Billy and Sidney need to learn to trust that connection, use it to overcome the differences that divide them—racial tension, cutthroat competition, ego conflicts, battles for local supremacy. Billy is an outsider, Sidney a local. For much of the plot they allow those differences to divide and weaken them, off of the court and on it, but they eventually recognize that their on-court similarities are a function of real-life similarities—they are both the same age, a little too old for the playgrounds, both trying to learn responsibility in their social connections, with their families, the women in their lives. For both of them, it is now time to put the court skills to work outside of the game, in the tough economic struggle, which itself requires the ability to think on one's feet, to make the best move possible in the conditions in which one finds oneself.

In one way the narrative of *White Men Can't Jump* works as a conventional story of male education. These playful, egocentric boys have to become responsible, other-directed men. But in that conventional story, maturation requires entry into an established social position in a recognizable hierarchy. In this film maturation involves making commitments to others who can then negotiate together the fluid social environment of contemporary culture. It means playing ball with people, relying on the connections that shared practices create, making up the game as one goes along, operating by the ethic and mind-set of basketball. To play pickup basketball is to live in postmodern culture, with few or no certainties, and to construct an unfolding reality through a social and cultural practice.

Inevitably, this cognitive mode conflicts with institutional requirements for predictability and discipline, embodied in the figure of the coach. Organized basketball is based on the premise that cognitive creativity must be subservient to hierarchically imposed performance goals. In contrast with the free play of pickup, organized ball subjects players to a network of institutional constraints—remember when they outlawed the dunk? Each coach has to decide how much free play will be allowed, how much the pickup game has to be harnessed and regularized. Some call a rigid play every time down the court, while some let the ballplayers play within general strategic guidelines. Mike Krzyzewski of Duke is probably the most successful coach who relies on the instincts of his players. Even in the last seconds of close games he often will not call a time-out, trusting his point guard and scorers to improvise in the moment. This trust in players' instincts makes Krzyzewski the sheer opposite of *Hoosiers'* Norman Dale, who wants to control every movement of his players. Dale is a coach from the old school, where top-down discipline imposes order on the chaos of the schoolyard. But even Dale learns that pure basketball creativity must be respected. As Spike Lee has pointed out, for all of Dale's talk of team-oriented discipline, he decides at the key moment to trust the individual talent of his star player. Instead of going with the clever set play that a coach would devise, Dale puts the ball in his star's hands, clears everyone else out, and lets him improvise, taking his man off the dribble. And even more out of character, the kids are the ones who convince him to trust the creative moment. When he calls the clever play in the huddle, a play that uses the star as a decoy in order to set up an easier shot for another player, the kids visibly lose their energy. They have been out on the court; they know who has the hot hand. And in pickup ball, you always go to the hot hand. At the key moment, that is, unquestioning obedience gives way to court instinct, to the feel of the game, to the creativity of the players. In *Hoosiers* this moment of resistance to authority is recuperated in conservative fashion as the attainment of maturity. Coach Dale tore them down, so now they have built themselves back up. They have accepted discipline, so now they are capable of making their own decisions, standing up for themselves. But the moment retains a disruptive quality. Throughout the film the messages of discipline and obedience are drilled on and off of the court. But at the key plot moment, the true culture of the game takes over, expressing itself even in this most institutionalized context. The cognitive culture of the game proves stronger than the institutions that try to master it.

PLAYER AND FAN COMMUNITIES

Basketball culture engages with questions of community on many levels. Players create communities out of their shared involvement in the practice; local games connect with local cultures and communities; school and professional teams come to represent various imagined communities; representations of the game are circulated through global media communities, allowing the game to interact with yet more local practices. Players' communities develop over time as they engage in the practice of the game. Our most common image of this process is an organized team that creates an intense community through its shared experience of practices and games, bus rides and locker room speeches. Beyond the world of organized ball, player communities are less visible, less easy to fit into a Hollywood narrative, but they exist in even the most casual backyard game and especially in long-term pickup games with regular players. In these local circumstances, in and through the practice of the game, players create informal but powerful communities, with shared ethical standards, movement styles, and mental strategies.

Basketball films often deal with pickup basketball, but this endlessly shifting community is less suited than an organized, competitive team to the dramatic narrative line required of the sports film genre. In pickup ball today's teammates are tomorrow's opponents, or perhaps they are never seen again. The dramatic moments are more momentary, more interpersonal. They are not public events that take on the dramatic weight that comes with the status of the spectacle. To tell the story of a pickup community would take the nuanced skill of a short story writer who could capture the dramatic significance of a brief encounter, or the social novelist's ability to tell multiple stories of many characters who connect in different ways with a local community and within a larger social fabric. In film terms, it would take a John Sayles or a Robert Altman, social realists with a sense of how complex communities work. Few basketball films deal with the pickup game in that larger cultural frame, but several films do provide some glimpses of the local communities that players produce in the act of playing.

A sentimental liberal version of this community of players occurs in *Grand Canyon*, in which a common interest in basketball and a session of driveway hoops help Mack, a white, upper-middle-class lawyer, and Simon, a black, working-class tow truck operator, "overcome their cultural differences and discover their common humanity," as the Hollywood cliché would have it. In their friendly game, Mack and Simon get to woof at each other a bit, talk about their women and their families, and bond as men who face the same problems in the same larger, American community, transcending the fierce divisions of race and class that threaten the social fabric. I say "sentimental" because their transcendence is all too easy and too total. I do believe that basketball as a practice can connect those who play, even if they are from radically opposed social groups. But those connections do not undo the oppositions—connection and opposition exist at the same time. Basketball as a shared practice does not bring us all to the Grand Canyon, before which we share a simple humanity. It can make the divisions more complex, less rigid and inevitable, but membership in the basketball community does not cancel membership in other communities or eliminate the tensions between them. It can open up a utopian vision of a world in which we recognize our everyday connections as well as our deep divisions, but it cannot magically produce that world.

Soul in the Hole takes a much more realistic look at the community of players, in this case streetball players from Brooklyn. For these players the community of ballplayers is an extended surrogate family, with intense loyalties and rivalries. Their team for the summer, Kenny's Kings, is the center of this network of relationships, though it is important to remember that all of these players play for other teams—high school teams, church league teams, pickup teams, local club teams, and so on. Kenny's Kings feels like a family, but it is only one of many such social structures that together constitute the fabric of community within the culture of basketball. Players go off to other games with other teams; they have histories with other players in other contexts. They are a tight group, but not a self-contained group. What gives Kenny's Kings the feel of a family is the presence of Kenny King himself, the coach and father figure. He and his wife develop a parental relationship with Booger Smith, the street ball legend and lost soul who haunts the film. Booger has great court skills, but he never seems present in the moment. He is always already somewhere else, back out in some other hustle. Kenny King, on the other hand, is a solid and commanding presence. He has connections everywhere in the community, through his jobs and moneymaking plans, but primarily through basketball. Kenny King is *known*, he is a figure in the community of players. *Soul in the Hole* shows us the on-court interplay and the off-court relationships within a community of players and between that community and the complex social world it inhabits.

Many basketball films also capture the ways that basketball teams can come to represent that larger community by depicting the relationships between teams and their fans. Movies as diverse as *Hoosiers* and *Soul in the Hole* are able to convey the powerful emotions of fans and the sense of community that basketball can create in a local context. In *Soul in the Hole* there are several games when neighborhood pride drives the fans ringing the court into outbursts of elation or aggression. They press on to the court, react visibly and viscerally to every move. They invest their bodies in the success of the local guys struggling against the outsider hotshots. The fact that their local community is scorned by mainstream society, seen as a center of crime and poverty and hopelessness, only increases the fervor of the identification. Here is one place we succeed, they say, and they stake their self-esteem and their identity on the outcome of the local struggle. A similar dynamic occurs in the very different community setting of *Hoosiers*. The local townspeople feel that they own the team, to the point of trying to unseat Coach Dale when they disapprove of his methods. They know their boys, and they are sure that their style of play works best. To them Dale and his style are aliens. They want to play zone and shoot jump shots. He wants to play man and move the ball. For the people of the town, these differences *matter*, and it is only after Dale convinces them that he has the best interests of the kids at heart that the town is willing to grant him the total authority he wants. It is a sign of how formulaic *Hoosiers* is, that once the team begins to succeed, all conflicts are forgotten, and the fans become unproblematically identified with the team, which they now see as the expression of their own local virtues. *Hoosiers* does not make any note of this irony; rather, it represents the fans in a wholehearted identification with the players. They suffer with the team, they are elated with the team, they are all members of an organic community taking pleasure in its own righteousness. *Hoosiers* appeals to audiences because it invites them to join that community. It imagines an organic, utopian community in which difference is eliminated and all practices express the same values.

Taken together, basketball movies represent the diversity of basketball communities. They take us into players' communities and fan communities, into elite, organized basketball and into casual pickup games. They show us basketball played in prep schools, ghetto high schools, prisons, schoolyards, and massive commercial arenas. Players in these films are black and white, male and female, urban and rural, rich and poor, gifted and ordinary, intense and casual, and professional and amateur. They form communities as diverse as the friends shooting a few hoops in *Finding Forrester*, the elite pickup teams in *He Got Game*, the summer league family of *Soul in the Hole*, and the incestuous, toxic teammates of *O*. And in all of these diverse social and cultural settings, the game itself looks equally diverse. On television, every game may look the same, but in basketball films the game is revealed in its beautiful variety, enmeshed as it always is in complex local circumstances.

RACIAL IDENTITY

One of the watershed moments in the history of basketball and its racial dynamic came in 1966 when Texas Western, with a team that featured five black starters, defeated Kentucky's all-white team, coached by the legendary Adolph Rupp. This famous game is the subject of the 2006 Disney film *Glory Road*. The film focuses on Texas Western's then-young coach, Don Haskins, who takes over an unsuccessful team and realizes that one way he can improve the team quickly is to recruit black players overlooked by major college teams that had imposed on themselves an informal but a widely accepted quota system that limited the number of black players that would be acceptable to the fans. Haskins, played in the film by Josh Lucas, convinces these black players that when he watches them play, he does not see race, he sees skill. The film then depicts his stalwart support of the players who prevail in the face of bigotry and harassment from white teams and their racist fans. Obviously race is the central theme of the film, and it does justice to the courage of the players and the coach who were able to focus on the game in the midst of a dangerous moment for American society. We see quite graphically the racism they are up against, and the film enlists our support for their defiance of the status quo.

But all is not harmonious within the team, and the conflict arises from the differences between "black ball" and "white ball," as they are defined within basketball culture. Haskins is attracted to the players precisely because of their "black" styles—the creative ball handling of Bobby Joe Hill and the powerful dunks of David Lattin—but then he tries to impose on them a set of "white" practices that would make Coach Dale proud: defense, passing, team ball, deliberate offensive play. The black players feel stifled and bored, and they force Haskins to realize that the solution is a negotiated synthesis of the two styles. In the climactic final game against Kentucky, Western plays fierce defense and handles the ball carefully, trying to control Kentucky's powerful fast break offense, but it also tries to physically intimidate its opponents, setting David Lattin loose for a powerful dunk on the first play of the game, confirming the Kentucky players' fears that they would be dominated by the athleticism of the black players. This insider awareness of the racial culture of the game gives texture to a film that might otherwise have become a true "Disney" story of racial uplift.

The film also succeeds to some degree in placing the racial identity of the team within the social and cultural context of El Paso, Texas, home of Texas Western (now University of Texas at El Paso). When they first arrive in west Texas from their city homes, the black players feel like they have traveled to the moon, and they simply do not fit into the culture of the place. They are surrounded by white cowboys and Mexicans, and they have to negotiate their place on campus and in the community. And then they have to face life in the still segregated South—restaurants and hotels that will not serve them, fans who feel entitled to hurl racial epithets at them, boosters who do not like the idea of a black-dominated team. *Glory Road* is in many ways a conventional sports narrative, with an underdog team winning the championship and earning the respect of its fans and opponents, but it does succeed in facing the facts of race at a time when black players still had to fight to create a space for themselves in the game.

Many basketball films deal with the issue of race in basketball culture in terms of the unrealistic "hoop dreams" that lead many young black players to believe that they can rise out of poverty on the strength of their basketball skills. Cultural critics have lamented the fact that because of the allure of media fame and wealth associated with the game, which seem in movies and on television so easy to attain, professional athletics, especially basketball, come to be seen as a workable plan—in fact, as the *only* workable plan—for a successful economic future, in spite of the overwhelming odds against making money from basketball skills. The playgrounds are full of guys who thought they could make it—still think they could—and who have no other viable plans for their lives, at an incalculable cost to

black social and economic life. *Hoop Dreams* is a film version of this critique, exploring the false hopes driven by media images that often divert
young black men from more substantial work on their futures. But many
other basketball films focus on young players with exactly that dream, who
ride it all the way to fairy-tale success. Basketball films, like many sports
films, have an unshakeable belief in the power of individual talent and
drive to overcome all socially constructed obstacles. They are what Bruce
Robbins calls in an essay on *Hoop Dreams* "upward mobility narratives,"
reinforcing the American ideology of individual achievement while ignoring the social forces that subordinate racial and other groups. Aaron Baker
agues that basketball films often are complicit in the media tendency to
turn basketball into a mythic narrative of black success in a white world,
one that reassures whites that the system works if you try hard while
teaching blacks that their success can occur only in and through the body,
displayed for white pleasure. I will argue, however, that films such as *Hoop
Dreams*, *He Got Game*, and *Above the Rim* provide a critique of that narrative, even as they play it out.

Television coverage of basketball has made the rags-to-riches stories
in the NBA a part of the national mythology. We have all seen the domestic
dramas of the NBA draft, in which young men in huge and beautiful suits
hug their brave and supportive mothers and promise to make up for all of
the sacrifices they made in protecting the players from the harsh realities
of ghetto life. This scene is the climax of the "upward mobility narrative,"
and it reinforces the myth that basketball is a viable strategy for success.
In this narrative, basketball is the antidote to the poisonous temptations of
street life, a way to become part of the larger world, with its lavish wealth
and media hype. *Hoop Dreams*, *Soul in the Hole*, *He Got Game*, and *Above
the Rim* all examine this narrative with a critical eye. And in all of these
films, the narrative is racially charged—in order to succeed, these young
black men will have to come to terms with the white institutions that
control access to that wealth and fame, and they will have to deal with the
local culture of basketball and of the neighborhood, which nourished their
skill but which can mix them up in dangerous pursuits—drugs and women
and hustlers and street agents—that will destroy the dream of success.
They will have to learn how to deal with white coaches, white universities,
white businessmen, white fans, and white media, all of which can be fickle
friends, while simultaneously renegotiating their connections to their own
black history and culture.

Above the Rim is the least critical in its use of this narrative. The
prospect of success in the NBA is treated as a realistic if difficult goal, the
institutions that support the elite game are benign and concerned for Kyle's
welfare, and his mother serves as a model of responsible, successful living.

In exchange for success in this narrative, Kyle has to reject his "black game," which is too selfish, too spectacular, too risky for the carefully calibrated college game. He has to accept the team concept, the authority of the coach, the white institutions that make the game possible, in order to fulfill his own fantasies of success. *Above the Rim* is about a "hoop dream" that succeeds, and the price required, submitting to rightful authority, is presented as the attainment of responsible manhood. In terms of racial politics, what is interesting about *Above the Rim* is that many of the authority figures who represent those white institutions are African Americans. The film evokes John Thompson, then coach of Georgetown, as the authority who validates the success narrative. His program showed that tough city black kids could succeed athletically and academically at an elite white university. If Kyle learns to play with the team, to play what the game calls "white ball," then his path through college to the pros is assured. But even more than Thompson it is Shep who has the local credibility of a once great player, who gives authority to the narrative. Shep has learned through bitter experience that playing with integrity is part of becoming a responsible adult, which for him will mean becoming the new local coach, where he can pass on the ethic of the game to the next generation. Shep is an argument for the contention that what gets characterized as "white ball" is in fact the ethic of the game, the way the game wants to be played, and that the error lies in believing that white people own that style of play and the ethic of responsibility that supports it. Shep does not need to repudiate his blackness in order to lead a mature, responsible life, and Kyle learns the lesson. What sustains this narrative in *Above the Rim* is an unquestioning belief in the white-dominated institutions that make this success possible. In this film coaches are caring, scouts follow the rules, and success in basketball serves as an entryway into the righteous social order they represent.

In Spike Lee's *He Got Game*, that belief is exploded. The business of the game is corrupt, and the corruption goes all the way to the highest levels of power. Lee contrasts the purity of the game with the hypocrisy of its official culture, and in the process he reverses the valence on the racial oppositions in the game. Lee believes in the righteousness of the improvised game, the "black game," over against the soulless system that preaches selflessness but practices selfish corruption. To be a responsible person in *He Got Game* is to live up to one's own principles, to play the game of life with the purity and intensity of the righteous pickup game. The tragedy of the film is that the father has to sacrifice himself in order for the son to have the opportunity to live his life fully. The black father in this film is the real model of selflessness, over against the white men in power who merely preach it.

The basketball success narrative also is central to *Hoop Dreams*. I think of *Hoop Dreams* as a great social studies project of a movie, carefully conventional and didactic. Its goal is to personalize the social problem of the black underclass turning in desperate hope to the promise of basketball as the way to gain affluence and celebrity. It follows two young players from the Chicago slums who get the opportunity to attend a private, Catholic high school because of their basketball skills. They and their families see this opportunity as the beginning of an inevitable rise to success, defined by making it in big-time college and eventually pro ball. They all also hope that the suburban atmosphere and the educational discipline of the school will rescue the boys from the failed public schools of their city. But no one forgets that basketball is the vehicle, in fact the whole point of the endeavor. The class benefits of associating with a school that creates educational opportunity and cultural capital are secondary to a much grander class desire—not to enter into the middle class but to leap to the fantasy wealth of the NBA. Part of the poignancy of the film is that the figures of William Gates and Arthur Agee, the film's protagonists, remind us that thousands of similar kids follow the same dream with the same naïve confidence. Although the film manages to take us into the distinctly personal details of their individual lives, they never stop being *examples* of the social problem the film is out to elucidate. They are case studies in an educational project designed to explain to white audiences the consequences of dangling images of great wealth and media fame in front of black kids who come from desperate poverty.

In "Neo-Colonial Fantasies of Conquest: *Hoop Dreams*," bell hooks (1996) describes the alienating experience of being a person of color in an otherwise all-white audience watching a film that claims to document the reality of black life:

> As the film began, a voyeuristic pleasure at being able to observe from a distance the lives of two black boys from working class and poor inner city backgrounds overcame the crowd. This lurid fascination with "watching" a documentary about two African American teenagers striving to become NBA players was itself profound documentation of the extent to which blackness has become commodified in this society—the degree to which black life, particularly the lives of poor and underclass black people, can become cheap entertainment even if that is not what the filmmakers intended. (1996, 78)

Her description casts the white people in the audience as hypocritical voyeurs, enjoying their privilege while indulging their liberal guilt. The audiende, hooks argues, gets to have its cake and eat it too: it recognizes that the film uncovers the cruelty of an exploitive system, but it is reassured that the American dream works, that even doomed dreams are inspiring and quintessentially American. Thus the American dream of individual progress is affirmed even in this story of failed dreams. Better to have hoped for more than to accept poverty and despair. And hooks herself is of two minds about the film: She sees it as confirming prejudices and stereotypes by displaying once again for a white audience the dysfunction of the black family, especially the black father, but she also admires the fact that it "acknowledges the positive aspects of black life that make survival possible."

I see the film as a more *critical* document than hooks does. At one point she says that "this film tells the world that the American dream works" (1996, 78), quoting the white coach of the prep school team who says to his kids: "This is America. You can make something of your life." But in the narrative of the film this coach is clearly the villain, the personification of the exploitive system that offers a false dream and then uses up the kids it seduces. Coach Pignatone appeals to the kids and their families with a rhetoric of uplift and belonging, but when Arthur Agee turns out not to be as good as the coach hoped, his scholarship help disappears, and when William Gates is injured, Pignatone pushes him back on the court before he is healed, causing a more serious injury that destroys his chances of playing at the highest level. Pignatone is revealed in the film to be a hypocrite and a user, so his assertion of the American dream rings hollow. He is the agent of the system that the film wants to unmask. In fact, he is such a villain that Bruce Robbins (1997), in " 'Head Fake': Mentorship and Mobility in *Hoop Dreams*," takes the film to task for being too hard on the mentors—such as coaches and school administrators—who Robbins sees as essential figures for underclass kids who want to find a path to any kind of success in a hierarchical society. This is not to say that the film flatly rejects the notion of upward mobility through basketball but that it documents the dangerous terrain that such mobility must negotiate.

I agree with hooks's analysis of the complex representation of black underclass society in the film. Both players have to deal with the weaknesses of their families, who have as much invested in their success as the kids themselves. Missing or weak fathers, families on the edge of financial ruin—just the figures to fulfill the expectations of a white audience. But *Hoop Dreams* also documents the courageous struggles of those families, overcoming drug problems, searching for jobs, finding faith, and getting training for working-class careers. Arthur and William do not live in a world of victimized, helpless black people. The young players and their families are not simply the passive victims of a corrupt white system. They are social agents who make complex decisions in a dangerous and racially divided world. Arthur Agee finds basketball success and communal belonging with his public school team, coached by a black man who understands the world his players face. William Gates finds happiness with his girlfriend and their child, who replace basketball as the focus of his life. Both players are depicted as living in a textured and layered social world, and the film succeeds to some degree in understanding basketball within the context of African American cultural life. *Hoop Dreams* wants to understand how basketball operates in that complex social world. Television images of the game are always present in the film, as the source of the hopeless dreams of kids who live in the bleak world that the film starkly represents. The contrast between the glamour of the big-time game and the harshness of black underclass social realities is powerful.

Hoop Dreams is clearly an outsider's view of that reality. It is a white film for white audiences. It focuses like a sociologist on *someone else's* problems. The documentarians' cameras descend from another world into the context that they want the audience to understand, and then they disengage and go home. I am not saying that no white filmmaker could possibly make a film that represented black culture accurately, but I am acknowledging that such an achievement would be very difficult within the context of a film industry that routinely plays to the least common cultural denominators, the clichés that audiences bring with them into the theater. Both black and white audiences know the stereotypes down to their bones, and even if they reject them, the stereotypes remain as familiar outlines that a film, even a black-produced film, must be tempted to fill in according to the prescribed formula. These financial and professional constraints explain why the record of basketball films as representatives of black culture is so mixed. The impulse to realism meets the need to work within formal and social conventions.

Nevertheless, the outsider's perspective of *Hoop Dreams* also is one of its strengths. The film never claims an insider's view—its middle-class, liberal perspective is easy for all to see, in its earnest conviction that something is wrong with a system that manipulates children for selfish institutional purposes. *Hoop Dreams* is a moralistic film, based on a humanistic belief that institutions and individuals in power ought to have in mind the interests of the children they serve, not their own. Because of the conventionality of the filmmakers' goals and methods, they were able to access *all* of the figures in the success narrative—the kids themselves and their families and friends, but also coaches, teachers, and school administrators. As a result of this comprehensive social vision, the film is able to unmask the narrative as a myth that serves the needs of white institutions while it jerks around the talented black kids who play the game. *Hoop Dreams* may have an outsider's perspective, but it compensates for that weakness by developing a broad and critical perspective.

Thus *White Men Can't Jump, He Got Game, Above the Rim,* and all of the others hope in their different ways to convey the reality of black life, even if they often confirm stereotypes at the same time. They take us onto the streets, into homes, to parties and family gatherings, and to restaurants and shops, into the daily culture of African American life, in a way that television coverage of basketball (and in fact television in general) rarely does. If TV keeps basketball and its black cultural style within the frame of the public spectacle, then movies can portray the texture and complexity of black life that surrounds the game.

CONCLUSION

Films about basketball give us access to local basketball cultures that we would never otherwise experience. No one in the audiences for these films has ever inhabited all of the cultural locations they represent. No one has played in prison and on a reservation and in a prep school and in an Indiana high school and in Brooklyn and in Venice Beach. All basketball players inhabit their own local communities, producing their own culture in that local context. We can forget how local our practices are, how determined they are by our own histories and relationships and unexamined assumptions. Basketball films take us to *other* local circumstances, other ways of playing and being, other social groups just as certain of the naturalness of their local practices as we are of ours. Taken together, they can serve the same function as the opening montage of *He Got Game,* to remind us of the diversity and "localness" of basketball, its entanglements in many and various American subcultures and circumstances. Because of their narrative and cinematic conventions, these films show us basketball in a personal and social context, never in the visual and symbolic isolation that television imposes on it.

Those conventions, however, also are responsible for the clichés and stereotypes that structure the narratives of basketball films. We cannot forget that these films also give us a highly *mediated* access to these cultures. They are representations, not direct experiences, of local realities. Their cliché plots and stereotyped characters domesticate differences for the purpose of mass consumption across cultural barriers. They cannot ultimately capture the lived complexity of local practices, but in this limitation they are not unique. All representations fail to represent; the other always remains other. Films take on the challenge of complex cultural representation in a way that television rarely dares, and if they fail, they fail at a useful task, the task of reminding local social subjects that other local social subjects exist, and that their differences matter. And at the same time they remind us that those differences are not absolutely beyond our ken. Those other local practices are truly different, but they are recognizably variants of the same practice. The game is different in Indiana and in Coney Island, but it is still basketball. We can see in both of those places how the game has adapted and evolved, but we also see common traits, habits of thinking and moving and feeling, that identify all of these variants as variants of *basketball*, a recognizable practice even in and through all of its local iterations.

Those guys over there, in that game in which I have never played, in a schoolyard where I never went to school, have a community to which I can never belong. The game they play makes sense to them through a set of experiences and expectations that I will never have. But if I got in the game, I would figure out a lot of things pretty damn quick. I would know who could play and who could not. I would know who to trust and who to fear. I would know whose head was in the game and who did not have a clue. I would know who had physical courage, or spiritual strength, or perfect skill, or dangerous intensity. I would know because we would be engaged in the same practice, for all of the local differences, and in that knowledge I would connect in a way that would insinuate itself subtly across those lines of differences. Basketball films remind us of how local our practice is, but also how deeply our practice inhabits all of us.

Works Cited

Anderson, Lars, and Chad Millman. 1998. *Pickup Artists: Street Basketball in America.* London: Verso.

Araton, Harvey. 2005. *Crashing the Borders: How Basketball Won the World and Lost Its Soul at Home.* New York: Free Press.

Archetti, Eduardo. 1999. *Masculinities: Football, Polo, and the Tango in Argentina.* Oxford: Berg.

Ardener, Shirley, ed. 1993. *Women and Space: Ground Rules and Social Maps.* London: Oxford University Press.

Baldwin, James. 1961. "The Black Boy Looks at the White Boy." In *Nobody Knows My Name: More Notes of a Native Son,* 216–41. New York: Dell.

Barrett, Lyndon. 1977. "Black Men in the Mix: Badboys, Heroes, Sequins, and Dennis Rodman." *Callaloo* 20: 106–26.

Bell, David E., Howard Raiffa, and Amos Tversky, eds. 1988. *Decision Making: Descriptive, Normative, and Prescriptive Interaction.* Cambridge: Cambridge University Press.

Birrell, Susan, and Mary G. McDonald. 2000. *Reading Sport: Critical Essays on Power and Representation.* Boston: Northeastern University Press.

Blythe, Will. 2006. *To Hate Like This Is to Be Happy Forever.* New York: Harper Collins.

Bourdieu, Pierre. 1977. *Outline of a Theory of Practice.* Trans. Richard Nice. Cambridge: Cambridge University Press.

———. 1990. *The Logic of Practice.* Trans. Richard Nice. Stanford, CA: Stanford University Press.

Boyd, Todd. 1997. *Am I Black Enough for You?: Popular Culture from the 'Hood and Beyond.* Bloomington: Indiana University Press.

———. 2000. "Mo Money, Mo Problems." In *Basketball Jones: America above the Rim,* ed. Todd Boyd and Kenneth L. Shropshire, 59–67. New York: New York University Press.

Bradley, Bill. 1976. *A Life on the Run.* New York: Quadrangle Books.

———. 1998. *Values of the Game.* New York: Artisan.

Brownell, Susan. 1995. *Training the Body for China: Sports in the Moral Order of the People's Republic.* Chicago: University of Chicago Press.

Burstyn, Varda. 1999. *The Rites of Men: Manhood, Politics, and the Culture of Sport.* Toronto: University of Toronto Press.

Cannon-Bowers, Janis A., Eduardo Salas, and Sharolyn Converse. 1993. "Shared Mental Models in Expert Team Decision Making." In *Individual and Group Decision Making: Current Issues*, ed. N. John Castellan, 221–46. Hillsdale, NJ: Lawrence Erlbaum Associates.

Caponi-Tabery, Gina. 2002. "Jump for Joy: Jump Blues, Dance, and Basketball in 1930's African America." In *Sport Matters: Race, Recreation, and Culture*, ed. John Bloom and Michael Nevin Willard, 39–74. New York: New York University Press.

Carrigan, Tim, Bob Connell, and John Lee. 1985. "Towards a New Sociology of Masculinity." *Theory and Society* 14: 551–603.

Carrington, Ben, David L. Andrews, Steven J. Jackson, and Zbigniew Mazur. 2001. "The Global Jordanscape." In *Michael Jordan, Inc.: Corporate Sport, Media Culture, and Late Modern America*, ed. David L. Andrews, 177–216. Albany: State University of New York Press.

Carroll, John S., and Eric J. Johnson. 1990. *Decision Research: A Field Guide*. Newbury Park, CA: Sage Publications.

Certeau, Michel de. 1984. *The Practice of Everyday Life*. Trans. Steven F. Rendall. Berkeley: University of California Press.

Clarke, Alan, and John Clarke. 1992. " 'Highlights and Action Replays': Ideology, Sport, and the Media." In *Sport, Culture, and Ideology*, ed. Jennifer Hargreaves, 62–87. London: Routledge and Kegan Paul.

Cole, C. L. 2001. "Nike's America/America's Michael Jordan." In *Michael Jordan, Inc.*, ed. David L. Andrews, 65–103. Albany: State University of New York Press.

Corner, John. 1995. *Television Form and Public Address*. London: Edward Arnold.

Daddario, Gina. 1998. *Women's Sport and Spectacle: Gendered Television Coverage and the Olympic Games*. Westport, CT: Praeger.

Danzin, Norman K. 2001. "Representing Michael." In *Michael Jordan, Inc.*, ed. David L. Andrews, 3–13. Albany: State University of New York Press.

Debord, Guy. 1983. *The Society of the Spectacle*. Detroit: Black and Red.

DuBrin, Andrew J. 1995. *The Breakthrough Team Player: Becoming the MVP on Your Workplace Team*. New York: AMACOM.

Dunning, Eric. 1986. "Sport as a Male Preserve." In *Quest for Excitement: Sport and Leisure in the Civilizing Process*, ed. Norbert Elias and Eric Dunning, 267–83. New York: Basil Blackwell.

———. 1994. "Sport as a Male Preserve: Notes on the Social Sources of Masculine Identity and Its Transformations." In *Women, Sport, and Culture*, ed. Susan Birrell and Cheryl L. Cole, 163–79. Champaign, IL: Human Kinetics.

———. 1999. *Sport Matters: Sociological Studies of Sport, Violence, and Civilization*. London and New York: Routledge.

Dych, Noel, and Eduardo P. Archetti, eds. 2003. *Sport, Dance, and Embodied Identities*. Oxford: Berg.

Early, Gerald. 1998. "Performance and Reality: Race, Sports, and the Modern World." *The Nation* (August) 10:17: 11–20.

Edmundson, Mark. 2001. "Fadeaway Jumper." *The American Scholar* (January 1): 61–75.

Eichberg, Henning. 1998. *Body Cultures: Essays on Sport, Space, and Identity.* London and New York: Routlege.

Ellis, John. 1982. *Visible Fictions: Cinema, Television, Video.* London and New York: Routledge and Kegan Paul.

Farred, Grant. 2003. " 'Theater of Dreams': Mimicry and Difference in Cape Flats Township Football." In *Sport and Postcolonialism,* ed. John Bale and Mike Cronin, 123–45. Oxford: Berg.

Feuer, Jane. 1983. "The Concept of Live Television: Ontology as Ideology." In *Regarding Television: Critical Approaches,* ed. E. Anne Kaplan, 12–22. Frederick, Md.: University Publishers of America.

Fish, Stanley. 1980. *Is There a Text in This Class?: The Authority of Interpretive Communities.* Cambridge, MA: Harvard University Press.

———. 1996. "Rhetoric." In *Critical Terms for Literary Study.* 2d ed., ed. Frank Lentricchia and Thomas Mc Laughlin, 203–22. Chicago: University of Chicago Press.

Fiske, John. 1987. *Television Culture.* New York: Routledge..

Foucault, Michel. 1995. *Discipline and Punish: The Birth of the Prison.* Trans. Alan Sheridan. New York: Vintage Books.

Fraleigh, Warren P. 1984. *Right Action in Sport: Ethics for Contestants.* Champaign, IL: Human Kinetics.

Gates, Henry Louis. 1992. *Loose Canons: Notes on the Culture Wars.* New York: Oxford University Press.

George, Nelson. 1992. *Elevating the Game: Black Men and Basketball.* New York: Harper Collins.

Gilligan, Carol. 1982. *In a Different Voice: Psychological Theory and Women's Development.* Cambridge, MA: Harvard University Press.

Gilroy, Paul. 2000. *Against Race: Imagining Political Culture beyond the Color Line.* Cambridge, MA: Harvard University Press.

Greenblatt, Stephen. 1995. "Culture." In *Critical Terms for Literary Study,* 2d ed., ed. Frank Lentricchia and Thomas Mc Laughlin, 225–32. Chicago: University of Chicago Press.

Gregg, Robert. 2004. "Personal Calvaries: Sports in Philadelphia's African American Communities, 1920–1960." In *Ethnicity, Sport, Identity: Struggles for Status,* ed. J. A. Mangan, Andrew Ritchie, 88–115. London: Frank Cass.

Gruneau, Richard. 1989. "Making Spectacle: A Case Study in Television Sports Production." In *Media, Sports, and Society,* ed. Lawrence Wenner, 134–54. Newbury Park, CA: Sage Publications.

Gubar, Susan. 1997. *Racechanges: White Skin, Black Face.* New York: Oxford University Press.

Gumbrecht, Hans Ulrich. 2006. *In Praise of Athletic Beauty.* Cambridge, MA: Belknap Press of Harvard University Press.

Haber, Honi Fern. 1994. *Beyond Postmodern Politics: Lyotard, Rorty, Foucault.* New York: Routledge.

Hardt, Michael, and Antonio Negri. 2000. *Empire.* Cambridge, MA: Harvard University Press.

Hargreaves, John. 1992. "Sport, Culture, and Ideology." In *Sport, Culture, and Ideology*, ed. Jennifer Hargreaves, 30–61. London: Routledge and Kegan Paul.

Hoberman, John. 1997. *Darwin's Athletes: How Sport Has Damaged Black America and Preserved the Myth of Race*. Boston: Houghton Mifflin.

hooks, bell. 1992. *Black Looks: Race and Representation*. Boston: South End Press.

———. 1996. "Neo-Colonial Fantasies of Conquest: *Hoop Dreams*." In *Reel to Real: Race, Sex, and Class at the Movies*, 79–82. New York: Routledge.

Huet, John. 1997. *Soul of the Game: Images and Voices of Street Basketball*. New York: Workman Publishing.

Huizinga, Johan. 1950, *Homo Ludens: A Study of the Play Element in Culture*. Boston: Beacon Press.

Ingham, Alan. 2004. "The Sportification Process: A Biographical Analysis Framed by the Work of Marx, Weber, Durkheim, and Freud." In *Sport and the Modern Social Theorists*, ed. Richard Giulianotti, 11–32. London: Palgrave Macmillan.

Jackson, Phil. 1995. *Sacred Hoops: Spiritual Lessons of a Hardwood Warrior*. New York: Hyperion.

Jameson, Fredric. 1991. *Postmodernism, or, The Cultural Logic of Late Capitalism*. Durham, NC: Duke University Press.

Janis, Irving L., and Leon Mann. 1977. *Decision Making: A Psychological Analysis of Conflict, Choice, and Commitment*. New York: Free Press.

Jhally, Sut. 1989. "Cultural Studies and the Sports/Media Complex." In *Media, Sports, and Society*, ed. Lawrence Wenner, 70–93. Newbury Park, CA: Sage Publications.

Kidd, Bruce. 1987. "Sports and Masculinity." In *Beyond Patriarchy: Essays By Men on Pleasure, Power, and Change*, ed. Michael Kaufman, 250–65. Toronto: Oxford University Press.

Kimmel, Michael. 1996. *Manhood in America: A Cultural History*. New York: Free Press.

Kryzyzewski, Mike, with Donald T. Phillips. 2004. *Leading with the Heart*. New York: Warner Business Books.

LaFeber, Walter. 1999. *Michael Jordan and the New Global Capitalism*. New York: Norton.

Lorde, Audre. 1984. *Sister Outsider: Essays and Speeches*. Trumansburg, NY: Crossings Press.

Lott, Eric. 1997. "All the King's Men: Elvis Impersonators and White Working-Class Masculinity." In *Race and the Subject of Masculinities*, ed. Harry Stecopoulos and Michael Uebel, 192–227. Durham, NC: Duke University Press.

Lumpkin, Angela, Sharon Kay Stall, and Jennifer M. Beller. 1985. *Sports Ethics: Applications for Fair Play*. St. Louis, MO: Mosby.

MacIntyre, Alasdair. 1994. *After Virtue: A Study in Moral Theory*. South Bend, IN: University of Notre Dame Press.

Mailer, Norman. 1957. "The White Negro." *Dissent*, vol. 4, no. 3 (Summer): 276–93.

March, James G. 1994. *A Primer on Decision Making: How Decisions Happen*. New York: Free Press.

Massey, Doreen. 1994. *Space, Place, and Gender.* Minneapolis: University of Minnesota Press.

McDonald, Mary G. 2001. "Safe Sex Symbol? Michael Jordan and the Politics of Representation." In *Michael Jordan, Inc.,* ed. David L. Andrews, 153–74. Albany: State University of New York Press.

Mc Laughlin, Thomas. 1996. *Street Smarts and Critical Theory: Listening to the Vernacular.* Madison: University of Wisconsin Press.

Mehrabian, Albert. 1976. *Public Place and Private Spaces: The Psychology of Work, Play, and Living Environments.* New York: Basic Books.

Mercer, Kobena. 1991. "Skin Head Sex Thing: Racial Difference and the Homoerotic Imaginary." In *How Do I Look? Queer Film and Video,* ed. Bad Object-Choices. Seattle: Bay Press.

Messner, Michael A. 1990. "Men Studying Masculinity: Some Epistemological Issues in Sport Sociology." *Sociology of Sport Journal* 7: 136–53.

———. 1992. *Power at Play: Sports and the Problem of Masculinity.* Boston: Beacon Press.

Miller, J. Hillis. 1996. "Narrative." In *Critical Terms for Literary Studies,* 2d ed., ed. Frank Lentricchia and Thomas Mc Laughlin, 66–79. Chicago: University of Chicago Press.

Mohrman, Susan Albers, Susan G. Cohen, and Allan M. Mohrman. 1995. *Designing Team-Based Organizations: New Forms for Knowledge Work.* San Francisco: Jossey-Bass.

Moran, Michael. 1991. *Nothing but Net: An Essay on the Culture of Pickup Basketball.* San Antonio, TX: Full Court Press.

Morrison, Toni. 1992. *Playing in the Dark: Whiteness and the Literary Imagination.* Cambridge, MA: Harvard University Press.

Morse, Margaret. 1983. "Sports on Television: Replay and Display." In *Regarding Television: Critical Approaches,* ed. E. Anne Kaplan, 44–66. Frederick, MD: University Publishers of America.

Nelson, Mariah Burton. 1998. *Embracing Victory: Life Lessons in Competition and Compassion.* New York: William Morrow.

Noddings, Nel. 1984. *Caring: A Feminine Approach to Ethics and Moral Education.* Berkeley: University of California Press.

Novack, Cynthia. 1990. *Sharing the Dance: Contact Improvisation and American Culture.* Madison: University of Wisconsin Press.

Novak, Michael. 1976. *The Joy of Sports: End Zones, Bases, Baskets, Balls, and the Consecration of the American Spirit.* New York: Basic Books.

O'Brien, Maureen. 1994. *Who's Got the Ball (And Other Nagging Questions about Team Life): A Player's Guide for Work Teams.* San Francisco: Jossey Bass.

Orwell, George. 1958. "The Sporting Spirit." In *Selected Writings,* ed. George Bott, 159–62. London: Heinemann.

Ostroff, Frank. 1999. *The Horizontal Organization: What the Organization of the Future Looks Like and How It Delivers Value to Customers.* New York: Oxford University Press.

Parker, Glenn M. 1994. *Cross-Functional Teams: Working with Allies, Enemies, and Other Strangers*. San Francisco: Jossey-Bass.

Perry, Lee Tom, Randall G. Stott, and W. Norman Smallwood. 1993. *Real-Time Strategy: Improvising Team-Based Planning for a Fast-Changing World*. New York: Wiley.

Peters, Tom. 1992. *Liberation Management: Necessary Disorganization for the Nano-second Nineties*. New York: A. A. Knopf.

Pratt, May Louise. 2002. "Arts of the Contact Zone." In *Ways of Reading: An Anthology for Writers*, ed. David Bartholomae and Anthony Petrosky, 6th ed., 605–19. Boston: Bedford.

Pruden, Vic. 1987. *A Conceptual Approach to Basketball*. Champaign, IL: Leisure Press.

Putnam, David. 2000. *Bowling Alone: The Collapse and Revival of American Commu-nity*. New York: Simon and Schuster.

Quinones, Sam. 2001. *True Tales from Another Mexico*. Albuquerque: University of New Mexico Press.

Ray, Darrel, and Howard Bronstein. 1995. *Teaming Up: Making the Transition to a Self-Directed, Team-Based Organization*. New York: McGraw-Hill.

Reeves, Jimmy L. 1989. "TV's World of Sports: Presenting and Playing the Game." In *Television Studies: Textual Analysis*, ed. Gary Burns and Robert J. Thomp-son, 205–19. New York: Praeger.

Rigauer, Bero. 1981. *Sport and Work*. New York: Columbia University Press.

Riley, Pat. 1993. *The Winner Within: A Life Plan for Team Players*. New York: Berkley Books.

Rinehart, Robert E. 1998. *Players All: Performance in Contemporary Sport*. Bloomington: Indiana University Press.

Rivers, Doc. 1993. *Those Who Love the Game*. New York: Harper Collins.

Robbins, Bruce. 1997. " 'Head Fake': Mentorship and Mobility in *Hoop Dreams*." *Social Text* 50 (Spring): 111–20.

Roche, Maurice. 1998. *Sport, Popular Culture, and Identity*. Aachen: Myer and Myer Verlag.

Rose, Nikolas. 1999. *Powers of Freedom: Reframing Political Thought*. Cambridge: Cambridge University Press.

Rouse, W. B., and N. M. Morris. 1986. "On Looking Into the Black Box: Prospect and Limits in the Search for Mental Models." *Psychological Bulletin*, 100, 359–63.

Rowe, David. 2004. *Sport, Culture, and the Media: The Unruly Trinity*. Maidenhead, England: Open University Press.

Russell, Bill, and Taylor Branch. 1979. *Second Wind: The Memoirs of an Opinionated Man*. New York: Random House.

Sartre, Jean Paul. 1995. From *Being and Nothingness*. In *Philosophic Inquiry in Sport*, 2d ed., ed. William J. Morgan and Klaus V. Meier, 110–13. Champaign, IL: Human Kinetics.

Scarborough, Vernon, and David Wilcox. 1991. *The Mesoamerican Ballgame*. Tuc-son: University of Arizona Press.

Scheflen, Albert, and Norman Ashcraft. 1976. *People Space: The Making and Break-ing of Human Boundaries*. Garden City, NY: Anchor Press.

Senge, Peter. 1990. *The Fifth Discipline: The Art and Practice of the Learning Orga-nization*. New York: Doubleday/Currency.

Silverstone, Roger. 1994. *Television and Everyday Life*. London and New York: Routledge.

Smith, Dean. 1999. *Basketball: Multiple Offense and Defense*. Boston: Allyn and Bacon.

Stam, Robert. 1991. "Bakhtin, Polyphony, and Ethnic/Racial Representation." In *Unspeakable Images: Ethnicity and the American Cinema*, ed. Lester D. Fried-man, 251–76. Urbana and Chicago: University of Illinois Press.

Sullivan, William M. 1995. "Institution as the Infrastructure of Democracy." In *New Communitarian Thinking: Persons, Virtues, Institutions, and Communities*, ed. Amitai Etzioni, 170–80. Charlottesville: University Press of Virginia.

Torgovnick, Marianna. 1990. *Gone Primitive: Savage Intellects, Modern Lives*. Chi-cago: University of Chicago Press.

Walzer, Michael. 1995. "The Communitarian Critique of Liberalism." In *New Communitarian Thinking: Persons, Virtues, Institutions, and Communities*, ed. Amitai Etzioni, 52–70. Charlottesville: University Press of Virginia.

Wegner, Etienne. 1998. *Communities of Practice: Learning, Meaning, and Identity*. Cambridge: Cambridge University Press.

Wellens, A. Rodney. 1993. "Group Situation Awareness and Distributed Decision Making: From Military to Civilian Applications." In *Individual and Group Decision Making: Current Issues*, ed. N. John Castellan, 267–91. Hillsdale, NJ: Lawrence Erlbaum Associates.

Wertheimer, Jon. 2005. *How Hoosiers Went Hip-Hop*. New York: G. P. Putnam's Sons.

Whannel, Gary. 1992. *Fields in Vision: Television Sport and Cultural Transformation*. London and New York: Routledge.

Wheeler, Daniel D., and Irving L. Janis. 1980. *A Practical Guide for Making Deci-sions*. New York: Free Press.

Whitson, David. 1990. "Sport in the Social Construction of Masculinity." In *Sport, Men, and the Gender Order: Critical Feminist Perspectives*, ed. Michael A. Messner and Donald F. Sabo, 19–29. Champaign, IL: Human Kinetics Books.

Wideman, John. 1994. *Fatheralong: A Meditation on Fathers and Sons, Race and Society*. New York: Pantheon.

———. 1998. "This Man Can Play." *Esquire* (May): 67–73.

———. 2001. *Hoop Roots*. Boston: Houghton Mifflin.

Widick, Richard. 2004. "Flesh and the Free Market." In *After Bourdieu: Influence, Critique, Elaboration*, ed. David L. Swartz and Vera L. Zolberg, 193–238. Dordrecht: Kluwer Academic Publishers.

Williamson, Thad. 2001. *More Than a Game: Why North Carolina Basketball Means So Much To So Many*. Cambridge, MA: Economic Affairs Bureau.

Woolf, Alexander. 2002. *Big Game, Small World: A Basketball Adventure*. New York: Warner Books.

Zettl, Herbert. 1997. *Television Production Handbook*. 6th ed. Belmont, CA: Wadsworth.

Suggested Readings

Axthelm, Pete. *The City Game: From the Garden to the Playgrounds*. Lincoln: University of Nebraska Press, 1999.

Ballard, Chris. *Hoops Nation: A Guide to America's Best Pickup Basketball*. New York: Henry Holt and Company, 1998.

Berkow, Ira, ed. *Court Vision: Unexpected Views on the Lure of Basketball*. New York: William Morrow, 2000.

———. *To the Hoop: The Seasons of a Basketball Life*. New York: Basic Books, 1997.

Blais, Madeleine. *In These Girls Hope Is a Muscle*. New York: Atlantic Monthly Press, 1995.

Caponi, Gina Dagel, ed. *Signifyin(g), Sanctifyin' and Slam Dunking: A Reader in African American Expressive Culture*. Amherst: University of Massachusetts Press, 1999.

Colton, Larry. *Counting Coup: A True Story of Basketball and Honor on the Little Big Horn*. New York: Warner Books, 2000.

Conroy, Pat. *My Losing Season*. New York: Doubleday, 2002.

Feinstein, John. *The Last Amateurs: Playing for Glory and Honor in Division I College Basketball*. Boston: Little, Brown, 2000.

———. *The Punch: One Night, Two Lives, and the Fight that Changed Basketball Forever*. Boston: Little, Brown, 2002.

Frey, Darcy. *The Last Shot: City Streets, Basketball Dreams*. New York: Simon and Schuster, 1994.

Grundy, Pamela, and Susan Shackelford. *Shattering the Glass: The Remarkable History of Women's Basketball*. New York: New Press, 2005.

Halberstam, David. *Playing for Keeps: Michael Jordan and the World He Made*. New York: Random House, 1999.

Jimerson, Jason. *Shirts and Skins: The Sociology of Basketball*. DVD. Directed by Ron Osgood. Princeton, NJ: Films for the Humanities and Sciences, 2005.

Maloney, John Fitzsimmons. *The Tao of the Jump Shot: An Eastern Approach to Life and Basketball*. Berkeley, CA: Seastone, 1999.

McPhee, John. *A Sense of Where You Are: A Profile of William Warren Bradley*. New York: Farrar, Straus, and Giroux, 1978.

Shields, David. *Black Planet: Facing Race during an NBA Season*. New York: Crown Publishing, 1999.

Telander, Rick. *Heaven Is a Playground*. Lincoln: University of Nebraska Press, 1988.

Index